Every Frame Counts

CW01558715

This book, written by an industry expert, covers the duties of an assistant editor over the course of an entire feature film.

Throughout the book, the author provides key insights and advice from years of experience, which will help assistant editors hit the ground running, keep up the pace, and continue thinking critically and creatively. The easy-to-navigate structure loosely follows that of the typical job by identifying and outlining four key phases: Dailies, Director's Cut, Screenings, and Finishing. Discussed therein are also passages that outline pre-production, the first day on the job, temp sound and VFX work, and turnovers as well as wrap and archiving.

Special features include detailed screenshots, advanced tips for interacting with Avid Media Composer (the industry standard for Non-Linear Digital Editing), editorial-specific use cases for automation using FileMaker Pro, and best practices regarding every aspect of the job.

This book is an intermediate resource for prospective and current assistant editors in the modern film and television editorial department.

Jared Simon is an industry-renowned editor and assistant editor with selected credits including *Ad Astra*, *The Piano Lesson*, *Chevalier*, and *Come From Away*.

Every Frame Counts

An Assistant Editor's
Reference Book

Jared Simon

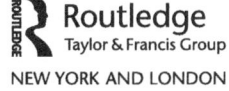
Routledge
Taylor & Francis Group

NEW YORK AND LONDON

Designed cover image: FILMOGRAPH

First published 2025
by Routledge
605 Third Avenue, New York, NY 10158

and by Routledge
4 Park Square, Milton Park, Abingdon, Oxon, OX14 4RN

Routledge is an imprint of the Taylor & Francis Group, an informa business

© 2025 Jared Simon

The right of Jared Simon to be identified as author of this work has been
asserted in accordance with sections 77 and 78 of the Copyright, Designs and
Patents Act 1988.

ISBN: 9781032850931 (hbk)
ISBN: 9781032843285 (pbk)
ISBN: 9781003516491 (ebk)

DOI: 10.4324/9781003516491

Typeset in Sabon
by Newgen Publishing UK

Access the Support Material: www.routledge.com/9781032843285

To my family, whose constant support means the world.
CL RL RR DSBL
SK MY AK SS

Contents

Foreword

by John Axelrad, ACE

An assistant editor once gave me some great advice: "You don't have to be the smartest person in the room—just the most useful." These words of wisdom encapsulate the mindset a successful assistant editor needs to embody in the television and film industry. Knowledge and experience come with time, but having the right attitude and instincts makes certain individuals stand out. As an editor, I want to hire humble and courteous people with the curiosity, ambition, and drive to get ahead. In a sense, I am looking for that "most useful person" in the room. I think any editor wants that quality from their first assistant.

One of my more recent assistants, Jared Simon, is one of the best hires I ever made. I hired Jared to work as a second assistant editor on the feature "Ad Astra" and was impressed with his attitude and ability to quickly learn how to anticipate problems and find solutions before the problems surfaced. Jared's talents were evident, so when my previous first assistant was unavailable on a lower-budget feature, I quickly hired Jared for the position. Jared started the job fully prepared and ready to take on the challenge. He possesses skills that can be hard to teach—intuition, anticipation, and problem-solving. Although he didn't have prior experience in this role, he did his homework and research and performed the job with both competence and excellence.

The thing Jared most impressed me with was his ability to take copious notes and write a "dossier" of the procedures and his skills as an assistant editor. Nobody asked Jared to do this; he was self-motivated to record his experiences and continuously refine his approach in the editing room. While writing his document, Jared also took the time to build a FileMaker Pro-based "codebook" database from the ground up. With his growing experience, his colleagues and I encouraged him to further develop his "dossier" into a book. Thus began a multi-year journey of writing the book you now have in front of you. It is filled with innumerable details and valuable insights into both existing and new methods of operation.

Getting firmly established in the world of post-production is greatly facilitated by having a mentor who is both experienced and generous. However, finding a mentor who will enrich you and help you grow can be a difficult endeavor. You must already be a motivated and knowledgeable person to even get noticed during a job interview. I truly believe Jared Simon's "Every Frame Counts" will give you a solid foundation and understanding of what happens in an editing room. It is the most thorough and up-to-date manuscript I've read on assistant editing. This book can serve as a "mentor in your pocket" and help you become the most useful person in the room and on the way to a successful editing career.

Acknowledgments

This book simply would not exist without **Robert Ivison**. Robert kindly invited me to speak at AFI, where he proposed that I publish this and subsequently suggested the title "Every Frame Counts."

One of my earliest mentors, **Chris Newman**, continues to be my North Star. His voice is forever in my head, and his lessons exceed the confines of any classroom. He introduced me to **Alan Heim** and **Walter Murch**, both of whom received lifetime achievement awards from American Cinema Editors, for which I was honored to cut reels. To have cultivated relationships with Alan and Walter has been beyond enriching, and I feel very fortunate and grateful to them for their time over the years.

To **John Axelrad** and **Leslie Jones**, two editors I work with most frequently: Thank you from the bottom of my heart for being so kind, generous, inclusive, and encouraging. The lessons I've learned from just being in the same room as you are immeasurable.

Marco Andrés Gonzalez is responsible for all the illustrations in this book. He is not only a skilled editor and assistant in his own right but, more importantly, an even better friend.

Footage in screenshots is provided courtesy of **Rich Camp**, from his short film "Pasta." Additional footage is provided courtesy of **James Bachelor, Alan Bachelor,** and **Javier Hernandez-Kistte** from a short film we made called "She Knocks."

My sincere thanks to everyone at Avid, especially **Rich Camp** and **Michael Krulik,** for their inclusivity and for welcoming me into the community over the years.

Thank you to everyone at **Taylor & Frances** for guiding me through my first publishing experience.

Finally, thank you to everyone who reviewed chapters, provided invaluable feedback, and have supported me throughout this whole process: **Adam Armus, Bob Berman, JC Bond, Z Taylor Bynum, Sushant Chaudhary, Len Ciccotello, Erica Frauman, Eddy Garcia, John Grenham, Natalie Haas, Quintin Harris, Steve Hullfish, Avo John Kambourian, Jan Kikumoto, Jacob Kirby, Alyse Kollerbohm Kerr,**

Dave Levinson, Ricki Reisner, Agustin Rexach, Stephen M. Rickert, Jr., Rich Rowe, Richard Sanchez, Sean Someroff, Jason Voss.

And, of course, thank you, dear reader, for picking up this book and giving it the time of day. I sincerely hope you find it helpful.

Introduction

Hi! My name is Jared, and I'm an assistant editor. I love watching movies as much as I love making them. I think playing with computers is fun, and that's how I found my way into this career. Modern film and video editing are at the intersection of what I love and what I'm good at. If everyone can find that intersection in their lives, their work won't feel like work.

My approach to assisting has largely been community-based. I feel strongly about paying everything forward. That's the mindset with which I wrote this book. I missed out on the era when first assistant editors would stand by their editor at the Moviola and learn on the job. Fortunately for me, I've been extraordinarily lucky to have developed close and meaningful working relationships with editors who have been generous with their time, skills, and feedback. They've encouraged me not only to be the best assistant *and* editor I can be but also the best *person* I can be. For that, I will always be grateful.

What you're holding in your hands is a collection of thoughts, observations, and notes I've been collecting throughout my career. I started writing everything down while working on various movies and TV shows to help keep myself organized. The first thing was dailies. I'd do dailies on one show, and then it would be a year before I got dailies again. To make sure I didn't forget any of the details, I wrote down what I called O^3 (which I thought was a cute and totally normal way to truncate "Order of Operations"). As I worked on more projects, my notes kept growing, and I added more and more to them every time I learned something new. So many details can fall through the cracks, and I wanted to ensure that never happened when I was around.

This book is structured in a linear order that a typical feature film digital editorial workflow follows. Pretend you're shadowing me, and we're going to go through the process of assisting on a feature film together. I'm writing this in my voice, so it's not your typical manual (if you're looking for that, right-click anywhere in Media Composer and click "What's This?"). I'm going to assume you're familiar with the tools on a basic level—and if you're not, I urge you to seek out introductory-level resources. The rest of this book

DOI: 10.4324/9781003516491-1

takes that foundation and builds on it in a modern and relevant way, accelerating your already existing knowledge by introducing you to other ways of working. Maybe there are a few tips and tricks in here you didn't know were possible. Maybe you already know it, and my writing here underscores and validates your already stellar methodology. Or maybe you hate it and will judge me for even considering publishing it. "How could you even *think* of pulling off a temp split screen that way, Jared?" you'll shake your head and mutter (p. 175).

So, it's not a Manual?

Nope! This book is also **not** a definitive and exhaustive guide for all things post-production, nor is it the "only way" to do things. Everything within this book (in this edition) is based on my experience and the way I used the tools available to me when it was written in 2024. Technology evolves rapidly. New workflows will emerge, augmenting or replacing some of the methods I have outlined. Does this make everything outdated? Absolutely not—the underlying principles and thought processes that led to the specific methodologies should remain relevant to any approach you choose to take, if not informative. Many principles and ideas can be transferred to any workflow because it's more of a mindset and a catalyst for critical thinking.

This book **is** the one thing I wish I had when I began assisting. It's insight into the mind of a first assistant editor, something I found difficult to obtain when I was finding my footing. I wrote this as a compendium of advanced and esoteric notes that I could only find buried within technical manuals, online forums, and through shadowing others. I intended to make it more conversational (and thus more approachable) than a manual and to create a resource that adds to the research you're doing in any particular area.

Navigating and Using the Book

This book originated from my notes, which was a hyperlinked PDF file—likely similar to how this is represented in eBook form if you have a digital copy. Also, in this book's digital and print versions, there's a glossary (p. 173) and an index for referencing. If you come across an unfamiliar term or abbreviation, and you want a definition (MDB, FFC, Perf Slip, etc.), odds are it's in the glossary.

Much thought and care has been put into making the print version just as accessible and easy to navigate. It's important to me that this be an actionable reference that allows you to cross-reference relevant sections as needed. Wherever I felt it was relevant, there's a parenthetical with a page number pointing to specific and relevant information on that page, like this (p. 265). I find it helpful to keep a finger on the page I'm reading, flip to the relevant blurb in another chapter, and then flip back to pick up where I left off.

I'd encourage you to use this the way I would have if I had it when I was in your shoes: **Annotate to your heart's content!** Highlight helpful sentences. Dog-ear pages. Scribble your notes in the margins and place sticky notes all over. Cover it in stickers and make it your own.

Prerequisites

This has been written as an intermediate-level resource with working assistant editors in mind. To get the most out of this book, I think it's best to be familiar with Avid Media Composer. If not, I once again urge you to seek out introductory-level resources (p. 266). Media Composer is the only non-linear editing software I discuss in this book and the only one I use professionally day-to-day. Sometimes, I'll refer to it by its proper name (Media Composer), but other times, I'll call it "the Avid" or just "Avid." Examples of concepts you should already know regarding Media Composer before continuing in this book include managed media vs linked media, how to restore a bin from the Avid Attic, and what a 3D Warp Effect is. If any of these seem new to you, the concepts in this book might be difficult to understand and use. The contents within are otherwise well worth exploring and keeping on your radar.

I primarily work on MacOS, and all keyboard shortcuts/file management tips are within the context of that operating system. Why? I like MacOS, and many editors feel the same way, so it's prevalent in the editorial circles. There are certainly editors who prefer Microsoft Windows and PC-based environments. While some keyboard shortcuts can be translated, and most of the applications I cover are cross-platform, it's something to keep in mind. Also, while there are a handful of review and approval platforms (p. 21), I generally use PIX. So, if I refer to "PIX," feel free to replace it in your head with whatever you're using.

If you've been in a cutting room or have the opportunity to shadow an assistant editor, that's the kind of experience that will enhance what you're reading about here. Please, bring the book along with you! It might give you some informed, detailed questions to ask.

1 Being a First Assistant Editor

The role of the first assistant editor is multifaceted. As I see it, I am the first point of contact in the department, just below the editor, acting as a sort of traffic cop. I coordinate with other departments and organize everything that comes in and goes out of the cutting room. I delegate tasks to my team, keeping everyone on schedule and completing tasks without letting anything fall through the cracks. I inspire my co-workers to do their best work and trust that they have my back. I know when to listen and when to share my opinion. Before I speak, I ask myself if what I'm about to say is helpful or if it only proves that I know the answer. To me, this is the difference between being the smartest person in the room and being the most helpful. These attributes serve one core goal: To allow the editor to work uninterrupted with the director.

Working as Part of a Team

Many editors get their start working by themselves or as the only editors on a small production. One of the biggest differences between simply *being an editor* and *working in this industry* is working with other people. It's important to recognize how a team of editors (picture editor, first, second, apprentice classifications, music, and sound editors, etc.) collaborate in a shared environment and your role in that. Let's explore what some of the other core team members do.

A second assistant editor's main role is to support the first assistant; this can mean creating outputs and turnovers, compiling lists, tracking VFX, and working on temp sound or VFX. A good second assistant editor takes direction well and reliably gets everything done exactly as the first assistant editor would.

An apprentice editor typically works on the digital lined script (which is a tedious but important job, especially during dailies) as well as various other editorial tasks. If the film has enough visual effects, you might have a VFX Editor whose main responsibility is to handle all the VFX coordination, tracking, and temps (p. 181).

DOI: 10.4324/9781003516491-2

A post-production assistant (post-PA) maintains the day-to-day operations of the cutting room. They're responsible for stocking office supplies and "crafty" (craft services, aka "the *good* snacks"), and they assist whenever needed. They're prompt, reliable, and interested in post-production. A great post-PA gets their job done without anyone else even thinking about it and shadows at every opportunity. They ask informed questions (p. 8) and are patient to know when best to do this so as not to interrupt the flow of work.

The post supervisor is my go-to regularly once the show gets going. I'll talk more about them in a later chapter (p. 12), but they're the liaison between all editorial and the studio. I confer with the post regarding the schedule, turnovers, my timecard, and anything I think the team might need.

Regardless of your position, it's an important virtue to be able to anticipate the editor's needs and exceed their expectations. Below are some minor technical and personal things that have helped me.

General Tips

- It may sound silly to note, but I think it's important to say, "Good morning" and "Good night" when you come and go. On one level, it's good to know who's in in the morning and when you're leaving—but it also shows care and respect for your coworkers. You're a team, and the team is more important than everything.
- If an email is actionable, act on it now. If you can't, create a draft so you remember to return to it later.
- Respond to emails to let everyone know you're taking care of it and to let the sender know their message has been received.
- When downloading a file, organize it immediately. Import it into Avid after organizing it.
- Keep your desktop clean. Both physically and digitally.
- Use keyboard shortcuts whenever possible.
- If you don't need to save new work into a bin, Option-open it; when working in a shared environment, bin locks are crucial, and you don't want to hog a bin when you don't need it.
- When you're done with a bin you have the lock for, close it!
- Don't forget to eat. Things can get busy. This sounds like a bizarre reminder for a book about being an assistant editor, but seriously, eat.
- **Write things down**. It's more about committing it to memory than referencing it later. I keep Field Notes notebooks on hand, which were the precursor to my digital notes, ergo, this book. I still use them daily to jot things down.

Time Management

Time management is key. The idea is to balance efficiency with efficacy: How will you get the most out of any process in the least amount of time? This can apply to everything, and I think it helps maintain a healthy balance of quality and quantity of work. You should be able to tell someone how long something will take—it can be the difference between the director waiting five minutes to see a new temp VFX shot or heading out for the day... and you do *not* want to keep anyone waiting for longer than you first advised.

Delegation

If you're used to being the *only* assistant editor, you might be likely to take on every request that comes in by yourself. As the first assistant editor on a team, you're likely hurtling toward manufactured chaos if you do this. Imagine a world where you're asked for four things, and a fifth comes in. You delegate that fifth task to your second assistant editor. Your head is still full of taking care of those first four tasks. Instead, I like to delegate tasks **before** my plate gets full. It frees me up to tackle quick requests and keeps my head clear. Those first four things? I'll give half the work to my second assistant editor, thus giving them responsibility, inclusion, and perhaps a learning opportunity. This permits me to still operate with enough headspace to manage whatever might be just around the corner. We work together to get everything done in a timely and efficient manner.

Thinking at Scale

As assistant editors, we are responsible for the overall editorial workflow. How might you be able to anticipate what could happen next so that you can work quickly and efficiently? Efficiency isn't only about the fastest way to do one thing. Being proactive can make you more efficient, and this can be accomplished by considering your routine, hourly, daily, and weekly.

Are there any parts of your routine that are recurring? If there is an opportunity to set up a system, thus being **proactive**, do so as time allows. When time runs short, as it most certainly will, we can only respond **reactively**, tipping the balance into manufactured chaos. As will be explored within later chapters, things like utilizing burn-in effect templates (p. 209), leveraging parallel encoding (p. 214), and setting up an auto-download system (p. 20) are examples of recognizing patterns and thinking about accomplishing tasks at scale.

Leadership

Your demeanor will differentiate you from everyone else. Though things may get harried, try to stay calm, cool, and collected. I want to avoid writing anything that explains "how to be." I'm a firm believer in being true to yourself and allowing your personality to shine. After all, assuming all candidates have an equal skillset, your personality is what gets you hired. There's a way to maintain your way of speaking, writing emails, and expressing yourself while also using common sense, thinking ahead, and reading the room.

Leadership can also be quiet. Setting an example of calm efficiency can dictate the tone of the working environment and create a more productive and happy cutting room.

Mentorship

Mentorship is a large part of what I think being a good leader is. I am eager to teach those around me, and I try to be patient. Some things are hard to learn until you're in the environment. One example is etiquette, like knocking on the door or listening for playback before entering an editor's or another assistant's room. An example of a smaller thing would be matching the volume of the person you're speaking with (like mirroring body language). I've learned that it's more helpful to teach in small bites, even if you know a faster (or more detailed) way because it makes it easier and less overwhelming for someone to grasp a new concept.

Morale

Keeping morale high is important. The cutting rooms I've worked in try to have a "happy hour" every week and take some time to talk about non-work-related topics over cheese and crackers, or tea. It's also important to allow the team to be as flexible as possible. This job requires demanding hours, so if someone needs to take off early or meet someone for lunch, I always try to help make it happen. All this is a two-way street because sometimes, I'm the one who needs to leave early, and it's a relief to know my team has my back just like I have theirs.

Growth

I always make a point of communicating with my team on every level. I like to periodically ask the other assistants and PAs what they'd like to learn and what their long-term goals are—or if there's anything they think we can change. I want to make sure no one feels stuck in one place or dismissed and that they, too, have a voice in shaping the work environment.

Asking Questions

The greatest compliment I've ever received was that I asked good questions. What does that mean, though? I hadn't thought about it before, but I've come to realize that the questions I tend to ask are both targeted and informed. I stray away from vague questions; I use correct nomenclature and specific terminology, and I don't ask about something without doing some research first. I'm not as curious about *how* something is done as much as I am about *why* it's being done. I've always believed that the reasoning behind why something is done informs the way we do it to begin with.

What does a vague question sound like? It's usually something directionless and uninformed. A vague question can come across as lazy. Here's an example: *"Is there anything else you think I should know?"* A better version of this question would involve thinking through the process being questioned and asking specifically about one possible aspect that could arise.

"Question Anything, Not Everything"

I operate under this mentality. To me, this means that nothing is off limits, but make your questions count; in other words, be inquisitive but not annoying. If you're having a tough time figuring out where to start (because, after all, you don't know what you don't know), start with a topic and drill down to something specific.

Think through a full day of work and all the possibilities of what could happen and who might need something. This might sound intimidating or overwhelming—how can you possibly be expected to think through every single permutation of how the day can go? It's more of a mindset than a tangible goal, and if these kinds of proactive and thoughtful tendencies become part of your standard operating procedure, they'll not only fall into the background and not feel like an encumbrance, but they'll demonstrate to others that you're mindful and holistic in your approach to learning more.

Now and then, I ask the editor if there's anything I can do differently or better. I have an innate sense of curiosity and a strong desire to continue to learn and grow, and I'm not resistant to criticism or change. These are attributes that I think have helped me get to where I am. When someone asks me a question, and I don't know the answer, that's not the end of the road. I'll try to find out.

2 Setting Up The Show

When starting a job, I try to take a macro-level look at everything. Once we're into the day-to-day operations, I tend to be laser-focused on the tasks at hand. The beginning is the time to establish connections with other departments, lay the foundation for the workflow pipeline, and set up an organizational system that fits the show. It's important to consider how files will be securely sent and received and if remote work is part of the plan. Let's begin by looking at who I'm communicating with from the start of the show.

Who I Talk to

It should go without saying that I am in constant communication with the editor. When I start on a show, the first person I talk to is the post-production supervisor and/or the head of post-production at the studio. Once I make my deal, I reach out to the director's assistant and a few departments, usually via email. The gist of each email is to introduce the editorial department and myself and outline/document the former's expectations in a friendly way. Here's whom I talk to:

Production Coordinator and Secretary

I ask them to include everyone in editorial on the dailies paperwork distribution ("distro"). I also ask if they can forward cast and crew lists, as well as an Avid Text export of the script from Final Draft. I ask about the art department logos, which usually puts me in touch with the art department directly. If the production office is local, I ask them to prepare hard copies of the script for the cutting rooms (their printers are usually faster, better and already set up). The production secretary handles the coordinator's assistant-level duties.

Studio Content Security

They usually contact *me*. Their bottom line: No photos, no videos, use the security title (if one exists), keep passwords rotating and meeting requirements. They enforce the use of encrypted drives (hardware

DOI: 10.4324/9781003516491-3

encrypted drives are usually provided by the studio). In addition, they advise you to lock any content in a safe or lockbox. Content security is of the utmost importance.

Studio Dailies Department

I'll ask about scheduling a workflow call, and what to expect from production regarding workflow. See below (p. 12) for details on what comes out of a dailies workflow call.

Dailies Lab Technician

Following the workflow call (p. 12), I'll summarize what was discussed and provide a template bin. The metadata must be accurate and precise, and I hammer home my appreciation for the technician's attention to detail in advance.

Camera Department

The editor might send this email and copy me. We ask them to share the shooting specs and camera info ahead of the workflow call, and we request that they slate every shot and provide a framing and focus chart (FFC) for each camera. We also confirm the frame rate, which has typically been 24.0 fps (not 23.98). Why 24.0? It's an even integer, which makes math easier, and 23.98 is a holdover from the NTSC broadcast TV days (for reasons I implore you to investigate, should you be so inclined).

Sound Recordist

Similar to the camera department and ahead of the workflow call, this call is mostly to confirm and discuss track layout, specs and anything else in that realm. What equipment are they using? Will they send master files on physical media (uncommon)? We confirm the frame rate as well.

Music Editor and Supervisor

If there's music playback involved, I want to know how we're planning to handle it and if they can send me the music master files. We discuss the click/thump tracks and audio timecode. I'll also ask if they know of anything the director might already have in mind for music. Lastly, I'll ask them to share anything they might have in mind for a temp score. If the composer is already attached, I'll ask if sketches exist or if there are any of their other scores we should plan on leaning on. All of this is just to gather information because the editor might already have some thoughts about the music they want to use.

Script Supervisor

The editor might send this email and copy me. We ask for a one-liner breakdown of the continuity, an Avid Script file exported from Final Draft (something that might ultimately come from the production office) and a short list of requests that are boilerplate regarding script supervision but always nice to confirm and get on the same page about. If your script supervisor uses digitals solution like Script-E or Lockit Script and PDF Expert, it's a good idea to request that they send Excel, CSV or XML files with each delivery of script notes. If the files are all manually lined and noted, that's fine too; you'll need to copy and paste (or transcribe) any relevant notes into a database if you're using one.

Assistant Director(s)

The editor might send this email and copy me. We ask for a one-liner breakdown *in scene order*. They might have a breakdown prepared in shoot order, but it's more helpful when you're setting up the continuity to have their one-liners organized as they are in the script.

Director

The editor will likely send this email, and hopefully, they'll copy me or at least keep me filled in on their conversation. It's an email with script thoughts and requests for clarification if needed. Perhaps the most important part of this conversation regards intention and how certain scenes or transitions will be shot. We'll also find out how the director likes to communicate and with what frequency—especially as it relates to reviewing cut footage during production (scene assemblies).

Post Facility

This is to confirm the rooms we have, square away parking information, and request furniture along with hardware and software. In addition, of paramount importance in the age of remote work is ensuring that the facility can provide the necessary bandwidth (p. 27). If I have tech questions, I like to discuss them with the post facility ahead of us starting, including testing out new equipment—see (p. 28) for more example specs.

Post-Production Supervisor

If the post supervisor has already started, I'll talk with them. There's a high likelihood that they won't join full-time until the director's cut begins, but I like to keep them CC'd and involved as early as possible. We work very closely throughout the show, so I need to foster that relationship.

Once everything gets rolling, the post supervisor is one of the people I talk to frequently. They handle scheduling, budgeting, and communication between editorial and the studio—not just those in the cutting rooms. I'm talking about the sound team, music editor, DI, VFX, and title vendors. The post supervisor corrals us all. I love my post supervisors. They are my *everything*.

Workflow Calls

These are conference calls for departments to get on the same page at the start of the show. Across all calls, three constants focus fundamentally, on communication, expectations and logistically, how we'll function together. Once the workflows are set in place, I ensure I'm set up on any file transfer services we plan on using—more will be discussed in the Media Transfer section (p. 19).

Dailies Workflow Call

The primary focus of this specific call is for each department to discuss the day-to-day operations during production and ensure all departments agree on specs. We usually begin with audio; the sound mixer will confirm they're recording 24 bit 48 kHz Poly WAV files at 24 fps. Master Timecode (time of day, or "ToD") is often used to jam sync, and it's broadcast to smart slates and on-camera timecode receivers. This call is a good time to talk about track assignments and settle on an order. The mix track is typically Track 1, and I advocate for including all booms, ISOs (lavaliere mics), and playback (when it exists), which is pretty standard. The ISO track labeling follows character script names listed in the CSV sound report and exists in the dailies metadata (p. 47). I also ask for the specific microphone models: What mics are being used for booms, lavs, and plants? I want this for down the road when we're recording ADR.

Then we move on to the camera department, who should let you know if they plan on framing edge-to-edge or a fixed percentage center extraction for safety. The latter is standard and referred to as "common center;" it's intended for subtle reframing or stabilization in DI if needed (p. 245). A framing and focus chart (FFC) (see Figure 11.2) should be shot open-gate for each camera detailing the resolution, intended aspect ratio, and any center extraction details. I'll ask about how the DIT is handling color, how many LUTs we have (p. 242), and what the turnaround time for getting footage to the dailies lab will be. I request that all this information be noted on the slate.

The lab will discuss metadata (p. 92) and footage processing (they should also send a workflow pipeline document). They confirm that they'll ingest, sync, and render out dailies for editorial (DNxHD SQ), review and approval (h.264 - mix track only), and marketing (ProRes). When they ask for my preferences for metadata I send them a template bin with the appropriate bin view—something I mentioned earlier when outlining those introductory emails (p. 9). I ensure their Avid version is the same as ours and that their project is set up as a film project so we can perf slip when syncing dailies.

The lab will back up the original camera files in two sets: One master and one backup. Dailies will be uploaded to editorial. Once editorial accounts for the footage each day, I'll send an email confirming all footage has been received and the cards can be released (p. 121). If there's a discrepancy (p. 96) (such as a missing angle or audio file), they can go back and check the cards. Once resolved, the cards can be released back into circulation. Editorial will generate a Dailies Report and send an Avid bin with a matching stringout of dailies to the studio each morning—more details on this in the Dailies chapter (p. 121).

VFX Workflow Call(s)

On the dailies workflow call, I briefly bring up VFX. We discuss what the expectations are on set, whether there will be blue/green screens, or what sequences we know ahead of time will need significant VFX work. This conversation is largely with the production team and on-set VFX supervisor.

Later, after production wraps and just before we start turning over preliminary shots, we will have another VFX workflow call with our primary vendor(s). We introduce ourselves and discuss the VFX shots in the film on a macro scale. The total number of shots is estimated, and we talk about the schedule and important dates (like preview screenings and what we anticipate needing early temps for), as well as specs for temp VFX shots to include in the edit as we are cutting.

This is a good time to settle on a naming convention for shot codes (p. 190), how submissions will be delivered (which codecs and file types, what color pipeline, CSV data and formatting, etc.), and who the point people are for creative feedback. The production designer might want to be involved, for example, in which case it makes sense to ensure they have their own line of communication with the VFX vendor(s).

While we discuss some of the bigger VFX events in the film (and those are turned over before any formal spotting session), this workflow call is separate from the VFX spotting session (p. 44). That will happen later and is more specific on a shot-by-shot level. We give the vendor a heads-up on which shots are challenging when creating temp VFX, and what areas we expect to see more VFX in when we do a formal spotting session.

Preparation

On a logistical level, once I have the one-liners from both the assistant directors and script supervisor, I begin building a continuity (p. 42). The one-liners help keep everyone on the same page and the beauty of having a database (p. 69) allows me to keep everyone's scene descriptions in the same place. I like to build a continuity as early as possible because I use it as a sort of shoot progress tracker (see Figure 4.6). I use FileMaker to build my continuity (p. 72). For each scene, I'll have a scene number, sort order, and separate fields for all of the different departments' descriptions. I'll print out a copy for the editor to review and create their descriptions if they haven't already done so. All descriptions end up on the printed forms throughout the show (with changes as needed) and are used to create wall cards (p. 43).

Next, I'll create the Avid Project (p. 32). I usually pick a word, name, or code that's four or five characters long. For no reason in particular, I like to keep the project name in all caps, which is strange for me because I otherwise avoid using all caps because it looks like I'm shouting. If this book were the Avid Project, I'd probably call it "FRAME." More details about project organization (p. 32) and settings (p. 36) are in the Media Composer chapter (p. 31), but here's a short list of what I do when prepping the project (a more in-depth checklist can be downloaded from www.routledge.com/978103 2843285):

- Set up the Nexis (p. 22); create workspaces.
- Create the Avid Project (p. 32) and check Project Settings (p. 36).
- Get the database up and running (p. 63).
- Calibrate the rooms (speakers [p. 155] and displays [p. 243]).
- Create head and tail leader (p. 221); this is not time-sensitive, but I'll get a head start.
- Import music and sound effects, especially if I've already spotted them (see below).

- Import pre-viz, stunt-viz or any storyboards that might exist.
- **Run a workflow pipeline test** (download, ingest, export, encode and upload).

Holistic Preparation

One prep step I enjoy is taking time on my own to spot the script for sound effects, music (needle drops in particular, but also where we could use themes), locations, any potential stock or archival footage, and anything that could be a visual effect. I'll build a continuity of my own after reading the script because it helps me better understand the story and use my words to describe the scenes. Sometimes, I won't even respect the scene numbers for this, instead choosing to list the events that are important to the continuity of the story. This helps me prepare for the project by getting deep into the story we're telling.

Remote Work (Jump and Evercast)

When setting up the show, consider whether your team will work remotely or not. My preference is to work hybrid when possible. This gives the whole team more flexibility than being physically bound to a desk and improves work/life balance by allowing you to start an export and go home to have dinner with your family—then log in to quickly upload and send a file. Remote solutions have been available for some time but became more prominent and reliable out of necessity during the COVID-19 pandemic. Three approaches exist: Logging into a remote location and accessing media there; having local media that all team members keep updated; and accessing all project files and associated media in the cloud. As of this writing, all my experiences have involved the first two methods mentioned.

As far as logging into a remote location goes, Jump Desktop is the simplest and quickest in my experience and, so far, my favorite. It feels a lot like a fully-featured version of the native MacOS Screen Sharing app. The biggest downside at this point is the audio limitation. You can't monitor in 5.1 surround. Thankfully, stereo suffices in most instances. I don't trust monitoring the mix remotely, though. The other downside is that it's a little more lightweight regarding security than rival offerings like Amulet Hotkey and Teredici, which some studios might prefer. When it comes to working locally, I tend to handle everything manually. There are solutions such as DNAFabric, Lucidlink, Resilio Sync, and Salon Sync, which automate keeping local files in sync across remote locations. I can't speak to those personally as I haven't used them. Whatever you choose, be sure it's approved and tested before production begins.

My manual process entails locking off my current "1" folder by timestamping it and then sending it to the editor alongside a transfer bin. I'll do this, for example, after importing music and SFX or rendering a complicated VFX temp shot. It's the old way of doing it, and it works; be aware, however, that bin file sizes can get big. They compress well, so I advise zipping all your bins before emailing.

Jump Desktop

Jump allows a machine in my dining room to "puppeteer" a computer in the editing facility. Once you sign up for a Jump account, the post house will provide a software seat for you and grant your account access to specific computers. I ask for access to all computers associated with our show. It's sometimes helpful to be able to *jump* into the editor's machine and run it or help point out where something is in the project or timeline. I have used Jump in a completely remote setting as well as in a hybrid setting, and below are some tips for the latter:

Jump Desktop Hot Tips

- In Privacy settings, enable "Privacy Mode." This will black out the physical screens so no prying eyes can look on as you work on sensitive material.
- Conversely, enabling "Observe Mode" allows you to view another person's screen without disturbing them. In general settings, you can enable "Start in Observe Mode." Always ask permission before viewing someone else's screen, but this is a great way to shadow someone and learn in a remote environment.
- In Display settings, select "**Same resolution as remote computer (with retina).**" This will prevent the resolution from changing when you remote in, which can cause Media Composer to crash as it rearranges windows to fit the new display resolution.
- Jump will change your Avid audio monitoring format to stereo. When returning to your computer in person, be sure to switch back into 3.1 or 5.1 if not monitoring in stereo.
- Consider creating a "Remote" workspace in Media Composer, and when you log in on your remote station, switch to that. This is helpful if you only have one display at home but two or more at the office.

- **Command-Option-Tab** cycles through displays. If you want to drag a file from one screen to another, start dragging it, *then* cycle displays.
- Use **Command-Option-F** within Media Composer to toggle full-screen playback on/off.
- In Avid, disable hardware using the toggle in the timeline window and **Option-click** the volume icon in the Mac menu bar (or go to Sound in System Preferences) to change the output from your hardware breakout (in my case, BlackMagic UltraStudio) to "Jump Desktop Audio." Remember to restore from these settings when you're back in the office in person.
  - This is usually automatic, but I mention it here to keep it in the back of your mind for troubleshooting purposes.
  - If you're troubleshooting: Close out of Jump on the remote machine when not using it. One less variable to think about.

Jump Desktop Alternatives

As mentioned earlier, technically, you could use **MacOS's Screen Sharing App**, but that's uncommon. **Splashtop, AnyDesk,** and **TeamViewer** are all serviceable, but they're not my preference. The more robust remote solutions (meaning they utilize VPNs and potentially hardware encryption) include **Amulet HotKey, Teradici,** and **HP RGS**. Some of these are exclusively Windows-based.

Evercast

Evercast is a way for us to output our video signal to a virtual chat room and review edits with the team in real-time. Briefly, the way it works is that everyone has an Evercast account, and when they sign in, they can select a "room" to enter. Each "room" is the video output of any given Avid station (via NDI source, in my use cases). When users enter a room, they can see and hear a stream from that Avid (assuming it's broadcasting) and choose to show themselves and speak just like on Zoom or FaceTime. They, of course, can choose only to observe if they want as well.

This isn't just a tool for remote work; it's a solution I gauge the need for at the beginning of a show. We might want a secure virtual meeting room for any team member to use. It can be used for sessions with a composer or VFX team. Everyone can annotate the screen, a feature that's helpful for VFX review sessions (p. 205).

The standalone Evercast application has evolved rapidly. You can use it as it was originally intended—creating a scene and sending an

NDI source to it. However, there's so much more flexibility now, including the ability for any participant to securely upload a file, which everyone can review in sync. In addition, anyone can share their screen with the whole room! Annotations can be made on top of the whole broadcast, regardless of the source. These are just a few examples.

Evercast Hot Tips

- Render all effects before your broadcast, if possible. You might not have time, but this rules out any potential Avid playback issues, such as stuttering due to unrendered effects.
- There's always a delay between what Avid is playing and what's on the broadcast. I use headphones with Avid while broadcasting and keep the Evercast broadcast muted.
- Try to use a bitrate of 3000 kbps. Go no lower than 1500 kbps; the image won't look as good.
  - Adjust this if there's lag or stutter.
- Broadcast in a higher FPS (60), so it's less noticeable if there are dropped frames. This is because your source is (likely) playing back at 24 fps.
- In Avid, make sure you're monitoring in stereo. As of publication, Evercast will accept a 5.1 stream, but it won't downmix it. So, it'll end up taking the left and right channels only.
- There are a few great features within the Evercast app under the "Stream" option. You can share your screen and upload a file that anyone on the call can start and stop (and it's deleted when you stop sharing the file) stream from DeckLink, NDI, or even your *phone*!
- Annotations are super helpful. By default, everyone has the same color, so you may want to change yours when the session begins.
  - There's a trashcan icon in the annotations toolbar that erases *only* **your annotations**. I prefer to use this instead of the eraser because it's faster and ensures no remnant annotations exist when moving on to another note.
  - I generally clear my annotations as soon as I receive confirmation that my feedback has been received and understood.

Evercast Alternatives

ClearView Flex is an alternative; however, it does require additional hardware. **Zoom** can be used in a pinch, although its security may be sensitive. Avid has released a new feature called **Avid Huddle**, which is a Microsoft Teams-based solution that's built directly into the application. It functions similarly to Evercast, and while nascent, it is more tightly integrated.

Media Transfer (Aspera)

Setting up a method to securely, reliably, and continuously send and receive media is imperative when setting up the show. The studio will likely have a system in place already, but you'll need to create accounts, sign in, and ensure everything is functioning properly. Much the same way the Avid Media Composer is the norm for NLEs, IBM's Aspera has been the preeminent service in my experience.

Aspera

IBM owns Aspera, and it comes in a few "flavors." I've mostly used Aspera Faspex, but in recent years, Aspera has introduced "Aspera on Cloud." This modern web-based UI uses Aspera Connect and allows you to upload, organize, and send files in much the same way you would with Dropbox or Google Drive. **Aspera Connect** is the helper app that facilitates file transfers behind the scenes. You can also use it to set upload/download speed limit defaults based on your connection speed and adjust it manually if a transfer is ping-ponging.

I tend to use Faspex through Aspera Drive, which is set up with a dailies account that auto-refreshes every minute. I request that the dailies tech use the same passphrase for all dailies Aspera transfers (this is standard protocol) so automatically downloaded files can be decrypted upon download completion.

My typical workflow for Aspera on Cloud is to create folders and subfolders that mirror the Turnovers workspace on the Nexis. For recurring collaborative work, like with a music editor, for example, I share a folder with them specifically and have "to" and "from" subfolders within that. I can then sign into Aspera Connect on our transfer station and set up a **one-way sync** so that whenever a file is uploaded from the music editor, it downloads automatically on our side. I emphasize one-way sync because it allows me to move the files out of the auto-download directory without Aspera re-downloading them. I like this because I know that if a file is still in that directory, I haven't organized it on the Nexis or imported it into Avid yet. As far as files and packages go, I tend to upload files and then "send in package." This allows me to organize the files in the workspace before sending them.

File transfers can be initiated from the Aspera Drive MacOS Menu Bar or, preferably, through the Faspex web browser. The latter is more flexible in allowing upload and download notifications. Also, depending on how the system administrator has their network set up, you might only need to add people to the Aspera workgroup if you want *them to be able to send files to you.* You should be able to send files to anybody without them being added to your workgroup. **Always send files encrypted with a passphrase.**

If you have any issues with Aspera, ask your facility to check their firewall settings.

Aspera Alternatives

Other similar services to IBM's **Aspera** include Sohonet's **Filerunner,** Signiant's **Media Shuttle, MASV,** and **WeTransfer** (in a pinch). Studios are looking for services that provide "encryption at rest," which Aspera certainly offers, but WeTransfer does not. Some departments will set up SFTP (SSH File Transfer Protocol) servers, allowing you to use apps like CyberDuck or FileZilla to transfer files to them.

Hard Drives

When Aspera can't be used, an encrypted hard drive will be the way to go. The studio usually provides the hard drives or, at least, the funds to purchase them.

Backup Drive: A large backup drive will be needed for the Nexis (p. 46). The backup drive should be a Raid that can hold all the media on the Nexis. This allows it to be used to rebuild the Nexis in the event of an emergency, as a working drive on the stage during the mix, and as a deliverable upon wrap.

Shuttle Drives: Make sure they have fast enough I/O and storage. At the time of this writing, a USB 3.1 Gen 2 SSD was my choice. A Thunderbolt drive with a 7200 RPM drive is a waste: The hard drive averages 180 MBps, while Thunderbolt 3 caps out at 40 GBps. Usually, 1 TB is enough, and 4 TB is great. Generally, I use these drives when we're making a DCP, when we have screenings, or if I need to send a lot of media to a department.

Thumb Drives: I use these for my daily backup and quick transfers within the editorial rooms. Sometimes, it's the fastest way to get files from one machine to another, especially if AirDrop is unavailable.

Formatting and Encrypting Hard Drives

All of these drives need to be software encrypted, at the very least. This can be done through Disk Utility. The alternative to software encryption is hardware encryption, for which Apricorn makes great drives. These have their manual to set up, but once up and running, you simply plug it in, punch in the code, hit the unlock key, and you're good to go. It functions like any other drive.

When formatting drives, APFS is preferred for flash storage; otherwise, MacOS Extended (Journaled) is fine. If MacOS's Disk Utility is only showing APFS options, it's likely displaying only the logical volume within the APFS container, not the physical drive. Change the view option in the upper left to "show all devices" from "show only volumes." Highlight the physical drive and format that. It should let you change it to something other than APFS.

Review and Approval

Review and approval platforms are heavily used during dailies to distribute footage to all team members. They're also extensively used throughout the post-production process to securely share cuts with people who are not in the cutting room. These should be set up before dailies start coming in. I will now list a few prominent platforms (alphabetically) for your reading pleasure:

- Clear (fka "DAX")
- Core
- Dropbox
- Flow Capture (fka "Moxion")
- Frame.io
- PIX
- Vimeo

As of this writing (and in my experience), PIX is perhaps the most prominent and frequently used in the industry. Check out the Outputs and Turnovers chapter for notes on file specs (p. 224). Regardless of the platform you're using, there are a few things to keep in mind.

Permissions

When you start on a show, the studio should spin up a new account specifically for it. There might be a few directories already created, one of which is named "Editorial." Ideally, this is a **private folder that no one has access to except for the editorial team**. This allows you to manage cuts for review privately without prying eyes. If such a folder doesn't exist, speak with an administrator and try to set it up.

File Organization

During production, the lab will upload dailies into a separate, private dailies folder. Depending on what is established on the Dailies Workflow Call (p. 12), either you or they will distribute the playlist.

I upload nearly everything to the private "Editorial" folder, further organizing it within subfolders. This generally matches the file structure in my Outputs directory on the Nexis. If I'm not uploading to the Editorial folder, it's usually a longplay into a "Cuts" folder ahead of a preview screening. Once the file has been uploaded, I'll let the studio know. They might take care of distributing the cut, and if not, I'll ask them to create distro groups. Distro groups make it easier for me to send to large groups of people without having to remember all their names.

Sending Media

Depending on your platform, you might have an option to generate a "playlist" or "review link" as opposed to sending a file directly. These options act as a vessel, allowing you to swap out the files within, even after sending. I like this functionality, as it allows me to quietly update an asset or revoke access if anything changes suddenly.

Nexis

Nexis is Avid's brand name for their shared storage server, which allows their proprietary bin-locking technology to be employed. It's scalable, robust and fast. Alternatives include offerings from Facilis, EditShare, and SNS (Studio Network Solutions), all of which can emulate bin locking. Avid's Nexis is more commonplace in larger productions and post houses.

The typical Nexis size I've used is 20 TB if not 40 TB. Remember, some of that space will be lost to drive protection. I've found, as seen in a few pages, that a whole show can take up around 12 TB of space. There are many factors—number of shoot days, the number of cameras shot, how much slow motion is planned, how VFX heavy the film is, and which editing codec will be used are good examples. The numbers I present are an average for reference from my experiences.

Users and Permissions

If your show gets a dedicated Nexis, you'll probably be able to administrate it. If not, ask if you can be set up as part of a "team;" teams allow you to administrate your little corner of the facility's Nexis. I'll create one user per Avid. Each is password protected, and I'll set the Nexis client app to Auto Log-In on our machines. Pro Tip: The Nexis client can almost always be on the latest version. At this point, I'll also name the computers in the Sharing tab of System Preferences. My computer is usually named "zJared". I'll prepend a "z" to all usernames to sort them together.

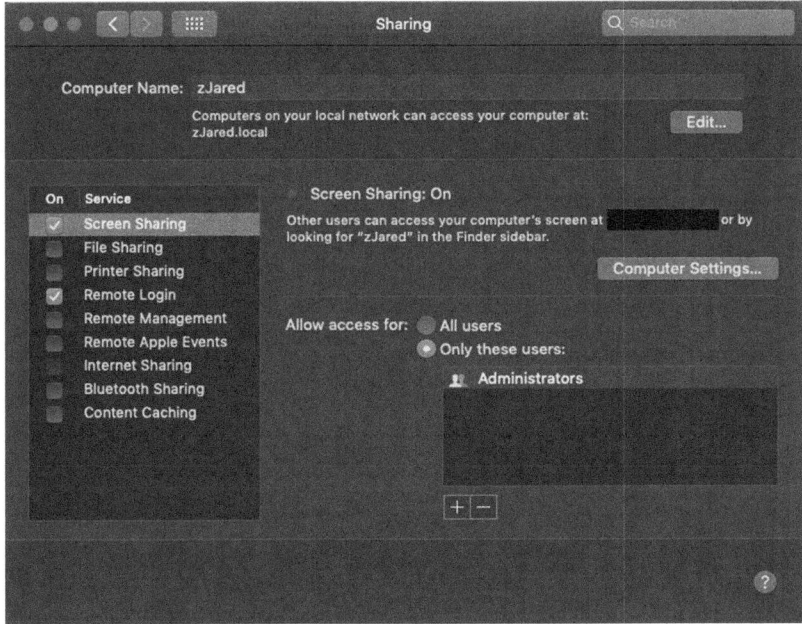

Figure 2.1 Sharing tab of MacOS System Preferences with modified computer name.

This is helpful when looking at the project user folders on the Finder level, the MediaFiles folders, finding our computers on the network, and seeing who has a bin open at a glance. The post facility will likely build the machine from a disk image, and the default name could be something like "admin" or "Avid182," which isn't very helpful when you're in the Avid project and trying to see who has the bin lock on the bin you need.

I'll choose to restrict write access to certain drives for the editor. This is to simplify where generated media can go. For example, there is no chance that the editor can accidentally import music or render media to the ADR_SND or Dailies Media drives because they don't have write access. This is an easy thing to change in a pinch if it's needed, but I've found it best to remove the variable altogether when possible.

Managed Media vs Linked Media

It's worth noting that I primarily work with Managed Media instead of Linked Media. Managed Media refers to the files within the Avid MediaFiles directory, which Media Composer creates upon importing a file. Linked Media is anything Media Composer references but does not re-encode, re-wrap, or copy into its managed media directory. As you'll see below, I store the original files I receive on their respective workspaces, but I also import them; hence, the media that Avid is reading resides in Avid MediaFiles.

It's possible that, in the future, as technology continues to evolve, we will embrace workflows that allow us to work with a mixture of these two kinds of media. Currently, working with Managed Media is faster and more reliable than working with Linked Media. I'd advise against working with a mix of Managed and Linked Media, as it can introduce unwanted variables into your workflow. Tools like MDVx (p. 222) can help you tame the Avid MediaFiles. Keeping the source files available on their respective workspaces and organized by the date they were received makes it easy to track down source files when needed.

Workspaces

This is an example of a Nexis partitioned into 12 workspaces. You can get away with fewer (generally, the fewer, the better for performance reasons), but this is how I like organizing the show. The figure shows how I visually lay out the drive icons on my desktop.

Here's a more detailed breakdown of how I decide what goes on each workspace. I list the allotted space along with the total amount of data that I averagely store on that workspace upon wrap:

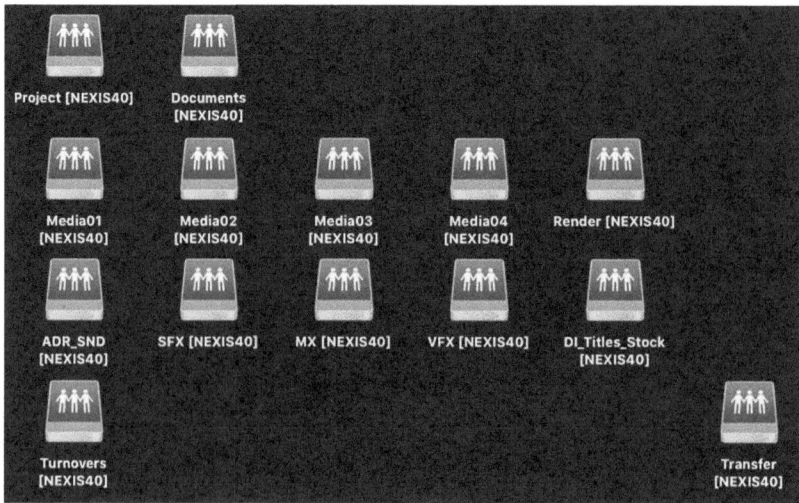

Figure 2.2 Avid Nexis partitions as displayed on desktop.

Project

Drive Size: 500 GB—Typical Usage: 250 GB

This only contains the Avid project and its associated Attic. Check your bin settings (p. 37) to manage your Attic size. If you run out of space on this drive, Avid will throw an error when anyone tries to save a bin (p. 59). Alarming at first, but just increase the workspace size, and the issue should be resolved. *This is the only workspace that should have **two-disk protection***.

I also keep a separate "Archive Project" on this drive for old screenings, outputs, turnovers, and work bins. The Archive Project can be used to siphon off some of the large, older bins that are rarely needed, take up a fair amount of room, and considerably slow down a daily Avid project backup. There is no media on this drive.

Documents

Drive Size: 100 GB—Typical Usage: 50 GB

Contains everything paperwork-related, like dailies reports, spec sheets, continuities, art department files, encoding presets and watermark (p. 210) files. This drive does not usually contain any media used in Media Composer.

Media Drives

Drive Size: 2 TB—Typical Usage: 1.9 TB (capped off)

Media 01, 02, etc., are for storing Dailies media. I cap them off at 2 TB each, which feels like an appropriate amount of space, and I create them as needed. For reference, we shot almost 67 hours of footage on

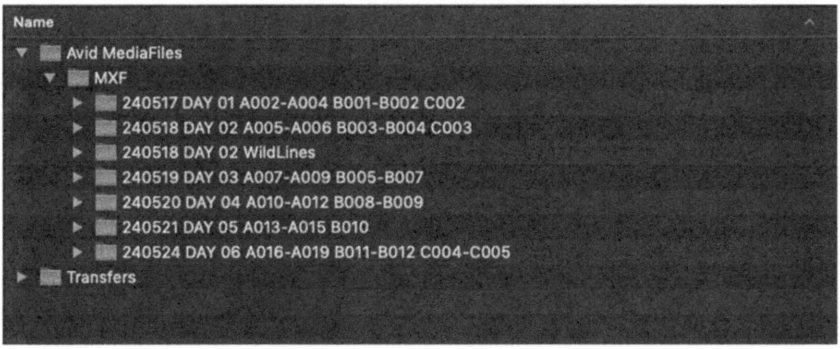

Name
▼ Avid MediaFiles
　▼ MXF
　　▶ 240517 DAY 01 A002-A004 B001-B002 C002
　　▶ 240518 DAY 02 A005-A006 B003-B004 C003
　　▶ 240518 DAY 02 WildLines
　　▶ 240519 DAY 03 A007-A009 B005-B007
　　▶ 240520 DAY 04 A010-A012 B008-B009
　　▶ 240521 DAY 05 A013-A015 B010
　　▶ 240524 DAY 06 A016-A019 B011-B012 C004-C005
▶ Transfers

Figure 2.3 Filepath/folder structure of a dailies media drive.

one show across 50 days and ended up with under 4 TB of DNxHD SQ media stored on three media drives.

Render

Drive Size: 1 TB—Typical Usage: 700 GB (expand as needed)

Render drives don't need to be separated into video, audio or editor and assist. One render partition for all is enough for a smaller team. If you go beyond four total editors (counting anyone with an Avid, like the VFX editor and an apprentice editor), then you should consider a secondary Render drive.

ADR_SND

Drive Size: 1 TB—Typical Usage: 400 GB

Any media from the sound department, including ADR, temp ADR, sound design elements, stems, and stems from the mix stage (p. 171).

DI_Titles_Stock

Drive Size: 1 TB—Typical Usage: 100 GB

This is anything from DI, title houses, or stock footage. Confidence checks (p. 252) can be linked instead of imported. The same applies to any audience capture footage from test screenings, which is also stored on this partition.

SFX

Drive Size: 1 TB—Typical Usage: 200 GB

This workspace is dedicated to our temp sound effects library. Temp SFX encompasses all imported sound effects that we expect the sound editorial department to ultimately replace. Some editors have libraries that they bring with them from show to show, which is why I like to separate SFX from other sound files, like the ones on SND_ADR and MX.

MX

Drive Size: 1 TB—Typical Usage: 200 GB

The Music drive contains all temp music, demos from the composer, and temp edits from music editors.

Turnovers

Drive Size: 4 TB — Typical Usage: 3.2 TB

I keep both Outputs and Turnovers on this drive. This also includes mixdowns created for preview screenings. Older files can be deleted, but I tend to hang on to files for as long as we can store them.

VFX

Drive Size: 1 TB — Typical Usage: 700 GB

This stores all incoming VFX shots organized by vendor. I also keep round-tripped temps in a "temp VFX" directory on this drive for anything exported from Avid to third-party compositing applications.

The Post Facility

When we first tour rooms, the editor and I discuss the merits of each option. We consider where the rooms are in relation to each other, other shows in the facility and what bandwidth is available, among other factors. I like to mock up possible layouts, which both the editor and the post facility appreciate. It's just a Photoshop diagram of where the furniture should go in the room (p. 29). Editors are different, and I like my layout to mirror theirs whenever possible.

Bandwidth

It's vital to confirm that the facility can provide the bandwidth you need. Increased bandwidth can impact the cost of the cutting room. Considerations should be made depending on whether your team is remote, how frequently files must be sent and received, and what service is physically available at your location. Most post facilities can offer great speeds, but ad hoc cutting rooms on location could be limited. During dailies, you might be able to request a temporary bandwidth increase, which will allow you to download footage faster (seeing as you'll be receiving a lot of footage regularly).

Equipment List

Below is an **example** of an equipment list I would provide (hardware and software) to the post house. This is constantly updating as new technology is released, and depends on budget; however, the core requirements haven't changed—CPU, 4 displays (two computer, one reference, and one client), speakers, and a breakout box.

Hardware

- Mac Pro (Late 2013) MacOS 10.14.6 (Mojave) 2.7 GHz, 12 Core Xeon E5, 64 GB RAM, FirePro D700 6 GB, 1 TB Storage
  - Also, a transfer machine: A standalone system that anyone on the team with outputs or large imports can use without tying up their main CPU. I use a Mac Studio or equivalent.
- 32" Computer displays (x2)
- 24" Reference Monitor
- 65" OLED Client Monitor
- Breakout Box (I have used a BlackMagic UltraStudio 4K Mini on many shows)
- 5.1 setup: 5.1 controllers, 5 speakers and a subwoofer
- Powered USB 3.1 hub
- Printer

Software

- Avid Media Composer Ultimate (latest version compatible with our OS)
  - This includes ScriptSync (p. 51), PhraseFind, and Symphony options.
- Avid Nexis Client (latest version)
- Boris Sapphire, Continuum and Mocha Pro plug-ins (p. 173)
- iZotope RX Advanced
- Filemaker Pro (p. 63)
- Apple Compressor
- Adobe Creative Cloud (specifically Acrobat, Photoshop, After Effects, and Media Encoder)
- Utilities: ChronoSync (p. 147), Jump Desktop (p. 15), MDVx (p. 222), Sublime Text (p. 57), Shutter Encoder, and VLC

MacOS System Settings I like to change:

- General: Dark theme, blue highlight color.
- Desktop/Screen Saver: Space images, mountain ranges, start screensaver after 10 minutes.
- Enable Night Shift.
  - This is a controversial setting, as it messes with the color on the computer displays. I can always disable it; even if I don't, this setting doesn't affect the reference or client monitors. I find that enabling Night Shift makes looking at the screen all day easier by reducing eyestrain.
- Security: Require password immediately.

- Keyboard: Full keyboard access uses Tab to move between All Controls, add app shortcuts for AvidMediaComposer (Mute/Unmute clips, f15 shutdown), and uncheck f14/15 under "Display."
- Sound: Alert volume south of center. Output is through the BlackMagic IO.
- Network: x3 Ethernet (dual connected Nexis, line out to web) + Wi-Fi for AirDrop file transfer.
  - All networking is contingent on meeting content security requirements.
- Finder Preferences: New window shows computer, open folders in new windows (not tabs), search current folder only, show connected servers on desktop, and add the computer as a location to the sidebar.
- TXT, EDL and ALE files open with Sublime Text (I avoid TextEdit—just my preference)

Furniture, Environment, and Layout

It's common to find variable height desks, Herman Miller Aeron chairs, bookshelves, a locking cabinet, up-lights and couches in most cutting rooms. Inquire about a whiteboard (or a corkboard; but whiteboards allow for easier annotations and work better with sticky notes) for yourself and your editor; a huge one can be used for wall cards (p. 143). Other furniture can be requested as needed, and when the post house doesn't supply certain luxuries (like a recliner, for instance), it's not unusual to bring in furniture of your own.

The things I find myself adding more often are pillows for the couch and additional soft uplighting. I install my own set of smart lightbulbs, which are on a timer, and they're programmed to be soft white by

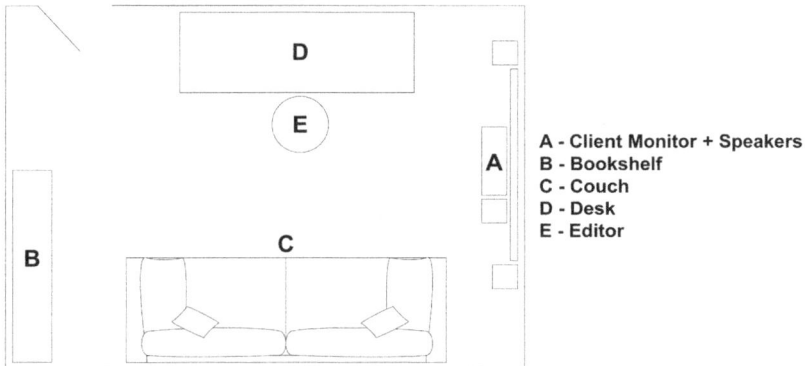

Figure 2.4 Example layout of an editorial office. See website for additional layout examples, figures 2.5 and 2.6.

default. They turn on before I arrive in my office and turn off late at night. In addition to making the atmosphere calm and welcoming, there's an added functionality to these smart lights: I have a remote that I give to the editor, which, when they press it, turns my lights blue. I've found this to be a sublime alternative to shouting between rooms, and it doesn't take the editor out of the flow of their work by requiring them to text me. Just one button press!

Part of creating a welcoming space is ensuring it's conducive to conversation. I like to sit so I am facing the wall with the door, with the client monitor to my right and the couch behind me, preferably perpendicularly.

I use a chair that swivels so I can review footage or cuts with anyone sitting on the couch. Another setup I've used is a more theatrical layout wherein my desk is placed at the very back of the room with the couch in front of it, both facing the same direction: Toward the client monitor. It was a great setup for monitoring 5.1 sound and presenting a cut, but I did find it more difficult to connect with whoever was on the couch since the back of their head would be facing me. There's no one way to set up a room, but these two examples might inform layouts you'd like to try to add some considerations to your plans.

3 Avid Media Composer

Let's take a moment to discuss the tool we'll primarily be working with: Avid Media Composer. What a name for a piece of software, am I right? At first blush, it's mildly musical. Then it's a little opaque, perhaps rigid. "**MEDIA**" sounds so very blunt. It's a thing of beauty, and the more I think about the name of the program I use day in and day out, the more I appreciate the thoughtfulness of its name. What is a sequence if not a composition? And what are we composing? That's right, video, audio… It's all media, baby! It's poetic!

As you're aware, this book is not an introduction to Media Composer. You likely already know Media Composer. When you first approached it, I bet there was palpable apprehension. There's a steep learning curve and a plethora of options. When I think about Media Composer and its limitations or quirks, I also consider the software's origins. It was built to bridge the gap between film and digital workflows. "Filler" is a concept uniquely tied to film. Managed media must reside on the root level of a hard drive. Clips can't be moved in the timeline during playback. These are concepts I embrace, and I'd encourage you to as well.

The process of editing film used to take much more time. Every time a cut was made, you'd have to walk to a film library and locate a piece of film. While the downside to this was the time it took to keep trims organized, the upside was that the same time could be used to think and reflect. This was a limitation that was embraced. The advent of digital non-linear editing has sped everything up, and there's less time to *think* now than ever. You know how I mentioned that Media Composer won't let you move clips in the timeline during playback? There's something to be said about taking your hands off the keyboard, kicking back from the desk, and watching your work without interruption. It gives you a second to think. In other Non-Linear Editors (NLEs), I've been guilty of being the guy who would hit play and then start nudging clips or adjusting keyframes. It was chaos, akin to laying tracks down in front of a moving train. I never gave myself time to think. The point is Avid Media Composer has been around for

DOI: 10.4324/9781003516491-4

a while. Many institutions rely on it for the infrastructure it provides, let alone the collaboration it allows and how robust it is. Good news, too: It keeps getting better every day.

Media Composer is purpose-built and evolving more rapidly than ever. As I've revised these notes over the years, so much has changed: The addition of the Universal Media Engine (p. 47), deeper integration with Pro Tools, the introduction of an SDK panel (p. 47) (the full potential of which has yet to be realized)—the User Interface. Certain ways of working will become obsolete with the introduction of new workflows and technologies. However, the bones of Avid Media Composer aren't likely to change, and that's one of the things I admire most about it; there's consistency, reliability, and peace of mind, knowing that there are resources from 20 years ago that are still relevant today. Some consider this outdated; I think it's the opposite—and part of the reason this particular software continues to endure and is trusted by institutions.

Of course, there are other NLEs out there, and everyone has their preference. At the end of the day, Media Composer is just that, a tool. We all use the best tool for the job based on what we know how to use. I've used other NLEs, and there are things I like about them. I spend most of my time professionally in Avid Media Composer, so that's the tool I will focus on. I'm not trying to convince you to use MY tool of choice—though doing so might make it a bit easier to understand what follows—but some elements can be translated to other NLEs if you're using something else.

Project Structure and Organization

Much of what I discuss in this chapter derives from my experiences working with several editors. This is the first of many instances where I emphatically encourage you to **check with your editor** about their preferences—in this case, to see how they want to organize everything. I usually go with numerics, as seen in Figure 3.1.

There's generally one folder that corresponds to each Nexis partition. Bins always sort the above folders, and I like to keep the root of the project free of bins when possible.

During dailies, the scene bins that need to be viewed will stay at the root level and bubble to the top. When the footage within them is viewed and marked, the scene bins get organized into the "Dailies by SCENE" folder. Otherwise, the only bin that stays at the root of the project is "•to [editor]", which serves as a transfer bin for assistants to quickly drop sequences into for the editor to grab (and vice-versa).

Any incoming items are organized into their appropriate subfolders, but anything going *out* gets categorized under Outputs or Turnovers.

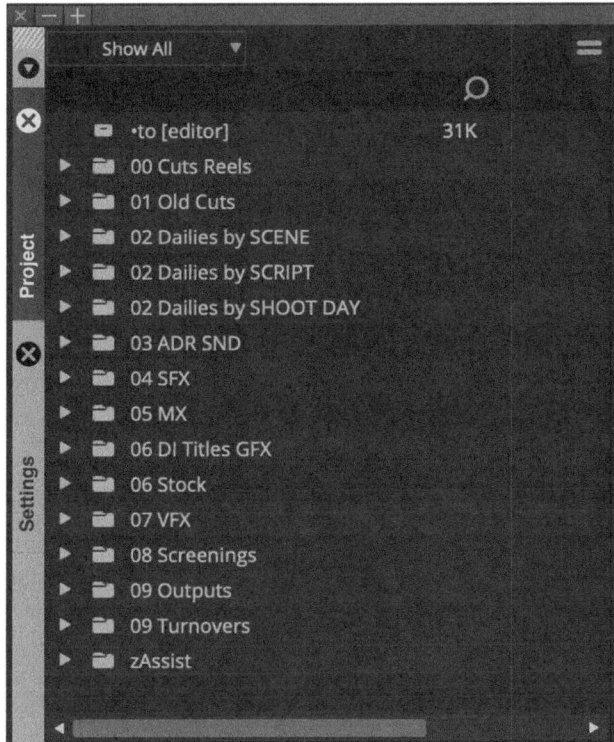

Figure 3.1 Example Avid Media Composer project structure for a feature film.

This will be explained below, but that's the general idea. Cuts, Scenes, Assets, and Exports.

•To [editor] (Transfer Bin)

There is always one "•to [editor]" bin at the top of the project, where I put sequences for the editor to review, cut in, or store somewhere else. This makes it easy for them to find what they need, especially in time-sensitive situations. I **always** drag a *copy* of whatever sequence I'm sending to the editor and then add the date to a date or notes bin column. I store the original in my "work archive" bin so the editor knows they can delete whatever is in the transfer bin when they're done with it, and nothing will be gone forever.

Also, I **never** clone or duplicate a master, sub, or group clip into the "•to [editor]" bin. This is because if the clip ever gets deleted; matchback will break (repairable, but a pain—you'd have to use the Media Tool to restore the clip in question, etc.) I *always* cut a clip into a sequence and copy the sequence into the bin.

Cuts Reels

The Cuts folder contains the current reel bins. I've worked in two ways that are equally as effective, just different in their organization. Versioning is expanded on in a later chapter (p. 138), but one way that has worked is having one bin per reel and maintaining one active current version of that reel at the top of the bin. Older versions of the reel live in the same bin, sorted below.

The other way in which I've worked is where we have one **folder** for each version and one bin per reel within that. This entails duplicating the sequence and adding the date every time a sequence is modified. When versioning up, a new folder is created along with new reel bins, and the most current reel sequences get duplicated into them. In this case, old cuts have their entire folder moved into the "01 Old Cuts" folder.

In either instance, the reels are displayed using a bin view which displays the sequence name, comments, duration, modification date, and Last Frame of Action (LFOA). If these bins get too big, I talk with the editor and move old versions into the "01 Old Cuts" folder. Some editors like to keep "Experiments" or "Alternate Cuts" bins for each phase: Directors Cut, Preview 1, Preview 2, etc. These hold alts, as outlined when discussing managing alternate edits (p. 136).

Dailies

I like to have three folders, all sorted under the number 2: "Dailies by SCENE," "Dailies by SCRIPT," and "Dailies by Shoot Day." The Shoot Day folder has the original dailies bins from the lab. The subclips generated from the master clips in these bins are sorted and organized into the Scene bins, which live in "Dailies by SCENE." Along with the subclips, Scene bins contain notes from dailies paperwork and early alternate cuts of the scene created during dailies.

On projects where we utilize script-based editing (p. 51), once these Scene bins are populated, the subclips are then used in script files, which are stored in "Dailies by SCRIPT." Each scene gets its script file, with exceptions being made depending on how sequences were shot. If multiple scenes were shot contiguously, I make one script that spans that range. This hierarchy of "Shoot Day > Scene > Script" is important to maintain matchback consistency. For example, using master clips from the Shoot Day bins in the Scripts will bypass the Scene bins (which have all the notes) when matching back.

ADR_SND

I keep a "temp ADR" bin in ADR_SND, and it also contains all ADR by Character (one folder containing a bin for each character) from recorded sessions. Anything received from the sound department or the Dub Stage is also organized here. This includes temp mix stems and bounces (a "bounce" is an exported section of audio) from the sound designer. I also have a subfolder for production sound where I import any production sound as needed during dailies. Each sound roll gets its bin.

SFX

SFX contains our temp sound effect libraries and anything temp imported on the show. Some editors will have bins and associated media from their libraries; others will rely on you to source sound effects. Some editors prefer to have bins organized per show they've worked on, as they associate certain sound effects with those shows and know where to look for certain sounds. They might fully utilize custom bin columns and have detailed, searchable notes. Other editors prefer to have multiple categorized bins for each type of sound effect (Ambience, Animals, Crowds, Foley, Nature, etc.).

MX

The music folder contains **all** music (temp and otherwise). I keep subfolders of our temp library next to subfolders of deliveries from the music editor and the composer. I also store music review sessions in this folder for when we receive new music cues, and we must cut them in or conform them before cutting them into the reel. More about music review sessions in the Audio chapter (p. 169).

DI Titles GFX

Anything from the DI lab or title house is kept here, as are any graphic elements (temp or otherwise). This includes confidence QuickTimes (p. 252), logos from production companies and the studio, temp titles, and graphics treatments.

Stock

Stock footage gets a folder because it can get pretty busy, depending on the show. I usually create one bin per source (Getty, Pond5, Shutterstock, FilmSupply, etc.) and then subclip the stock master clips to organize them into more content-specific bins. I think of this akin to dailies, wherein "Dailies by Shoot Day::Stock Source," and "Dailies by

Scene::Stock Content." Color coding clips help differentiate temp and unlicensed shots from the high-resolution, purchased shots. I mention this because some people may elect to create separate bins for temp vs licensed, but I tend not to do this.

VFX

This starts out containing anything that comes from an on-set VFX supervisor. Then, as we continue cutting, I have a "temp VFX" subfolder containing one bin per scene for which I do significant temp VFX. It's great for working in while the editor is working in the reels, storing presets, and saving old versions for reference.

As we receive versions of VFX shots from the vendor(s), **I'll create one bin per vendor** containing all VFX version submissions. I find that there's no need to separate by delivery date—by using a custom bin view, it's possible to sort by creation date (which is when a version was imported and by the transitive property when it was likely delivered).

Screenings, Outputs, and Turnovers

Any time we have a screening—internally, at the studio, or a preview—a copy gets saved in the Screenings folder.

An **Output** is anything that's destined for a review and approval platform. Sometimes, there will be a crossover of screenings and PIX uploads, and a duplicate will exist in both locations for posterity.

Turnovers get separated into subfolders by department and consist of anything that is to be worked on by another department. These bins can be archived outside the project to reduce bloat once we get deeper into the show.

zAssist

A folder for all assistants to store whatever they like. I use it for my work bins, notes bins, archive bins, etc. I even have some effect presets saved there. I also like to keep leader, mattes, and calibration materials in bins within this folder.

Avid Project Settings

I like to check certain settings at the beginning of every project. They vary between user, site, and project-level settings. Below, in alphabetical order, are the settings I use and my reasoning behind choosing them.

Audio Project

I typically work in 3.1 or 5.1, so I set that up in this dialog box and ensure it's set to use PCM-MXF media. Under "Effects," I typically set the default to Equal Power, which adds 3 dB to the dissolve curve. The difference between options and implications of your choice are discussed in the Audio chapter (p. 157).

Bin Settings

Auto-save every three minutes (inactivity of 1 second) with forced auto-save at five minutes. Max files in Attic set to 2000 (max versions 100). One thing to note is that while not everyone on your team needs to have the same autosave settings, they should all have the same "Maximum Versions" setting to avoid wiping out archived bins from other users who have their settings at a higher number.

The other setting to note is "Always keep at least one version in Attic." It's wise to keep this *unchecked* because it can lead to a bloated Attic since it'll save one version of *every* bin, even bins that were created temporarily or erroneously. Afraid of losing bins? Make sure to back up your whole project every day (p. 146). Think of the Avid Attic as a buffer, not an archive.

Using the above settings: (**Autosave@3 x MaxVers@100**) = **300 minutes (5 hours) of backups for open bins.** Between these settings, daily backups, and a consistently refreshed and archived Attic (if needed), you should never lose more than three minutes of work at most. Personally, it's been years since I've lost any work. The downside to these particular settings is the frequency of the "Save As" dialog

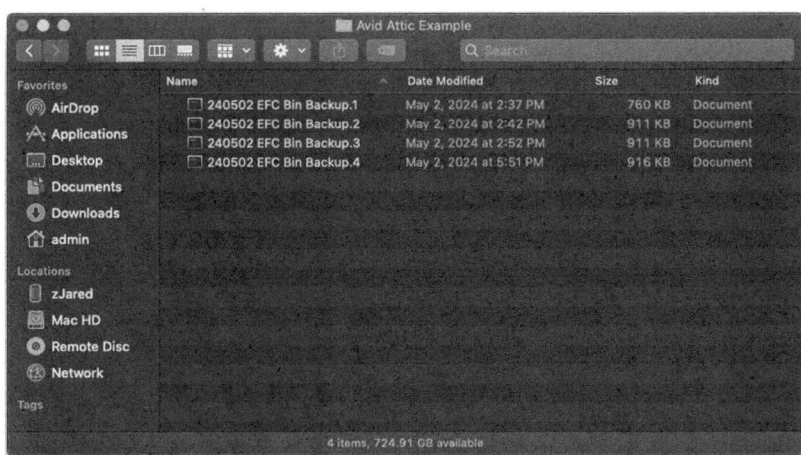

Figure 3.2 Avid Attic on the Finder level.

box pop-ups when working with a locked bin. There's a setting to override that pop-up, but I wouldn't risk that (because I'd *absolutely* accidentally lose work). I'd sooner open a locked bin, take a copy of what I want to reference or use, and close that locked bin.

Composer Settings

I disable "Auto-enable Source Tracks" when working on a project where the subclips have all audio tracks, not just the mix track.

This ensures that after setting up dailies, not all tracks are re-enabled each time a clip is loaded in the source monitor. The mix track will remain selected, and others will not. It's advised that all users in the project match this setting because if one person has it turned on and loads a clip, they essentially reset the enabled tracks.

Mask Margins

This is set in the Format tab instead of the Project or User tabs. I match our Aspect Ratio and then check the Video Output settings to ensure that Mask Margins are applied. Then, in the Composer window, I can set the target mask on the record side to "Black Mask." I don't usually apply Mask Margins in the Composer window personally because I like to see the metadata and the Mask Margins are applied in Fullscreen Playback and on my reference and client monitors. Also related to Mask Margins, I then set up some export presets that enable usage of the Mask Margins (despite not using these either; reasoning explained later [p. 214]).

Media Cache

I believe Media Composer relies more on the CPU than the GPU and creating a media cache can reduce latency when playing back in the timeline. The GPU might also affect how Media Composer handles effects. The larger the cache, the better the performance. It's a good idea to clear the cache from time to time.

Recommendations for any system with 64 GB of RAM or more	
Thumbnails	1024 RAM, 2048 disk
Source Browser	1024 RAM, 2048 disk
Video Memory	8 GB
Audio	1 GB
File	8 GB

Media Creation

I usually set everything to write to the Render drive across the board, and I ensure that it's all MXF media (not OP-1a or WAV—again, this is per my usual workflow). I set the codec to match the dailies. The import location changes frequently, but I usually access that via the Source Browser window (which also contains a shortcut to the Import Settings window).

Search Index

This may not be in the Settings window, but it's definitely in the bottom left corner of the Find window (see figure 3.3, below). Nowadays, the default is to store the search index locally. Check to ensure this is the case because there's another default option: Project Default. If this is selected, a search index will be created within each user's user folder at the project level. This can bloat project size and slow down the project. Keeping the index stored locally on the machine allows for faster recall and smaller projects.

Transcript Settings

Upon project creation, there's an option to "Include new bins in transcription," which is checked by default. Depending on how much you plan on using transcripts, you may want to disable this and transcribe as needed (particularly if you're importing a lot of non-transcribable audio, like music and sound effects). Bins can be toggled on for

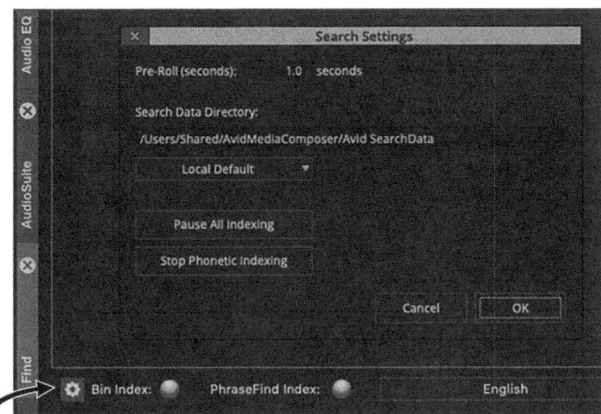

**Click the cog in the Find Tool
to open "Search Settings" window**

Figure 3.3 Find Window with search index stored locally.

inclusion in transcription indexing by right-clicking them and selecting "Include bin in transcription."

The other relevant transcript setting resides within the Find window in the Search settings. The Search Index can also be changed here, but that does not pertain to transcripts. If PhraseFind indexing is turned off, clips will not be actively transcribed. Some people choose to turn off PhraseFind indexing to improve performance. Two conditions need to be met to use transcripts: A bin must be included in bin transcription, and PhraseFind indexing must be enabled.

Timeline Settings

Disable "Auto-Monitoring." This helps by not monitoring a track that is different from what you intend after loading a series of different clips in the source monitor.

Important: Once you're finished adjusting your settings, quit Media Composer and relaunch the application because if your system crashes before you do this, your user settings won't be saved.

User Interface

The recent User Interface (UI) change of Media Composer came with a few new ways of interacting with the software. While it may look slightly different at first, it's fundamentally the same (save for the introduction of Bin Containers). Once your user settings are loaded up, you only have to make a few tweaks to feel right at home.

Many people feel more comfortable with a layout that matches 2018's Avid version (which is no longer officially supported). One feature that was introduced not too long ago is the option to create a new user profile with "classic" Avid features enabled, which closely resembles the 2018 version. Feel free to take this route, and I'll cover some of those settings below if you want to poke around and cherry-pick settings to add to your already existing user profile. Here are some tips to try out to familiarize yourself with new options within the UI, how to get it to behave in a similar manner that you might be used to, and the settings I like to change to speed up my workflow.

- Disable the second Host panel.
  - It blocks you from accessing the desktop, and if you panel bins on it, they're always in the background and get covered by floating windows too frequently.

- Take the one host panel you have and put the Composer and Timeline windows in it.
- Collapse the Workspaces bar too.
- Call up the project window, then tab the settings window in the same panel.
- Save this as a workspace. Boom, classic Media Composer!

• In Composer settings, select "Display Middle Composer Button Panel." This restores the classic insert/replace/overwrite buttons. Magnifique!

• Tab and/or panel certain tools together.
  - I like having my Audio Tool paneled with my Timecode window. Invoking one of them brings them both to the foreground (Command-1).
  - I tab all my audio tools together: Mixer, EQ, AudioSuite. I also have the Find window tabbed with these as well.

• You can have multiple Tool palettes. Using the new UI, these can be docked with windows where the buttons are most useful.
  - Dock one to the left of your Timeline to mimic where Smart Tools used to be.
  - I take advantage of all the added button space at the top of the Timeline.

• "Command - ~" will cycle through all open windows. **Control-Tab switches between tabs!**
  - The former is an operating system shortcut not limited to Media Composer.

• **Bin Containers**: I'm still trying to figure out how best to use them, but I keep three open: One for reels (all reels tabbed), one with a bunch of tabbed/paneled utility bins (effect presets, work bins), and one which I use to open all other bins.
  - If you name them, they are saved as part of the workspace.
  - Sometimes, I use the bin sidebar to open bins and have them tab into the bin container. Other times I'll open a bin from the Project window to float it (or it will open the bin tabbed in the last used bin container).
    - Command-opening the bin inverts the setting in Bin Settings, which allows this.

The Keyboard

Everyone seems to want to know how other people map their keyboards. My philosophy is to start with the default layout and then build on top of it by adding functions I regularly use. I'll share my keyboard here and explain my thought process, but I encourage you to start from scratch and add/replace functions as you *need* them, not just because it "seems" useful. That's what's great about being able to customize your keyboard; it's custom to you.

I try to avoid starting with a keyboard layout that mimics another program. If you're migrating from, say, Premiere, you might be inclined to map your Avid keyboard to match more closely to Premiere. In my opinion, that's largely unhelpful. I hold this stance because it's a different program that is fundamentally interacted and operated with differently from Media Composer. Trying to force one application to behave like another tends to lead to frustration. So, take that thought for what it's worth and do what works for you.

Let's discuss what you *can't* customize: The Option and Command keybindings.

What You Can't Customize, Part 1: Option

Avid has built **much** functionality into adding the Option key to keyboard shortcuts. For example, "Add Edit" adds an edit in all selected tracks at the Time Position Indicator (that's the official nomenclature for the playhead), but adding Option to "Add Edit" will *only* add edits to Filler—not any clips. Adding Option to "Mark In" will change it to "Go to in Point." Add Option to "Source Record Mode", and you'll toggle in and out of the Single Viewer Composer window.

What You Can't Customize, Part 2: Command

Command bindings are hard coded into the software and less enumerable than the Option modifier offerings. Things like Command 1-9 have very useful navigation features you can't change. Command-E sorts the selected column when in a bin, and Command-T will "tighten" (align to the grid)—holding down Command while scrubbing will snap your playhead to edit points (or invert the setting if you have snapping enabled already).

My Keyboard Customizations

As you can now see, there are only two layers of customization: The base keyboard layer and the Shift modifier layer. I try to embrace this "limitation" by avoiding mapping in functions that are already hard-wired to the keyboard. This isn't always the case, and if you look at my keyboard, you'll see I have two instances of "Mark In." Truth be told, I use them both depending on where my hand is on the keyboard. In large part, I find my hand resting on the left side of the keyboard, which is where many of my frequently used functions are mapped.

The first thing you'll notice on my keyboard is that my function keys are completely stacked. I make full use of those. The keyboard I use physically separates the function keys, making them easier to access without looking. I like to think of each group of four function keys as if they're all performing similar functions. This is especially notice-able under the Shift modifier, where F1-4 are bin-specific commands (different bin views), F5-8 are the inverse of their default layer functions, and F9-12 are all audio-related; adding the Shift modifier to those makes them media and effects-related.

I love having "Export to File" mapped to F13, which is a key that's out of the way. I view exporting something as a function outside my normal editing procedure, so mapping it to a key that's out of the way makes sense to my wacky brain. I hide the List Tool under the same key with a Shift modifier because, in my mind, it's a similar function (exporting a document, like exporting a media file).

I like having my six favorite timeline views be Shift 1-6, and then my four most used workspaces are mapped to Shift 9, 0, -, and =. This lets me navigate through the software with ease. I often use match frame and find bin, so those live next to each other. I only have one marker color mapped because I can easily tab through the "Add Marker" dialog box and change the color. I have keys that remain unmapped

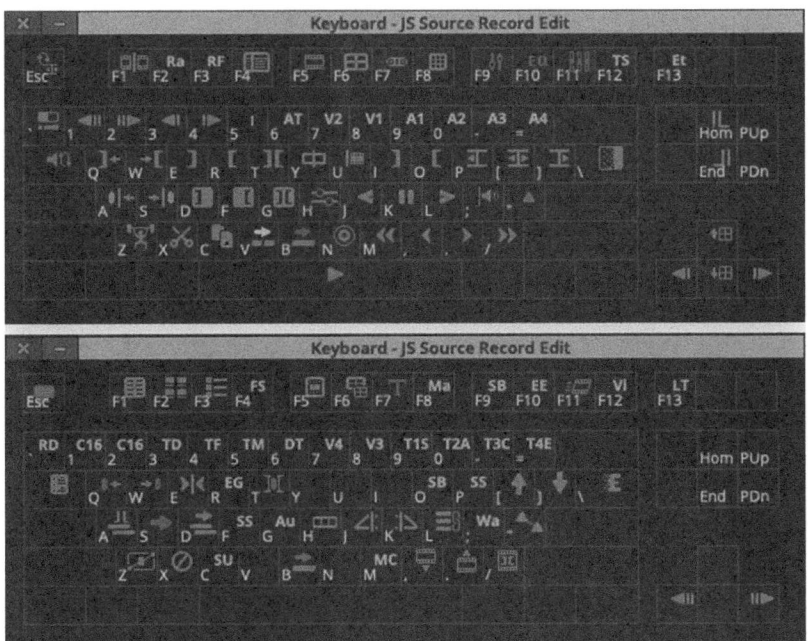

Figure 3.4 My keyboard settings: The top image shows the base layer; the bottom image shows the keys with the shift modifier active.

and some that change depending on where we're at in the process. During dailies, I like to have my "6" key be a second marker color for convenience. After that, I change it to "Add Timeline Clip Note" because I use that more frequently. The function I use more than anything else is "Toggle Source/Record in Timeline" (`).

PS: I'm a total nerd (obviously) and a huge fan of mechanical keyboards. I use a Keychron Q6 with Cherry MX Brown switches. Highly recommend.

Good Stuff to Know (Tips and Tricks)

Here are the tips and tricks. Let's start with some general ones:

- The shortcut to **force** a "Save All" is **Option-Command-S**. This works even when a bin is active, unmodified, and the "Save Bin" menu item would otherwise be disabled.
- Source Browser filter/search bar: Switch to "Search" and type "." to **import** all files in the directory. Use with "Create bin based on folder" for added efficiency. **Linking** (instead of importing) works more intuitively and does not need this "period search" workaround.
- Adding Shift while dragging any slider (in the Effect Editor, for example) increases precision.

Bin Tips

- "Snap to Grid" in the Bin Fast menu is great for bins during dailies.
- Right-clicking on a bin column presents many options, including "Set column to."
    - For all selected clips, this is an easy way to enter the same data in that column.
    - If you right-click on a column that already has a value, that value will be auto-entered in the ensuing dialog box.
    - If you Option-click on a column, a list with all values found in that column for clips elsewhere in that bin will appear.

Timeline Tips

- Command-Option-U lets you add a custom track to the timeline: Audio, video, or data. This track can also be **inserted anywhere**, not just appended to the bottom.
- Command-Shift-Drag locks your selection in time. It's helpful when reorganizing audio tracks.

- I use "Restore Default Patch" a lot. Like, *a lot,* a lot. I just wanted to share.
- Command-double-click a track patch to match frame on the clip where the playhead is parked.
- Command-click on the video track monitor to solo that track. It's helpful for split screens.
- Option-Find Bin from a sequence is like performing a match frame + find bin in one step.
- Selecting all to the right, then Shift-Option clicking the same function **selects only Filler** (inverse).
- Bonus points if you have the yellow "Segment Insert" smart tool active and hit "Delete." This is great for creating a quick stringout of VFX in the right circumstances (p. 247).
  - Consult the Edit tab within Timeline Settings to check whether "Select Filler with Segment Tools" is on.
- Hidden tracks: Command-Shift-H will hide any active tracks. I've found it best to use this feature temporarily to focus on one thing, like audio.
  - Extractions affect hidden tracks, but lifts and trims do not.
  - Switching to a saved timeline view will restore any hidden tracks—assuming the timeline view wasn't saved with any hidden tracks.
- Trim tip! If you want to open up space without creating a bunch of hacked-up edits (as "Add Filler at Position" would do), perform an Option-Add Edit and use those as the primary trim point.
  - Do not select the video tracks; just select the audio.
  - As the edit opens, Filler will be added to the video tracks, and the audio pre/post laps will maintain sync.
  - Insert the new material and close the edits using trimming as well. Voila!
  - Don't forget to remove match frame edits.
- Don't allocate more than 1.5 GB to waveform cache—diminishing returns.
- I don't mind updating Media Composer in the middle of a show. That's because I don't mind the possible inconvenience of having to roll back to an earlier version. Is this advice I give to you? Not necessarily—the juice might not be worth the squeeze for everybody. I like taking advantage of new features and bug fixes as they become available.
  - Mind you, I read the "Read Me" and "What's New" documents, so I'm aware of possible issues that could arise.
  - I test the version on my machine before it gets installed anywhere else.

- I generally stay on the same major version release and update to minor point increases/bug fixes.
- If there are big changes that could affect our workflow, I abstain.
- This is not a priority of mine, and I will postpone updating if I have any reservations.

Newer Features (as of 2024.6)

Yeah, this became outdated immediately after I wrote it. That said, many people using Media Composer might be coming from an older version and are unaware of newer features. Perhaps these get lost among more substantial features that have been introduced over the years. Consider these a continuation of "General Tips and Tricks" as this book ages.

- The **Batch Subclip Tool**, as mentioned later when discussing subclips during dailies (p. 100), is a welcome new addition. Select a handful of clips, and you can create subclips from them without all the ugly ".sub.01" extensions, and you can even specify tracks and handles.
- **Bulk Edit** is great for renaming a bunch of clips all at once. I rarely need to use this, but it's usually to do something like append the date to the beginning of a bin of clips. The date is the "Specified Text" with a space, and then the "Name" column data is appended to that. Or use it to add a counter.
- **Find and Replace** is what I often use. Beware: It will replace all instances of found text, so maybe switch bin views before executing one. For example, I'll import a bunch of files and dupe the name into a custom "Import Name" column. If I then perform a find and replace the "Import Name" column will be affected. Any columns not displayed aren't affected, so I switch the bin view to something else that hides the "Import Name" column first.
- The AAF export option to "**Exclude all Media from Previous Sequence**" works wonderfully in a standard environment. By this, I mean sequences that are iterating up and changing slightly, with new and additional dialogue or music being added.
  - It's basically a "Copy all Media" AAF that only takes the new stuff.
  - I imagine it wouldn't work great if whole scenes were constantly being added and removed. In that case, it might be more lightweight to stick to a standard "Link To" media workflow and then use something like MDVx to preemptively corral new imported and rendered media (p. 222).

- Similarly, the new **Pro Tools Session File Export** is primed to replace AAFs altogether. I've used it instead of an AAF, and the sound department seemed to favor it.
- The Command Palette now has a quick find field, which allows you to search for a function instead of clicking through all the tabs and trying to remember if markers are considered "Other" or "More." Long-time Avid users just let out the largest collective sigh you can imagine.
- **Bin Map and Timeline Map:** I think these are cool ideas, and people seem to like them, so you should be aware that they exist. I don't use them all that often. Enable or disable them in their respective fast menus.
- **"Display Source Track Name in Timeline"** is a phenomenal new feature! It allows the metadata from the audio track name columns (originating on the production sound mixer's recorder) to flow through the bin and, ultimately, into the source track patch. This means that instead of looking at "A1, A2, A3, etc.," you could see something like "Mix, Boom, Brian, Marco, etc." It's helpful when cutting in ISO tracks.
- **Sequence Templates** are a great new feature that allows you to pre-name tracks. Even better, you can retroactively apply Sequence Templates to existing sequences.
- The **Transcript Tool** is new and powerful (p. 49). Words highlight live as playback occurs, and the tool is automatically ganged to the composer window. You can select text, which automatically creates in and out points, enabling you to edit a selection into a sequence and assemble it easily.
- The **Universal Media Engine** has been introduced to replace the dependency on Apple's QuickTime framework. It's fast, flexible, and poised to enable more efficient workflows.
  - UME is 64-bit.
  - "DNxHD 115" is the same as "DNxHR SQ" *in 1920x1080*. When the raster is 1920x1080, you might see this codec labeled **"DNxHD SQ"** since it is still High Definition (and not High Resolution... HD vs HR).
  - MOV export uses a different engine than MXF export.
- The **Panel SDK** is an interesting one to watch. It'll allow other developers to integrate their apps deeply into Media Composer.

Media Composer Panel SDK

What is it? A Software Development Kit (SDK) is something provided by the developer (Avid) to other developers who can use it to create applications (including plug-ins) that are more deeply integrated into the host application. This has caught my eye regarding the future of Media Composer because it allows developers outside of Avid to add functionality. The first example of this has come from Doom Solutions (p. 266) and their plug-in "Marvin Jr."

One action from Marvin Jr. is the ability to batch-edit markers in clips and sequences. This plug-in also allows for auto-numbering (which is great for assigning VFX shot codes [p. 190]) and consistent formatting of markers (which can be used for ADR markers [p. 158] and DI markers [p. 248]). This tool is to metadata what the Boris plug-ins are to VFX. It makes us more efficient, and the results are clean. As of the publishing of this book's first edition, the SDK panel is still nascent, and Marvin Jr. is the best use case I've seen put into action.

I'm just brainstorming here but, imagine a panel in which you have a chatbot-type dialogue where you can ask it to apply a 3D Warp (and specify parameters!) to all clips on track V3 and place a DI marker in the center of each one. The sky's the limit, though, and it's good to keep an eye on what possibilities are out there.

User Settings

As you've guessed or assumed (correctly), I archive my Avid user settings. I don't wait until the end of a show to do this; I'll archive them periodically. I will now come clean and admit that I am guilty of dragging and dropping my user settings folder into the Avid Users directory, and things have been, by and large, pretty, pretty good. For the record, **it's advised that you create a new user**, open your **old** user settings, and then drag and drop any settings you want to preserve into your new user.

Whatever you decide to do, know that the Avid User is the first stop on the troubleshooting train (p. 58). Certain settings are largely safe to migrate over (bin views, timeline views, keyboard, list tool, some export settings [read: anything *not* QuickTime dependent]), but others, I'd advise against (workspaces specifically—things can get wonky).

Creating Room Tone from Production Audio

First, cut an entire take of production audio from which you want to extract room tone into a sequence. Then, duplicate it onto an adjacent track. Select only the top track, mark the clip, and run "Strip Silence." Then, go to your in-point and "Select all to Right" (not selecting filler—you might need to add the Option modifier to accomplish this). Move the clips down to the lower track and then back up. You can delete these clips now and (if needed, turn off the sync lock) extract the

Filler between all the silence you found. Remove any breaths and add some dissolves as needed.

Spotting Audio Changes

Create an audio mixdown of your sequence (or segment in question) and apply an "Invert" AudioSuite effect. Invert flips the audio phase 180°, like how noise-canceling headphones work. This means the original audio will be canceled out when played back with the inverted audio, and all will be silent... except for the different areas.

Using Scripts and Transcripts

Scripts have been around for a while within Avid as a representation of a scripted scene. As of this writing, transcripts are still nascent, but rapidly evolving. The way I've found it best to differentiate between the two is as such:

Script: The creative intent of what was scripted to be said.
Transcript: The objective truth of what has been said in the audio clip.

When a master clip is transcribed, the audio is analyzed, and its information is indexed in a database, which can be managed through the project transcript settings (p. 39). This transcript ripples through the project and becomes accessible in subclips and group clips. It represents the dialogue the software has determined was spoken. Actors, being human, after all, may improvise, reset, or flub a line. This is where the script comes in: We line the script (p. 51) to represent the different takes and alts that exist. In other words, **the transcript is data, and the script is the story**.

Right now, it seems that the most relevant use cases for transcripts are in unscripted and documentary environments. As the use and development of transcripts continue to evolve, the concept of "data vs story" will likely inform how we interact with and continue using them.

Titler+

A brief history of Titler+: For the longest time, a helper app was installed alongside Avid Media Composer, and it was simply called "AvidTitleTool." It was a 32-bit app hidden within the Supporting Files folder inside the operating system's Applications folder. This helper app became obsolete on Macs when Apple went full 64-bit on their operating system (every OS after Mojave). However, it is still available on Windows machines and older Macs if you download the legacy installer package. Avid's replacement for this helper app is future-facing: An effect named **Titler+**.

I say future-facing because the old helper app was pretty limited; it took you away from the Media Composer application and generated new media whenever you needed to edit the text. The switch from an external app to a native effect was a big deal. Long story short, Titler+ had a rough start as the transition was weathered, but we've arrived at a new foundation, which is substantially more capable, multiple times more flexible, and significantly more stable.

Using Titler+

Titler+ can be applied from the effect palette, the default timeline button labeled "**T+**," or from a mapped button on your keyboard (p. 42). Regardless, you'll first have to mark an in-out region in the timeline. That's perhaps the biggest difference between the old title tool and Titler+: Most people used to load a title into the source monitor and mark a region there before cutting it into a timeline. Once you adapt to marking a region in the timeline *first*, you'll get used to it. After the effect has been applied, Media Composer enters Effects Mode (heads up: Clicking in the timeline will exit Effects Mode—so keep your scrubbing within the timeline *just under* the record-side composer window) and displays a dashboard in addition to the Effect Editor.

From there, simply click anywhere in the record-side composer window to start typing. You might find it easier to use a workspace that shows a single composer window (or toggle it using **Option-Source/Record Mode**) to increase the screen real estate. When you're typing, you're in what I'll call a "micro-mode" within Titler+: Text mode. When finished typing, click outside the text to pop into the "move" micro-mode. This is one way to start moving the text around on the screen. You can add multiple text and shape objects within the same effect, group them together if you please, and animate their keyframes. Saving a template is as simple as dragging the effect icon from the Effect Editor into a bin—just like any other effect.

One use case of what I like to do is create templates for ADR and VFX. The position on-screen and text color are saved, so when I want to banner a shot, I can "mark clip" in the timeline, simply drag the saved effect from the bin into the timeline track I desire, and then edit the text.

Alternatives to Titler+

If you don't want to use Titler+ and don't have access to the legacy Title Tool, I suggest using the SubCap effect. Create a template and turn off global sync so your titles don't synchronize across the sequence (or reels). This goes against the premise of using SubCap, but it's part of the workaround. You can save the effect preset in a bin, apply it to a region of filler, and quickly change the text (just like Titler+). You'll be slightly limited on what you can do with the text, but it's fast and lightweight. I've predominantly used this for on-screen ADR line slugs—more on titles later in the DI section (p. 250).

Media Composer will keep evolving well past the publishing of this book. To keep your finger on the pulse of new features and how best to use them, check out some of the Avid-related recommended resources (p. 266) at the end of the book.

Digital Scripting (ScriptSync)

Let's start with the analog: A script supervisor's lined script is a copy of the shooting script annotated with lines denoting camera angles and takes. The lines are drawn on the script, covering the dialogue and action recorded for a take. Squiggly lines are drawn over parts that were performed off-camera. Lined scripts have been indispensable tools for editors throughout history, as the script supervisors are our eyes and ears on set, and their notes are referenced throughout the editorial process. "Did we get that? How many takes?" Let's check the lined script. Yes, we did—and we have five takes. The digital lined script (an Avid-exclusive feature) lets us re-create a physically lined script to make it interactive. The idea of a digital lined script within the editing application is that you can highlight a region of text, assign a clip (or clips) to that region, and then mark the intersection of time within the clip(s) with the corresponding line in the script.

A quick digression: I see many people calling this "ScriptSync," but I primarily see scripts lined manually in the context of the cutting room. *ScriptSync* is the software option used when running the phonetic indexing engine on the script. *ScriptSync* analyzes the text and creates script marks. I don't think you're "doing" ScriptSync if you're manually scripting the scene. Regardless, the whole process takes a lot of manual labor, even if you're using the ScriptSync option because you usually must adjust the analyzed marks. It's semantic, and I'm a stickler for these things, but that's why this section is titled "Digital Scripting" and not "ScriptSync."

Technical Details

A script file is created by selecting File > New > Script and importing a text file formatted specifically for the application.

The formatting is important to understand because it impacts how you edit the text later—it's all indented by spaces, left justified. There are 15 spaces from the left for action, 35 for a character name, and 25 for dialogue. There are no tabs in a text file formatted for Avid, and although you can use them when editing the text, I advise against it just to keep everything consistently spaced and indented—more on editing the text later (p. 57).

The script file (**.avs**) is identical to a bin file (**.avb**) as far as Media Composer is concerned. It holds clips like a bin; it's saved as a bin (even in the Attic, although Avid does separate bins from scripts, which is convenient.) There's even a script counterpart to the "find bin" function (you'll never believe this, but it's called "find script"). A script file contains slates, takes, and script marks. A slate is a collection of takes, and a take contains several script marks.

My script settings are set to the margins, font size, and typeface the editor prefers. Within the script, there are slates and take tabs. A slate represents a setup, and a take tab has a line that corresponds to a take. Usually, a take with a pickup or reset will be split into two take tabs—one for the first part of the take and a second line that begins at the pickup or reset. The take line heights should be adjusted by hand accordingly. You might choose to create separate subclips for each pickup/reset instead, and if you're using "ScriptSync" proper, you'll need to.

I break the script into small chunks that don't necessarily correspond to the scene bins. Using "Scene 30" as an example, imagine it has so many clips that I broke it into three scene bins. I then opt for one "Scene 30" script containing clips from **all three Scene 30 bins**. Many times, I'll opt to combine a few scenes into a single script because the coverage overlaps enough to warrant it.

For each script file I create, I also create a new script in Media Composer and import the entire Final Draft export of the script. Then, I enter text edit mode and delete everything irrelevant to the scene(s) I want to include. The benefits of having multiple small script files over one large "hero" script are that the scripts are smaller files and, thus, open and respond more quickly, and the editor can work in one script while an assistant works in another.

Lining the Script

During dailies, I have our apprentice editor and second assistant create the digital lined script within Media Composer. The digital lined script proves to be an invaluable addition to scene bins while cutting, especially down the road as a research tool when working with directors and producers. For this reason, it's imperative that the assistant lining the script is incredibly diligent and notates every-thing (every reset, flub, pickup—every region that's out of order). They need to find a way to communicate what was scripted and not shot, and what was not scripted but indeed shot. It needs to be crystal clear which takes are multicam and which are off-speed or MOS. I cannot overstate this: **Everything must be noted.** The editor will use this as the definitive guide to find all the footage; every line read, and every significant action. This way, when someone asks to see something and asks if anything exists, we can say, "It's all right here."

There is a balance to lining the script, however. While you want to notate as much as possible, you must maintain the signal-to-noise ratio. The rule of thumb I use is to mark each thought (usually every two or three sentences or on the rhythm of the dialogue—whatever feels right.) I mark all the blocking beats and significant actions (someone getting shot, an item being thrown, or someone running past a certain point) and keep the moments consistent across takes where possible. If I mark an item being thrown in Take 1, I'll mark it in all subsequent takes. When lining a script, I think about how I'd want to use it as an editor.

Color	Script Take Line
	Line delivered slightly differently, but the same idea
	Out of order - each mark will jump around in time
	MOS
	Off-speed, match back for slow-motion
	At the head and tail of the take—group clip
	Director's select
	Editor's select

With everything above said, here's how I handle lining our script: The colors I've used loosely correlate with the source side marker colors, and the table below outlines them. If there's an improvised line that's different enough from what's scripted, then I add it in <carrots>—this also goes for blocking and action.

Let's take a look at what a scene from a digital lined script looks like. (turn the page)

We can see that the 4A setup is multicam because the tops of the take lines are orange. There are some improvised lines and some out-of-order lines, and it's clear which lines are off-camera, thanks to the squiggles. There's a note to the editor about the order (and occasional overlap) of "Cheers!" and we can see that there are sections of 4A-3 that the director and editor have favorited different parts of.

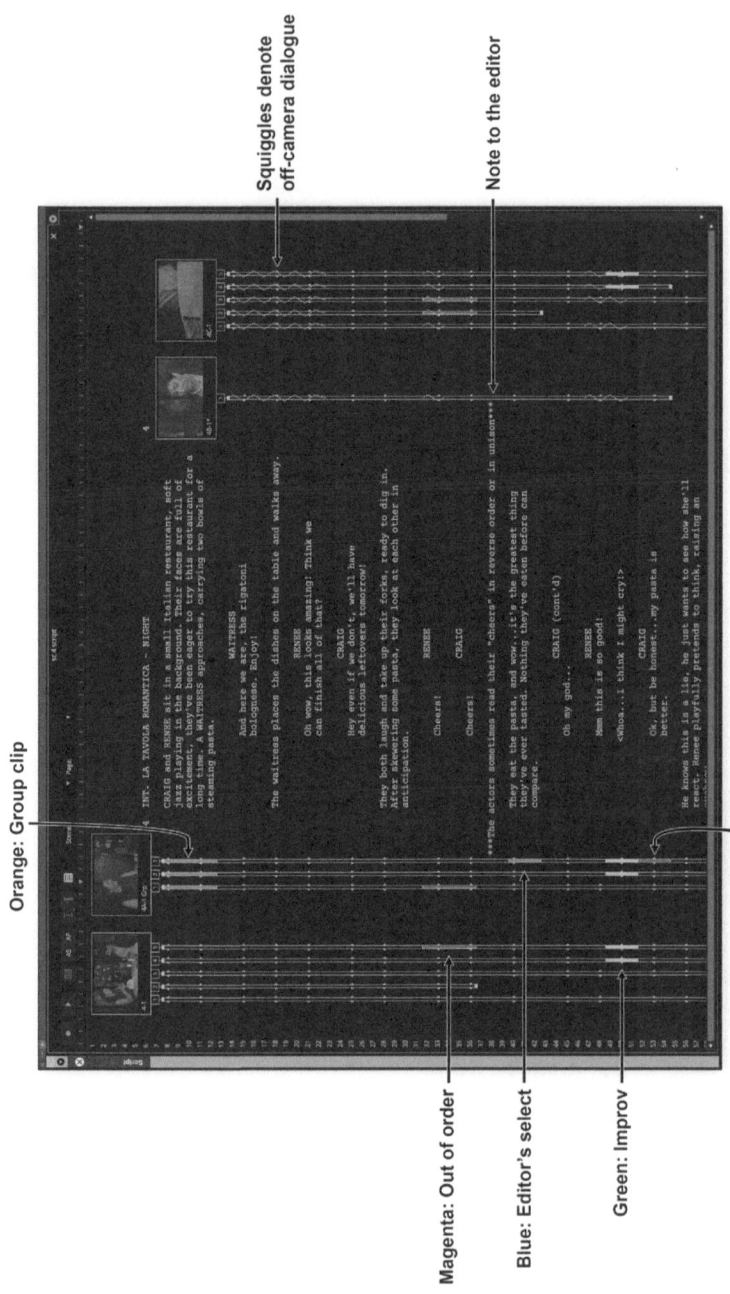

Figure 3.5 Fully lined and annotated script within Avid representing a scene with four setups.

Scripting Improvised Lines

Looking at one of the improvised lines (line 50): The scripted line is
Renee saying, "Mmm, this is so good!" Since there are takes where
Renee said, "Whoa... I think I might cry," in place of the scripted line,
it gets transcribed, added to the script in <carrots>, and labeled green.
The carrots have been added, accounting for the margin, so they visu-
ally grab the editor's attention.

If Renee said, "Mmm, this is so *tasty*!" that might not necessarily
need to be transcribed because it's similar enough to the scripted line.
Your editor will want to weigh in on this decision because perhaps
they don't need it typed out but *do* want the green-colored take for
that line.

Let's consider a nonverbal example of improvisation: Craig slurping
noodles. It's hilarious, and in every take, he does it differently and
intermittently—not at the same time in the scene. The editor might
want to opt for a scripting approach in which they **add a script line**
that reads: "All Craig Slurping Alts," and then add as many script
marks from as many takes and angles as you'd like, allowing the editor
to toggle through all variations that might exist, regardless of their
placement in the context of the scripted scene.

There are many ways to approach lining a script and organizing
footage, so get creative!

Avid Lined Script Workflow

It's time for another one of my famous disclaimers: There is no one
way or right way to do this; as long as you get it done on time. Here's
how I line an Avid script:

I highlight the region the clip covers, then drag the first take of the
first setup (or the master wide, usually the same) into the script. You
can adjust this region later by **command-clicking and dragging** the top
or tail of the take to the desired line of dialogue. I like starting with
the wide because it gives me a baseline for what to expect, and they
usually cover most of the dialogue. I don't add all takes from the same
angle to this slate *immediately*—I add them as I go, so it's a bit easier
for me to add resets and pickups (don't worry, we'll get there).

Starting with the first take, I hit record and run through the scene,
marking each line with my mouse cursor while my other hand rocks
the J and L keys (not K; that stops the recording process) [I'm referring
to my keyboard mapping (p. 42)]. I click on the line just before they
say it, sometimes rocking J-L to get it right. If something is blocked
completely differently, said out of order, or improvised, I color that
part of the take (or edit the chunk of text) accordingly (usually once
I'm through the take).

For a reset or pickup, I adjust the end of the take and drag **the same clip back onto the same slate**. This creates a second take line, which I adjust to start from the top of the take or just the reset line. If the next instance takes it back a line or two, I add a red marker before the yellow marker (in the clip) and a point increase in the clip name. If they take it back to the top, a whole number step is taken (**1.4 -> 2.4**), and I add *another* red marker. If the scene bin is unavailable, I'll write a note to myself to circle back and add these notes later.

Then, I resume scripting. After all the takes in a setup are complete, I'll mark any of the offscreen ranges since they are oftentimes consistent across all takes in a setup. Rinse and repeat for all takes until the whole scene is accounted for.

Matching Back from Scripts

At this point, I'd like to note the relationship of the clips. By dragging subclips in from the scene bin, we're maintaining the parent-child relationship thus allowing for matchback from the script to the scene bin.

One could theoretically mark a region within a subclip loaded in the source side composer window and drag it into the script as previously described. **This is not a good idea** because it will create what I'll call a "ghost subclip." It exists *only* in the script, and when you try to match back, you're prone to receive an error message. Media Composer can't find the subclip used in the script **because it doesn't exist** as far as the software is concerned.

As mentioned earlier, you might choose to create new subclips per reset or pickup, which will avoid the ghost subclip issue, and, depending on your editor, they might want these subclips re-labeled and included in the scene bin or sequestered into a "Multicam Subclips"-type bin. One benefit of creating these distinct subclips is that it allows the ScriptSync automation to work. Without these subclips, ScriptSync's engine will look at the whole clip duration, which includes all pickups and resets, so it'll likely only ever mark the first instance.

Adding Notes

As previously identified, there's a note to the editor about the order and occasional overlap of "Cheers!" in our example scene. To add this note, we had to edit the script. Editing the script text within Media Composer is easier now than ever. However, using a third-party text editor like Sublime Text is still faster. I like how this application visually identifies spaces and tabs and how slick it looks and behaves.

My best practice is to use the text editor as a scratch pad—to store different lengths of indent spacing to copy and paste. I also like to use it when manually transcribing—I'll play a section on a loop and keep typing and filing in the gaps until it's all written down.

Manual ADR Transcription

There was an instance where I had a long take of ADR I needed to script, even though it was unscripted initially. This meant transcribing the audio and marking it up. I accomplished this by going through the take and adding script marks arbitrarily at breaks in the waveform. I had copied and pasted filler text into the script window, so the formatting was correct. I went to the second line down, marked out, and clicked the line above it. This highlighted a range to transcribe in the timeline. I would play it back on a loop while typing what I heard in real time using a text editor (Sublime Text). When I finished typing, I would copy and paste the text into Avid's script window, adding a return wherever it would automatically wrap the text (this way, each line was an actual line in the script window). Once all was transcribed, I could record the script marks for each line of the paragraph I transcribed into the script window by following the "bookmarks" I had made (or I could run ScriptSync).

If you don't have the ScriptSync option enabled on your copy of Media Composer, then that's how you'll likely handle it. Otherwise, there's an excellent new feature in Media Composer 24.6, where you can right-click on a clip and select "Create Transcript" (p. 49). This will handle all the above for you; it's remarkably fast on Apple Silicon Macs.

Text Editing Tips

- The arrow keys move the cursor by one character. Adding Option will move the cursor by one word and adding Command will move it to the beginning or end of a line. Add Shift to any of the above, and you'll have a selection.
- Command-X/C/V are cut, copy, and paste (respectively) for the uninitiated.
- When moving text from a third-party app into the Avid script, I find it's easier to keep all the text for a section on one line and then add the carriage returns at the desired margin within the Media Composer script.

PhraseFind

This seems like a good time to bring up PhraseFind, as it's often bundled with ScriptSync, and they use the same underlaying phonetic engine. PhraseFind allows you to use the find window to search for an audio clip based on the sound of the clip instead of the text associated with it. For example, if you search for "*this is a line of dialogue*," the results will be any clip that phonetically matches that string.

Because this is a phonetic engine, a good tip is to **use and leverage phonetics.** Spell out everything and separate the letters of acronyms. There's a difference between searching for "ok" and "oh kay," "vanilla," "vuhneluh," and "vahnilah." It doesn't recognize any punctuation or abbreviations. Like most other search engines, everything entered will be searched for. If you want to narrow your search down, using quotations around a couple of words will find those **exact** words in that **exact** order.

Troubleshooting: Bugs and Workarounds

What is a bug? It's a problem that leads to an incorrect or unexpected outcome in software. There are hardware issues and software issues, and sometimes, the answer to those software issues is that it's a **bug.** Some bugs are detrimental to workflows, and the software should be updated ("patched") or rolled back, but others are small and inconsequential. These smaller bugs can be dealt with by coming up with **workarounds.** For example, if Media Composer constantly crashes when you click on the marker window after saving but activating the composer window *before* bringing focus to the marker window doesn't result in a crash, the workaround is to select any window *other* than the marker window after saving. These workarounds are uncovered through a process called **troubleshooting.**

My approach to troubleshooting computer issues is to start with the most basic question and work my way down. The first question I always ask myself is: **Is the problem hardware or software-related?** If I think it's hardware-related, I'll physically check connections and look up known limitations related to compatibility. If it's software-related, I start with the specific software and ask myself how it communicates with the operating system or related programs. With Media Composer, my first stop is the user profile—if I make a new user profile (or trash the project user settings) and the issue is resolved, I know it's a user-related problem. Sometimes, it's a project setting or a media creation issue—which could be operating system-related (if the permissions change.) I just go down the list of possibilities and probabilities, changing one thing at a time and noting what changes. Almost always, a restart of the software or the machine will help.

When helping someone else, be mindful of how you ask questions. It's easy to accidentally place blame on someone, even when you have positive intentions. Try to keep your questions impersonal—for example, instead of asking, "Did you turn off the computer?" try, "When was the last time the computer was turned off?"

To demonstrate the troubleshooting mindset, here are some limitations, bugs, and errors I've encountered in Media Composer over the years, including their workarounds (even if they've since been resolved):

"DOMAIN_COPYIN_FAILED" on Save

This is an error sometimes associated with corrupt media or bins. It pops up when you try to save a bin. In our case, we ran out of space on our project drive (Attic archives were taking up too much room), and the bins couldn't write to the Nexis.

Fix: I trashed old archives and increased the workspace capacity.

Importing Markers to Source Clips

It's not yet possible to import markers to a source clip. The workaround is to create a sequence of your clips *using auto-sequence* (that way, the sequence has the same timecode as your markers). Once you auto-sequence the clip(s), import the markers. They should appear in the correct spot. If you have auto-sequenced multiple clips, the next step is to make a subclip/subsequence of just ONE clip. Open the subsequence (which should still have all the markers). Open your marker window, select all the markers, and copy them (Command-C). Match back to the original master clip, open its marker window, and paste (Command-V). Creating a subsequence of the full master clip length ensures that the copy-and-paste function maintains all your markers' locations.

Trim Mode Mix to Black

We sometimes had issues with trimming being sluggish, delayed, and unresponsive. It was puzzling: Was this an overload on the CPU, a limitation of our Nexis connection, or an issue with the media? After replicating the issue on our local backup drive, it was clear this wasn't a Nexis problem. We trashed the project user, and the problem disappeared. The setting in question was Target Mask > **Mix to Black**. When in trim mode, the software must render the 50% opacity on the fly to three outputs: A side, B side, and the Video Output. This slowed the whole system down, which was likely a limitation of our CPUs at the time.

Workaround: Don't use "Mix to…" target masks. Opt for no mask or a solid color mask.

Bin Status Bar Inaccuracies (21.6)

Command-clicking to select and deselect clips in the frame view lags by one click in reference to the information displayed in the bin status bar.

Workaround: Command-click on the background of a bin to update the bin status bar.

SYS_ERROR on Launch

Before the Project window would pop up, I'd get a small box that said "SYS_ERROR." This usually has to do with illegal characters in a folder or filename on the root of a connected drive, or it could be related to the permissions settings of a project folder.

Workaround: Double-clicking the .AVP file I wanted worked, but after fiddling around for a bit, it was a combination of trashing MC State files (site and user) and resetting the read/write permissions in the project directory (local and connected). It might have been a .pList issue.

SYS_ERROR -5000 on Export

This error only appeared on a Mac Studio upon initiating an export. We were able to narrow down the cause of this error to effects that were applied to muted clips. Perhaps they were corrupted somehow; I don't know. This has both a workaround AND a fix:

Workaround: Perform mixdowns and export the resulting sequence.
Fix: Remove all effects applied to muted clips.

AudioStreamReader::UpdateWithStreamStatus Invalid statusReturn (23.12)

This happened when exporting via UME on the Mac Studio. I haven't found a true fix yet.

Workaround: Brute force! First, try renaming your export, then restart Media Composer and the Nexis Client. If all that doesn't work, then try restarting the computer.

Nightmare Fuel

Keeping a cool head in the face of a malfunction is imperative. I'll quickly share two real-life stories that no longer haunt me but go to show that this stuff happens, and how you deal with it makes all the difference. It was a Thursday; the week was almost over. Everything was smooth sailing. I was browsing the web when the editor called me into their office. **They couldn't save their bin.** *What!* I went back into my office to see if it was happening on my machine, too; sure enough, it was. That told me it wasn't specific to their computer, but holy cow, what do you mean, *"We can't save bins?"* The editor was rightfully concerned about losing the work if the bin closed. First, we saved the bin to the desktop as a backup. That put us all at ease for a moment, but the editor was in the middle of working with the director, so the clock was ticking. I started thinking about *why* a bin wouldn't be able to save. Was it a corruption? No, that was too vague. I stopped thinking intensely and simplified my question. *Where* was the bin being saved? We saved it to the desktop, after all. Ok, the next step was to look at the Nexis. *There was no space on the Nexis project drive!* I immediately logged into the Nexis management console (through a web browser, not the Nexis client app) and increased the drive's capacity. We were then able to continue working and save bins as normal. Occam's razor!

I've alluded to an in-house screening room, and there's more on that later (p. 234). The obvious benefit is that we can open Media Composer and play our sequence back in real time instead of exporting a self-contained video file ahead of time. The drawback: It's real-time; anything could happen, just like on Saturday Night Live. It's a calculated risk mitigated by testing the system beforehand, rendering the timeline before playback, and trusting the system. **The video began to stutter** 10 minutes into one screening. Horrified, I hesitated to touch anything lest I made it worse. But I had to. We simply could not continue watching the film in that state.

Was it the breakout box? Possibly. I went to the Finder level to ensure all the workspaces were mounted. It took forever to open the window. *"What's up with the Nexis?"* I calmly asked the room for patience as I ran into the cutting rooms to see if our second assistant editor had any issues. They did! Their system had frozen up. *"What were you doing when it froze?"* I asked. They were exporting an AAF (as assigned—we were multitasking). They said it was taking an unusual amount of time. *"Exporting? Using what settings?"* I asked. They couldn't answer. I asked them to force quit the application and ran into my office to attempt playing back the timeline. *No issue.* I went back to the screening room and tried playing back. *No issue.* I apologized profusely, restarted the film, and the screening continued. Afterward, I asked the assistant to show me their AAF export settings. It wasn't one of our usual presets but one they brought from a previous show. Our typical AAF export for that specific turnover was a "Link to AAF," which simply exports metadata about the timeline into an AAF file.

The preset they were using was a "Copy All Media AAF," which copies, well, all the media in the timeline. Not just what's in the timeline either, but the entire source media files. A consolidated media AAF would have only taken what was in the timeline, plus handles, but this monster of a file was pulling **everything** because the assistant had also selected **all the video tracks**! This pulled so much bandwidth from the Nexis that nothing was left for any other system to read media. Lesson learned, albeit the hard way. Was the lesson to stop multitasking? NO! It was to ensure you knew your export settings and not blindly use a preset from a previous show. Ouch!

4   FileMaker Pro

I don't identify as a FileMaker developer, and this is not a book about FileMaker; I never intended to explore the depths of FileMaker Pro. Yet here we are. Over the years, many people expressed an interest in how I use FileMaker, so including a chapter covering it made sense. There was no better place to put this chapter. If it were at the end of the book, you'd spend a lot of time reading about how I use "my database" without knowing what that even meant. I'll spend a fair amount of time referring to my database as part of my workflow, so it's only fitting to cover the fundamentals and provide an overview of the tool.

I view the database I developed as a by-product of my primary focus: Editing. In this section, I'll discuss my process and techniques as it relates specifically to FileMaker Pro. As with all software, there are alternatives and an ever-changing landscape. I hope the principles I apply within the context of FileMaker can translate to any solution deemed fit for the job. Whether it's Microsoft Excel, Google Sheets, Airtable, or some yet-to-be-invented tool, the goal is to leverage automation to reduce mental strain and free you up to do more creatively fulfilling work.

The Big Disclaimer

FileMaker Pro is a robust tool that *anyone* in *any industry* can utilize. It's so extensive that there aren't many resources available that are specifically tuned to filmmaking, let alone editing or assisting. While I've done my best to make this chapter accessible, it's somewhat advanced and still dense. I wouldn't blame you for skipping it until you absolutely need to reference it, or if you haven't already started to dive into FileMaker. If at any point you get overwhelmed, know that I felt the same way when I first began learning FileMaker. Though advanced, this chapter is inserted into the book at this juncture to continue the continuity of where and how it fits into my workflow timeline.

This chapter aims to expose you to how I made the tool work for me and how I use it in the context of the cutting room. What you'll likely find available online are tutorials that lean on customers, products, line items, and invoices. That's pretty dry and far removed from

DOI: 10.4324/9781003516491-5

filmmaking unless you consider the possibility of a customer being a **character**. What if a product was an **ADR Line**? What if an invoice was an **ADR cue sheet**? Now, that might start to make more sense!

What I've learned from teaching myself FileMaker is that abstracting concepts helps translate them into ideas I can use. I kept this in mind while watching tutorials and troubleshooting my script steps. Even if you find a forum post from 10 years ago about a flower shop sorting records and their inventory, see if you can find the core truth behind the problem they're trying to solve. The odds are that there's something applicable to you there.

Automation Disclaimer

One thing I feel strongly about establishing is that at the end of the day, automation (a database running scripts, in this chapter); is just another tool that reduces human error but never *eliminates* it. Therefore, **your utmost attention to detail is required**. Automation is not an excuse to blindly perform any task or not check any work.

The Absolute Basics

Here are the boilerplate basic elements of FileMaker:

Tables

Think of a **table** like a spreadsheet. You can make as many tables in your FileMaker database as you want, and they can be related to each other based on specified criteria.

Records and Fields

Tables contain **records**, and each record has a given number of **fields**. If you're familiar with a spreadsheet, think of a record as a row and a field as a column. Fields are defined by type (most common are Text, Number, Date, Container, Calculation, and Summary).

Layouts

This is the visual representation of a table. Who likes looking at spreadsheets? Maybe you and my favorite accountant (Hi, Stuart!), but not me. You can certainly make a layout that looks like a standard spreadsheet, but I prefer to place fields in certain areas on-screen, color code fields with conditional formatting, and add tooltips to objects so I don't forget certain things. I find it creatively satisfying to design something that looks exactly how I want. I generally make two layouts

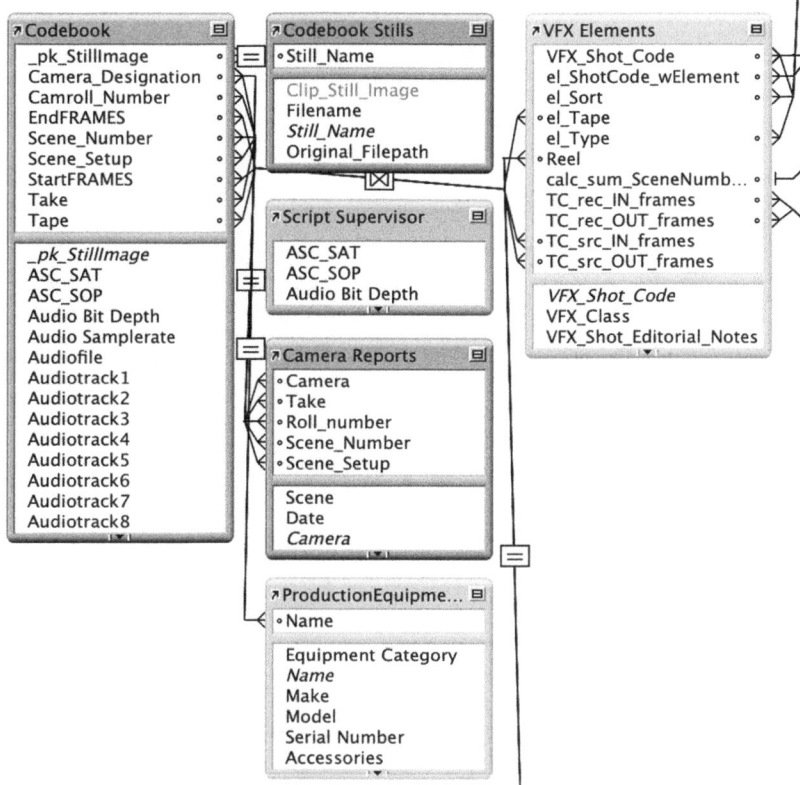

Figure 4.1 Custom FileMaker table graph.

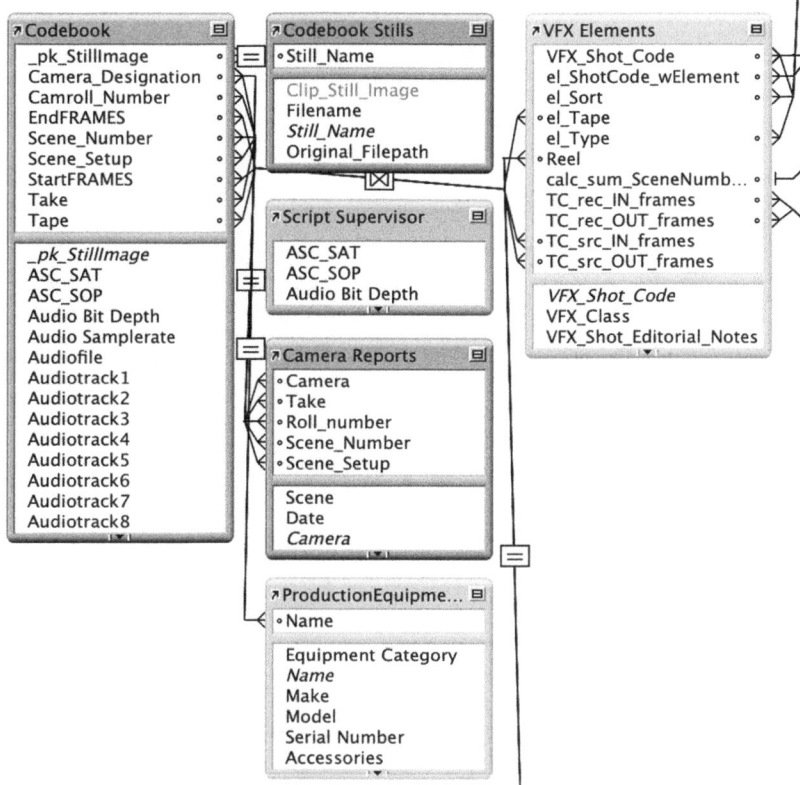

Figure 4.2 FileMaker table view layout, displaying records and fields.

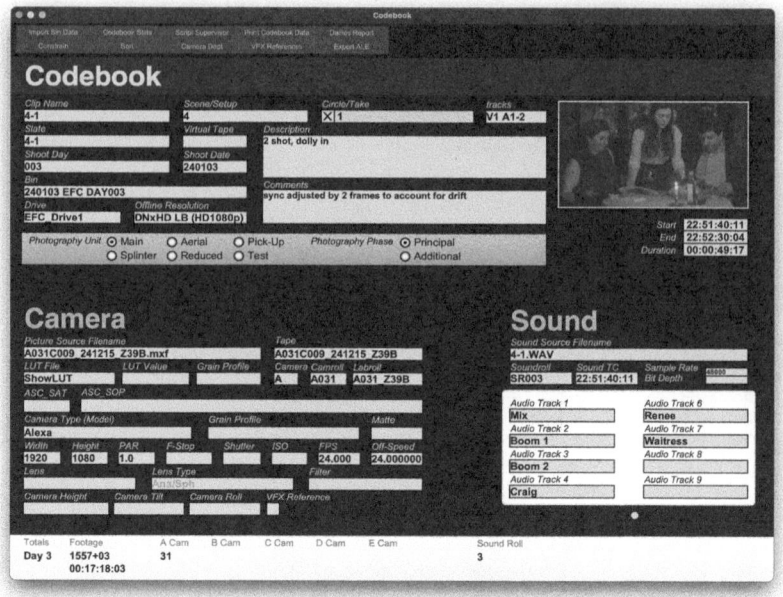

Figure 4.3 Custom codebook layout.

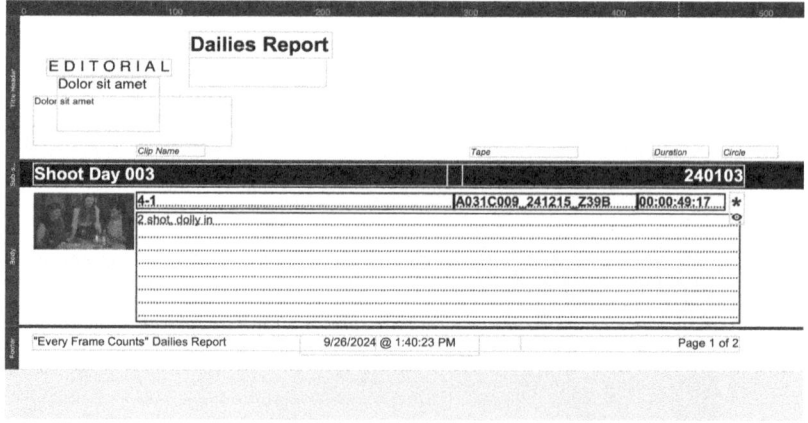

Figure 4.4 Custom print layout.

for any table: A UI layout (which looks like a computer program) and a print layout (formatted for a printer or digital PDF).

Scripts

Scripts are a great way to tell FileMaker what to do. Anything you find yourself doing manually can usually be done within a script. Anything you're routinely doing *should be* in a script. For example, if you're

constantly going to the codebook layout, searching for today's date, and sorting by tape name. That's a lot to do repeatedly. What if you wrote a script that did *those* things in *that* order?
Here's a simple, barebones script which does that:

```
#opens a new window on the Codebook layout
New Window [Style: Document; Using layout:
"Codebook" (Codebook); Close: Yes; Minimize: Yes;
Maximize: Yes; Resize: Yes; Menu Bar: Yes; Dim
parent window: No; Toolbars: Yes]

#finds all records from today
Enter Find Mode []
Set Field [Codebook::Shoot_Date; Get (CurrentDate)]
Perform Find []

#sorts found records
Sort Records [Keep records in sorted order;
Specified Sort Order: Codebook::Tape; ascending]
[Restore; No dialog]
```

Now, you can do a few things; for example, you can add a button that performs this script to one of your layouts or attach it as a script trigger (a trigger executes a script) upon opening your database. Imagine the time you can save when thinking about this at scale. We haven't even discussed variables, expressions, functions, or even loops!

Variables and Global Fields

Okay, since I teased you with variables, let's touch on them briefly. A **variable** is something that can be changed—in this case, a little morsel of data. FileMaker allows you to define a variable within a script (and elsewhere, but let's stay focused) and then use that variable in other steps within that script. Using the example above, instead of setting the field to "Get (CurrentDate)," we could have used another script step before then to define the variable "$DateCurr" (variables within FileMaker are formatted with a $ symbol). The "Set Field" step would have looked like this:

```
Set Field [Codebook::Shoot_Date; $DateCurr]
```

Another kind of variable is a **global variable**. The difference between global and non-global variables is that a global variable exists outside the running script. Regular variables are "sandboxed" within the script, and then they disappear when the script ends. Perhaps there's a startup script you want to trigger upon launching your database, and one of the script steps is to define a global variable with the current date. This allows you to write the scripts and calculations referencing this global variable, which will exist until the database is closed or the global variable is cleared.

I'm mindful of using global variables. They're helpful when you have subscripts within scripts or in the example mentioned above, but if you don't clear them (using a script step that sets the variable to " " [double quotes mean "empty"]), they can affect the way other scripts or features within your database function.

Lastly, since we're talking about global variables, we must also touch upon the concept of a global **field**. As we've established, each record has any number of fields. A global field contains **one value for all records**. This can be helpful in a pinch, but it's advised to avoid them, especially in a shared environment, as they'll only update to match the host machine once the host machine (or server) closes and reopens the database file.

Whoa, we almost got a little too far in the weeds there. Feel free to skip ahead now or continue into the abyss.

Why FileMaker

I initially chose FileMaker Pro because it allowed me to do two things I couldn't accomplish using Microsoft Excel or Google Sheets: Design layouts and write scripts. Layouts make it easier to interact with and look at data and design beautiful PDFs. Scripts automate repetitive or complex tasks—take VFX pulls (p. 198), for example. I wrote a script that generates an EDL of plates to pull for VFX. It creates per-shot line-up sheets with dailies metadata and CSV files. Without the database, I'd have to manually collect all this information, build a sequence within Media Composer, and find a way to get the vendor the necessary data. That could take a while, create mental strain, and prevent me from doing more creatively fulfilling work.

That's just one example. Kicking out ADR cue sheets broken down by character and status takes seconds. Creating a continuity form is as simple as a one-button click. This is all predicated on consistent data formatting (through parsing EDLs and formatting Avid markers). I created keyboard shortcuts within FileMaker, which perform these scripts even faster. However, it wasn't an easy or fast process to create this infrastructure. It was informed by years of experience in cutting rooms and knowing what to anticipate. Since I built it, I know exactly how to change it and what can break it. It continues to grow and change as the circumstances demand, which should be the most significant takeaway from this chapter: **Your greatest strength is your ability to adapt and be flexible.** Building tools to support yourself in that endeavor gives you the power to do exactly that.

My Database

As I mentioned, there aren't many resources regarding FileMaker that directly target assistant editors. I wanted to write about my approach to building my database, how I constructed a few key tables and relationships, and then demonstrate how I made it work for me. There are many ways to accomplish what I've done, and no one way is the "right" way. That's the beauty of building your solution: You can keep improving it.

The database I built has many tables, layouts, scripts, and calculations. Tables include the codebook, continuity, reel versions, music cues, DI events, ADR, a dynamic to-do list, a VFX tracker with elements, versions and vendors, and other odds and ends. I built relationships between these tables to leverage the power of automation. Scripts are mapped to buttons within interfaces that look and behave the way I want them to. Calculation fields host all the math that breaks timecode down into total frames, and then a handful of different fields reconvert the total number of frames back to timecode (or footage, in the case of ADR).

Data Import

How I get information into my database depends on where it's coming from: Is it metadata of clips in a bin or details about clips in a timeline? If it's dailies metadata, then it's coming from a **bin,** and I need specific columns of metadata. Within Avid, I switch to an appropriate bin view and export a tab-delimited data file, then import that into the codebook table of my database. If the data comes from the **timeline,** the next question is whether I need information from **markers placed within clips** (e.g., an ADR line) or **information about the clips the markers are in** (e.g., a VFX shot).

Markers within clips, like ADR lines, have little to nothing to do with the clip that the marker is in. I include the scene number in the marker text. I need the marker text and timecode; therefore, I export the markers as a text file (this is a tab-delimited file) and import *that* into FileMaker. You might think, "Well, if you extract the scene number from the clip name, then you can surely use that, Jared." You wouldn't be wrong. But what happens when a clip from **Scene 18** is used in **Scene 76**? Or, if the continuity scene number doesn't match the clip's scene number (**sc 16-20** might be a montage in the continuity, which wouldn't match "**18**," from the clip name). These considerations must be made because we're introducing automation into the workflow.

On the other hand, VFX shots require information from the clip that the marker is in—tape name, timecode in, and timecode out. The placement of the marker within the clip is less important in this context than in the example mentioned above. To get this data into the database, I export an EDL from Avid (which FileMaker views the same as a plaintext file) and import it into FileMaker. This requires a bit more than a standard import because, unlike the previous examples, an EDL is not delimited in any specific way. It needs to be parsed by looking for patterns in the text and collecting data using variables. The data in these variables are entered into the appropriate fields using loops within scripts.

Data Export

How do we get the data *out* of FileMaker? Mostly, it's via scripts that ask a few qualifying questions and then save a file. I usually execute a "Find" command and a "Sort" command before saving a CSV or PDF with the data. Those are natively supported file types, as is XLSX (Excel). ALEs and EDLs can also be generated via custom scripts. They're not native export options, but by analyzing the structure of these (and other) plaintext files, you can write scripts that utilize variables and loops to emulate (and thus create) any file you need.

One thing worth remembering is that using automation doesn't mean you don't have to check your work. Apologies for the double negative, but automation is **not** an excuse to cut corners. I know what my scripts are doing and where everything should be, but I **never** blindly put markers through the database and kick out PDFs without spot-checking them at the very least. Maybe I formatted a marker incorrectly, or there's a typo—the point is, there's always room for human error. Automation reduces that for sure, but it's never eliminated.

The Codebook

I make sure ahead of time, on the workflow call and subsequent communication with the dailies technician, that the metadata I need is coming through in the bin columns I expect.

I request:

- Comments column: Please notate where possible—False Takes, Slates, VFX_Ref, No Slate, Tail Slate, MOS, Off Speed (preferably with framerate, ex "36 fps" or "96 fps")
- Camera type (Venice, Alexa, RED, GoPro, etc.)
- Width and Height of the negative
- Tape Name (p. 93)
- Camera Roll
- Original File Name
- AudioFile
- Audiotrack 1–8 (or as needed)
- Soundroll
- Scene
- Take
- Shoot Day (DAY001)
- Shoot Date (YYMMDD)
- As much camera data as possible: ASC SAT, ASC SOP, shutter angle, gamma, ISO, focal length, and lens.
- LUT Name
- AuxTC 1 could be the Sound Timecode
- AuxTC 2 could be Playback Timecode (if it exists on an audio data track)

I have a custom codebook bin view (which I share with the lab) and manually add any information (like duping the Name column into the Slate column) before exporting a tab-delimited file of the bin from Avid and importing it into FileMaker. This way, when I import it into the codebook, the field order stays consistent. The camera data spreadsheet I export for the post-PA gets re-imported again (once they've filled it out by referencing the handwritten camera reports [p. 120]) and merged with existing records based on the Tape name (p. 93).

This began as a simple data repository for the VFX table, but other uses have emerged over time. One great example is a Dailies Report ("Custom Dailies Report generated from FileMaker database" can be downloaded from www.routledge.com/9781032843285), a summary of all recorded takes for a given day of dailies. It has a cover page and as many pages as needed, which show the takes, their shot descriptions, and any relevant metadata (usually tape name and timecode). I also have scripts that manipulate the dailies data and reformat it into new ALE files, which I use to make subclips. One script generates an ALE file that makes subclips expressly used to export still images from Avid to import into the codebook. Another script runs which generates a different ALE file that creates subclips used in the scene bins and the digital lined script. The differences between these two ALEs are in the Name, Tracks, Start, End, Mark In, and Mark Out columns.

For the "**Stills**" ALE, the Name column is modified to include the tape name and the Mark In/Out columns are modified to calculate the exact center of the clip and place a one-frame range there. When the subclips are exported from Avid, they'll all be parked (hopefully) on a representative frame. I can extract the tape name from the filename to build the relationship in FileMaker.

The "**Subclips**" ALE has modified Tracks, Start, and End columns. Changing the data in the Tracks field allows me to specify which tracks I want to include (or omit), so I can specify that it *only* uses audio track A1, which is the mix track. Modifying the Start and End timecodes allows me to pad the clip with a small number of handles so I can perf slip if needed.

The codebook table is related to the VFX Elements table via matching tape name, $\leq$ Timecode In and $\geq$ Timecode Out.

The Continuity

I go over building and updating the continuity in a later chapter (p. 142), but here's a bit about how I built the functionality to interact with it in FileMaker. I have quite a few layouts for this table: A form view, which lets me enter all data; a list view, which allows me to view all the scenes sorted in a list by sort order and broken down by reel; a print layout for PDFs, and a wall card layout (a different kind of print layout).

The resulting PDF of the wall cards can be printed from the Mac Preview application using the following steps: Load the 3"x5" inches cards into the printer and set the paper type. In the printer dialog box, select 3"x5" inches **borderless** as the paper type and make sure it's set to **landscape**.

Each scene record has a sort order field with a number counting in increments of 10 (automatically entered upon creation), so I can alter this number after the fact when the scenes need to be re-ordered. I can also make reel assignments that are left empty until the first assembly. I generally use the list view for continuity, changing the sort order and reel as needed.

I build the continuity from the one-liner breakdown the script supervisor provides. That gets entered into a secondary field. I'll then add the assistant director's one-liner to another secondary field. I also reserve the primary field for the editor's preferred verbiage, then condense their one-liner into something much shorter for the wall cards (p. 143). However, I perform most continuity-related tasks manually, although scripts expedite the process of marking a scene that's been lifted or combined by changing other fields (clearing the reel field and changing the status to "Deleted" or "Combined").

While we're shooting, part of my dailies workflow is to search for all scene numbers that the production report lists and change their statuses to reflect whether they're partially or completely shot. Any

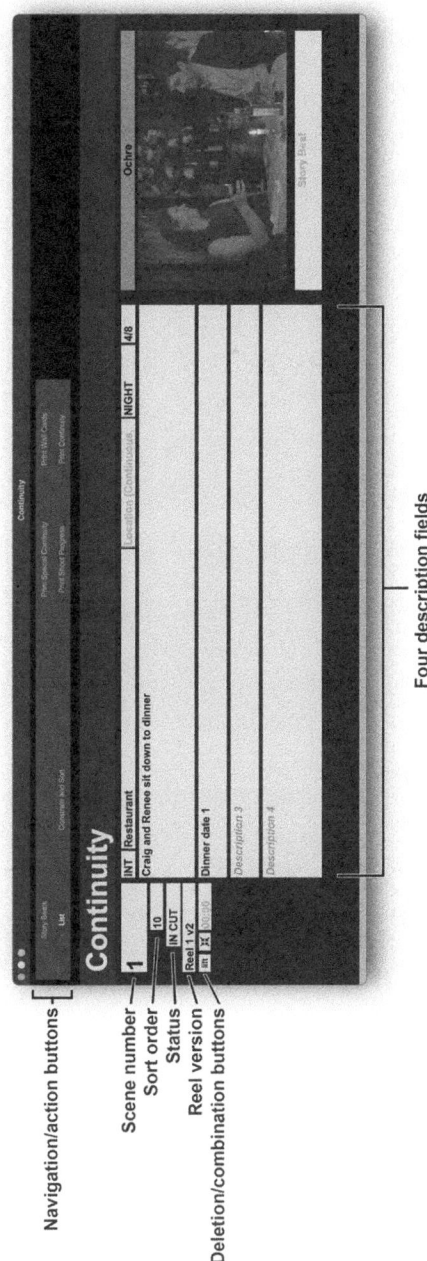

Figure 4.5 Continuity table as viewed in form view. Note the scene status and still images.

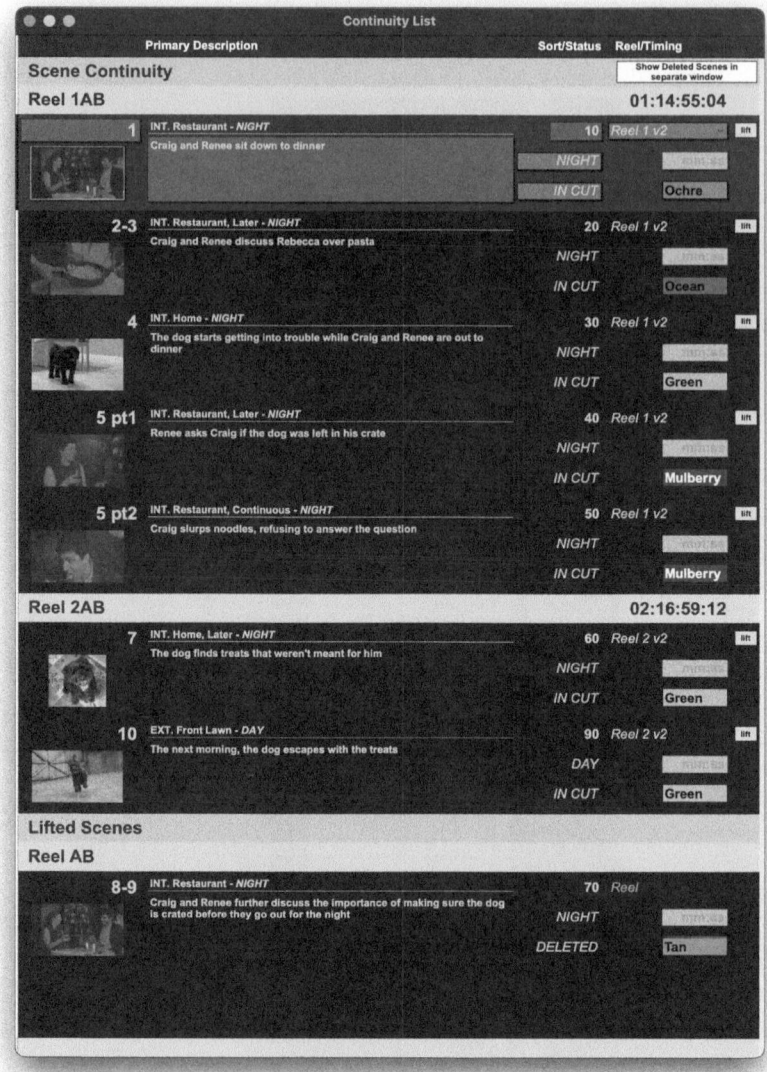

Figure 4.6 Continuity table as viewed in a list layout.

notes are added to a notes field. Upon wrapping production, all completed scenes have their status changed to "In Cut," and scenes that were not shot get changed to "Omitted."

I'm usually asked by the editor not to share the scene timing and TRT initially (or until specifically requested.) This is because, during the director's cut, we want to avoid any notes based on a number at the top of the page or next to a scene. If I must measure scene timing, I usually ask the second assistant to go through the show and manually add it after I've taken a pass to ensure the scene order is accurate. Some ways to automate this involve carrying clip comments or markers that denote a scene's beginning or end (or both). Still, sometimes, these clips and markers get deleted, which becomes more of a headache than a benefit to me. Besides, I like the added benefit of keeping myself engaged with the film and familiarizing myself with the changes. **Automating everything isn't always the answer.**

Given that I chose to forego relying on scene timings, I had to devise a solution for measuring the TRT. I decided to measure it using a sum of the length of all reels and leverage a relationship between the Continuity and Reels tables. The relationship was already there since I assigned a reel to each scene. This also allowed me to display the scene range of any given reel in the Reels table. Pretty cool, right?

The Reel Tracker

The Reels table only contains the number of records as reels that exist. I have a separate table where I archive old versions of the reels before updating them. I extract the reel number from the hour number in the timecode of the duration of the reel. This becomes the primary key to all other tables, including that Reel Archive table I just mentioned (see the below section on Relational Databases for more on primary keys [p. 84]). The cut itself is versioned using a global field in the dashboard, but the reels version up independently. This means reel 1 can be v16.1, reel 2 can be v16.2, and reel 3 could still be on v16 if we haven't updated it; but the whole cut is referred to as "version 16". I can keep

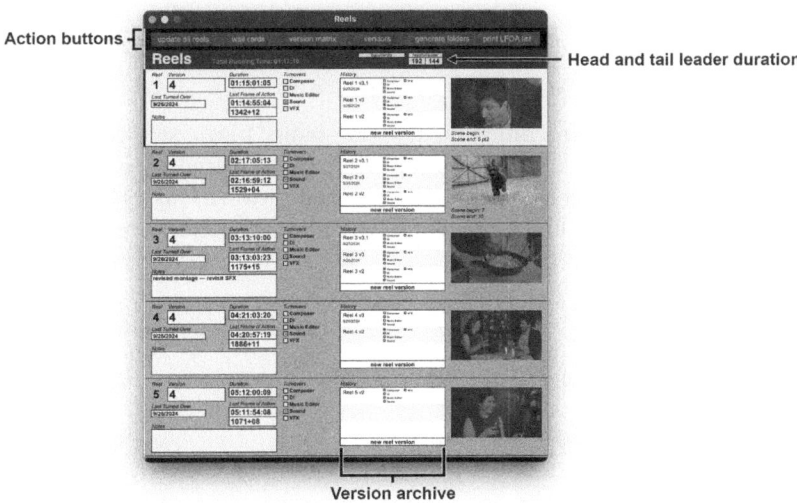

Figure 4.7 Custom reels layout, detailing the reels in the film and their associated runtime data.

notes and check off boxes per reel indicating which departments have received which turnovers.

To use the Reels table as a means of calculating the TRT, I disregard the hours from the reels and subtract the head and tail leader (192 and 144 frames in my case, respectively). I also have an override for logos at the head of the show and for credits at the tail. Duration is measured from the first frame of action (FFOA) after logos to the last frame of action (LFOA) before the first credit, except when the final credits are added, at which point I disregard the override. I simply input the duration of the sequence, and the calculations are done from there to calculate both an LFOA list and TRT.

The Marker Driven Tables

My ADR and DI tables are both marker list-driven tables. They rely on me exporting marker lists from the Media Composer Markers Tool and importing them into FileMaker Pro. This is different from the codebook (which gets its data from bin metadata exports), The Continuity and Reels (largely manually entered data), and VFX and Music tables (which parse EDLs to extract data). There *are* markers in the EDLs, but we'll get to that.

Regardless of where the markers are, they **absolutely must** be formatted in a specific way to make the most of them—with delimiters. I use equal signs to delimit information so chunks of the markers can be directed into specific fields using script steps: A method passed down to me while working with John Axelrad. An example of a basic ADR marker comment is:

> ADR=Brian=I'm running a marathon, so we can't get burgers.=end

In this "formula" (technically, it's a "string"), we see a classification, character name, and dialogue line, all separated by equal signs. FileMaker will replace each = with a pilcrow (a carriage return), turning it from one line of text into a **value list**, where each line is a new value.

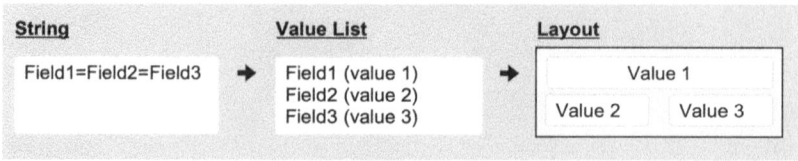

Figure 4.8 A breakdown of how a string of text is reformatted into a value list.

Value 1 is "ADR," Value 2 is "Brian," and Value 3 is "I'm running a marathon, so we can't get burgers." If the markers are formatted correctly and consistently, these value lists will route information to the correct fields and then reports (like ADR cue sheets, DI effect lists, music cue sheets, etc.) can be sorted and saved to PDF with calculations being done along the way.

These calculations can be anything from the total number of cues, or how many kinds of cues, to what type of DI effect and at what timecode (in TC or footage). One thing to consider: Create macros for your markers! You can tab through the marker dialog box to change the color and marker name, and most importantly, you can make sure the correct number of equal signs are typed out.

The Music Cue Sheet

This one is specifically unique because I have two scripts that can run to import data, and they're not the typical markers or EDLs I've outlined. Once the data is imported, the table formats and calculates all the same, but I've built it to import either ProTools Markers or a Media Composer EDL. With the ProTools Markers, there should be two markers (one at the beginning of the cue and one at the end) per cue; both should be formatted the same way. These markers use = delimiters just like I use in the Media Composer markers.

With the Media Composer EDL import, the information is stored elsewhere: Timeline Clip Notes.

You can segment-select a music clip (or clips) and tag them all with the same timeline clip note. This timeline clip note contains both the scene and cue type, like this: **"MX54=Source."** Timeline Clip Notes

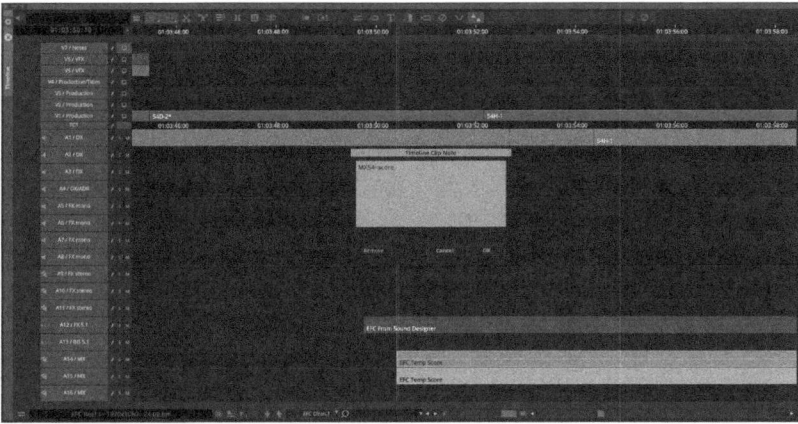

Figure 4.9 Avid Timeline with clip notes window pop up, displaying a formatted music cue identifier.

come across in an EDL with an asterisk in front so that FileMaker will look for the following pattern: "*MX" and then it will parse the number before the equal sign as the scene (54), and the word after the equal sign as the type (Source). The script that imports a music EDL will take the "Record TC In" of the first clip in the cue and the "Record TC Out" of the last clip in the cue, then list all unique clip names between the two timecodes. This effectively summarizes all clips used in a temp cue and calculates a duration.

The Visual Effects Tracker

I go into detail regarding tracking visual effects later in the Visual Effects section (p. 181). For now, I will outline how I built my tracker on a technical level. The minutiae of accounting for the shots can be discussed separately and on their own merit. The VFX tracker contains a record of every visual effect shot in the film. A shot has two statuses (see figure 8.4):

- **Cut Status**: Active or inactive (it's either in the timeline or it's not)
- **Shot Status**: A range of statuses for the stage of work it's in (Temp, In Revision, Avid Review, Final).

Those are two separate fields. Another field is the work order, which describes the scope of work to be done on the shot. I have fields that act as flags that I add to keep track of how many types of shots we have. These flags are **Cosmetic, Graphic, Re-Speed, Comp, Key**, and **Paint**. It was important to me to separate these flags because I'd often have a shot, which would be a couple of these—such as a "key" and a "cosmetic" shot. Separate vendors would do these different work orders. It's helpful to find all the "key" shots and then from those, forward the approved cosmetic shots to the second vendor for cosmetic work. Conversely, consider the need to find shots flagged *only* for cosmetic work and switch their vendor. Additional flags I use include **Matte**, which denotes that the final shot should be delivered with a holdout matte for color correction, and **Sound**, which denotes that there's sync sound associated with the shot (like gunfire).

Every VFX shot is comprised of one or more plates, otherwise referred to as "Elements." Likewise, each VFX shot will ultimately have at least one version submitted from the VFX vendor. Both VFX Elements and VFX Versions have their own tables and are related to the tracker using the shot code as the primary key (p. 84). Leveraging portals on the VFX Tracker layout allows me to view all related elements and versions for any given shot. More detail about how the VFX tracker operates can be found in the VFX chapter under "Lifespan of a VFX Shot (p. 187)."

Scripting in FileMaker Pro

I believe the best way to begin learning about scripting in FileMaker is to start being mindful of what you're doing manually in the program and then write scripts that do those things. The previous example in the Absolute Basics section highlights a perfect use case (p. 187). The resource I've found most helpful is the FileMaker Functions Reference on the Claris' website (https://help.claris. com/en/pro-help/content/functions-reference.html). I'll cover some examples of scripts I've written and their contexts to give you an idea of what's possible and to get you thinking about the scripts you might want to write.

First, here are some best practices. Notice in the example that I added comments describing what each chunk does. **Comments are Step 1 in scripting**. It's a good practice to get into, whether you're sharing your database with others or just opening a script you wrote a decade ago and need to remember *why* you did something or wrote it in a certain way. Comments also help you get your head in the right spot before writing any "code;" they force you to think about your goal in writing that small section.

Name and organize your scripts. I like to duplicate a script and *rename the duplicate* with a version, leaving the original as the "live" script (since it's usually already mapped to buttons or called out by name as a subscript). I archive the duplicated and versioned script.

Let's look at a few examples. First, read through the script and see if you can get a feel for what it's trying to do. I'll follow each one up with some details and an explanation.

Codebook: NAV- Codebook New Window

```
#opens the codebook in a new window, form view
Set Error Capture [On]

#exits the script if the permissions aren't high enough
If [Get (AccountPrivilegeSetName) ≠ "[Full Access]" and
PatternCount (Get (AccountPrivilegeSetName); "[Lesser
Access]") ≠ 1]
        Exit Script []
End If

#Does a fun little pirate thing if command-shift is
held down
If [Get (ActiveModifierKeys) = 17]
        Show Custom Dialog [Title: "ARR!"; Message: "Ye
    found me buried treasure! enjoy your
        metadata "; Default Button: "...what?",
        Commit: "Yes"]
```

```
End If
```

```
#opens a new codebook window and resizes it
New Window [Style: Document; Name: "Codebook"; Using
layout: "Codebook" (Codebook); Top: 15; Left: 50;
Close: Yes; Minimize: Yes; Maximize: Yes; Resize: Yes;
Menu Bar: Yes; Dim parent window: No; Toolbars: Yes]
Set Zoom Level [200%]
Adjust Window [Resize to Fit]
```

```
#omits test days from found set
Constrain Found Set [Specified Find Requests: Omit
Records; Criteria: Codebook::Photography Unit: ""
Test""] [Restore]
Go to Record/Request/Page [Last]
```

There are a couple of things to unpack here. This is a relatively simple script, and I use it for navigation. It's attached to a button on my main dashboard layout, and executing it opens a new window using the codebook layout. It then omits records from test days. I tend to start all my scripts with "set error capture" on so the script can run unencumbered. If there's an issue, I'll find it in the debugging process and figure out how to handle the specific error code being thrown.

Next, we run into an "if" statement. I do this for data integrity and privacy. Only a user with the correct permissions can run the script.

The following "if" statement is a little goofy but a good illustration of what's possible: You can check to see which modifier keys the user is holding down. In this script, it's inconsequential. In other scripts, it can be the difference between running one branch of an "if" statement or another.

The next chunk opens a new window and specifically positions and resizes it. Finally, the found set is constrained to all non-test shoot days, and the script navigates to the last record (which should be the most recently shot footage.)

ADR: Re-Parse ADR Marker

```
#re-parses marker text and places updated values in
ADR fields
Set Variable [$ADR_Values; Value:Substitute
(ADR::Import Text; "="; ¶)]
Set Field [ADR::ADR_Tag; GetValue ($ADR_Values; 1)]
```

```
#sets the status as OMITTED if "OMIT" is found in
the tag
If [PatternCount (ADR::ADR_Tag; "Omit") > 0]
      Set Field [ADR::ADR_Status; "Omitted"]
```

```
End If
Set Field [ADR::_fk_CharList_Abbv; GetValue ($ADR_
Values; 3)]
Set Field [ADR::Dialogue; GetValue ($ADR_Values; 4)]
Set Field [ADR::Reason; GetValue ($ADR_Values; 5)]
Set Field [ADR::Note; GetValue ($ADR_Values; 6)]
Set Field [ADR::ADR_Cue_Code; GetValue ($ADR_
Values; 7)]

#places the scene number into the scene field from the
note if it finds "sc "(this MUST be the last thing in
the field)
If [PatternCount (ADR::Note; "sc ")]
      Set Field [ADR::Scene; GetValue (Substitute
      (ADR::Note; "sc "; ¶); 2)]
End If
```

This is another relatively simple script: It re-parses a string of text. It showcases some interesting uses of "if" statements, variables, and a value list. The script starts by defining a variable that is formed from a calculation. It takes the string of text and replaces all = with ¶, thus creating a value list (p. 76). Each field is then filled with data from the values.

Did you notice how each line uses the "GetValue" function, and the number increases by one each time? The "if" statements only execute if a pattern of text is found.

Codebook: Create ALE for still subclip generation

```
#creates an ALE file for the shoot day with marks in the
center of clips to export still images
Freeze Window

#confirms script should be run and asks for filename
Set Variable [$Export; Value:Codebook::Shoot_Day]
Set Field [Project Dashboard::Export_Filename_g;
$Export & " subclips for stills"]
Show Custom Dialog [Title: "PAY ATTENTION!"; Message:
"Make sure your shot log import settings
      are set to merge events with known sources and
      automatically create subclips "; Default
      Button: "OK", Commit: "Yes"; Button 2: "Cancel",
      Commit: "No"]
If [Get(LastMessageChoice)≠1]
      Exit Script [Result: "User abort."]
End If
Show Custom Dialog [Title: "Create ALE for Subclips in
   "& $Export; Message: "This will create
   an ALE that represents the dailies bin for still
   frame creation. "& ¶ & ¶ & "Enter a name
```

```
        for your groovy new file here: "; Default Button:
        "OK", Commit: "Yes"; Button 2: "Cancel",
        Commit: "No"; Input #1: Project
        Dashboard::Export_Filename_g, "ALE Filename"]
If [Get(LastMessageChoice)≠1]
        Exit Script [Result: "User abort."]
End If

#initialize file with file header info
Set Variable [$title; Value:If(IsEmpty(Project
    Dashboard::Export_Filename_g) = True;
    "Untitled"; Project Dashboard:: Export_Filename_g)]
Set Variable [$file; Value: $title & ".ale"]
Set Variable [$Dir; Value:Get (DesktopPath)]

Create Data File ["$file"; Create folders: Off] Open
Data File ["$file"; Target: $FileID]
Open Data File ["$file"; Target: $FileID]

Set Variable [$line; Value:"$$ALE_Header"]
    Write to Data File [File ID: $FileID; Data source:
    $line; Write as: UTF-8; Append line feed:
        On]

#constrain to Shoot Day
Go to Layout ["Codebook" (Codebook)]
Find Matching Records [Replace; Codebook::Shoot_Day]
Sort Records [Keep records in sorted order; Specified
    Sort Order: Codebook::Tape; ascending]
        [Restore; No dialog]

#gather ALE clip data, set as variables, write string
to text file
Go to Record/Request/Page [First]
Loop
        #data
        Set Variable [$name; Value: Codebook::Tape & "
        Still Image"]
        Set Variable [$srcTape; Value: Codebook::Tape]
        Set Variable [$startTC; Value: Codebook::StartTC]
        Set Variable [$endTC; Value: Codebook::EndTC]
        Set Variable [$tracks; Value: "V"]
        Set Variable [$frame; Round((Codebook::EndFRAMES
        + Codebook::StartFRAMES) / 2; 0)
        Set Variable [$markIN; Value: $frame]
        Set Variable [$markOUT; Value: $frame + 1]
        #write data to file
        Set Variable [$line; Value: $name & " " & srcTape & "
            " & $startTC & " " & $endTC &" "&
            $markIN & " " & $markOUT & " " & $tracks]
```

```
      Write to Data File [File ID: $FileID; Data
             source: $line; Write as: UTF-8; Append
             line feed: On]


      Go to Record/Request/Page [Next; Exit after last]
End Loop

#close data file
Close Data File [File ID: $FileID] Unsort Records
Go to Record/Request/Page [First]
Show Custom Dialog [Title: $title; Message: "ALE
   exported to " & Get(DesktopPath); Default
   Button: "OK", Commit: "Yes"; Button 2: "Cancel",
   Commit: "No"]
```

This is the last script I'll include. It's another one from the codebook that creates an ALE text file from codebook metadata. It begins by asking a couple of qualifying questions, and if the answer is no, the script is exited. These steps serve to ensure the script is not run unintentionally.

The script then creates a data file on the desktop with the ALE header information (notice I'm using a global variable here that stores the ALE header). The found set is then constrained to one shoot day, and most notably, we enter a loop.

A loop is repeated until a condition is met; for example, in this script, when it reaches the last record in the found set. In this case, the loop gathers all necessary metadata as variables and then concatenates them into one line of text, which is written into the data file. It goes to the next record and continues until it reaches the last record.

Finally, the script closes the data file, returns to the first record, and shows a dialog stating that the script has finished running.

Scripting Conclusion

From the examples presented here, you should be able to start poking around and playing with "if" statements, loops, variables, and setting fields. If there's something you feel you should be able to do, research it online to see how other people are accomplishing it. Odds are you're not the only person who has ever needed to, say, include a summary of all records while only displaying a found set. The answer you find online might be from a printer salesman who asked a question in 2013 about his script; if you keep an open mind, you'll find that their solution may work for you, too.

Building a Relational Database

As outlined above, FileMaker Pro can be extremely powerful when its relational capabilities are combined with its scripting and automation tools. I've barely scratched the surface myself and continue to expand my database with each project I work on. Workflows change, and it's important to be able to adapt. I encourage anyone interested in building a database to look into an introductory FileMaker Pro course (p. 266), as it will lay out the fundamentals of how the software works on an elementary level. It can be difficult to untangle, but the results can provide easier and more reliable workflows, so don't be discouraged!

Unlike a program like Media Composer, which has a comparatively singular purpose (editing video), FileMaker Pro can be one person's personal budget app and another company's event tracker. The point is, you can use it however works best for you. It's also vital to abstract ideas and repurpose them, like with the examples I used of the flower shop and the printer salesman. My VFX tracker, which is easily my most complex set of tables and scripts, was built with previous experiences using Google Sheets, Excel, and Flow Production (fka "Shotgrid") in mind. By learning the core program and leaning on personal experience, you give yourself the ability to adapt and create on the fly. That alone is more powerful than any inherited database.

Primary Keys

If I could impart one concept pertaining to related tables, it would be the notion of a "primary key." For each table in your relational database, there will be either a primary or foreign key. Your primary key field should contain uniquely identifying information that is used to "link", or "**relate**" the record in that table to records in other **related** tables. In a way, a foreign key is the opposite of a primary key. It's an identifying field in the related table. The best examples of primary key use in my database would be the VFX Tracker and the VFX Elements tables. The primary key is the "Shot Code" field in the VFX tracker. It is related to the "Shot Code Element" field (which is the foreign key in this relationship) in the VFX Elements table.

Relationship Examples

I've provided a few examples of relationships I've created in my database. In the relationship outlined earlier in the codebook section, the qualification of the relationship between the codebook and VFX Elements is a record with a matching tape name, $\leq$ Timecode In and $\geq$

Timecode Out. This means that all the above criteria must be met to display a related record.

If I import an EDL, it will contain the following data about a clip from my timeline at a minimum: Tape name, source timecode in and out, and record timecode in and out. When this data is parsed, and in the VFX Elements table, the Timecode sets go through a series of calculations:

21:55:48:10	Field 1: Source TC In [text]
1894762	Field 2: Source TC In Frames [calculated number using **Field 1**]
1894754	Field 3: Source TC In with Handle Frames [calculated number using **Field 2** and handle field]
21:55:48:02	Field 4: Source TC In with Handle [calculated text using **Field 3**]

I'm transforming the data by adding frames to the timecode fields (in this case, it's to add handles to a VFX shot). Since the relationship between the codebook and VFX Elements tables is based on timecode, if I add too many head or tail handles, I could push the timecode of the proposed scan past the available recorded footage. However, this would invalidate the relationship. The above example adds eight frames of handles. My database would flag it if, say, the clip in the timeline started at the very beginning of the recorded take.

Another relationship I maintain is for thumbnail images in the VFX Elements table. Using a trick similar to the Codebook Stills ALE, I create subclips that are named to reflect the Element ID ([shotcode]_[element]). When exported in bulk, I get a bunch of JPEG files, and when I import those into container fields within a VFX Stills table, I'm left with two pieces of data: An image and a filename. The problem is this filename doesn't match anything in my VFX Elements table due to that pesky file extension.

A couple of approaches to remove it: You could have the field set up to auto-enter and replace itself, substituting ".jpeg" with "", or you could create a new calculated field that performs the same substitution function and use that as your primary key in the relationship. I chose the latter simply because it is not destructive.

Next Steps

This is a dense subject to write about. The hope is that this chapter has provided context for how an assistant editor uses FileMaker in a cutting room. I encourage you to look up any terms that are foreign to you and try to bridge the gap between what's written here and other resources referencing other contexts.

Try starting by building a 1:1 codebook from dailies bins, which only has dailies data. Play with getting data in and out of your solution by creating import and export scripts, then map those to buttons. It's easy to feel overwhelmed when presented with a tool that can do seemingly anything. I still feel intimidated by what I've seen other people do with FileMaker.

Know that while FileMaker may have a lot of answers, what's more important is knowing what questions to ask of it—those questions will come with experience and time. You're now better equipped to stay alert and start collecting questions to answer with FileMaker or whatever tool you decide to use.

5   Dailies

Cameras are rolling, sound is speeding, and Editorial is beginning to receive footage. Exciting! How do we handle this? What follows will go step by step through the dailies process, starting with the paperwork, organizing the media, prepping scene bins for the editor, and finally, distributing dailies to the studio. Each section has a little checklist-style bullet-pointed list which you can use as a quick reference (that's what I do; see "dailies checklist [downloadable]" on www.routledge.com/9781032843285), and they are all followed by an in-depth explanation for *why* I operate this way.

Some aspects can be skipped over in certain instances: Grouping clips (p. 106) is unnecessary if you only have single camera takes. Syncing off-speed footage (p. 102) is similarly irrelevant if there's no footage that's been shot at a different frame rate. Nevertheless, the steps necessary to handle these kinds of things lie where they belong in the order of operations which I would process them in if they were to exist. Note that this workflow accounts for working in 5.1, so you can ignore any of those steps if you're working in stereo.

I'm going to repeat myself once again before we dive in: Talk with your editor about their preferences for how they'd like you to handle marking clips and laying out bins. You can always make suggestions, but these are all highly personal choices that vary depending on the project and the editor.

Dailies Paperwork

- Add all documents to dailies paperwork folder named with the shoot date and day
  - Example folder name: 250509 DAY001
  - Include script supervisor notes (from the script supervisor), camera, sound, and transfer reports (from the dailies technician email), ALEs and bins (included in the same email as well), call sheets, and other notes or files pertaining to the day.

DOI: 10.4324/9781003516491-6

- Folders are: Bins (Bins and ALE files), Camera Crew Reports, DIT Reports Cam Roll, DIT Reports Daily, EDR (End of Day Report), PRR (Posthouse Receiving Report), Script Reports, and Sound Reports.
- Print production reports, editors' logs, facing pages, and camera reports for yourself (the PA might do this). Store them in a binder when finished with dailies for the day.
- On a Post-it note, write the shoot day, shoot date, camera rolls shot, sound rolls recorded, scenes shot (noting partials), and any notes for the dailies tech as you go through. Place this Post-it on the production report.

The dailies paperwork I expect to receive includes:

- Call Sheet
  - *From the production office; arrives the day before the shoot.*
  - *Outlines the scenes planned to be shot.*
- Camera Report
  - *From the camera department through the dailies lab (request CSV if possible).*
  - *Details the camera rolls shot, takes recorded, and associated metadata.*
- Sound Report
  - *From the sound recordist through the dailies lab (request CSV if possible).*
  - *Details the takes recorded and track assignments.*
- **Script Supervisor Notes** (Production Report, Editor's Log, Facing Pages, Lined Script)
  - *From the script supervisor directly and through the dailies lab.*
  - *Request CSV of Facing Pages or Editor's Log, if possible*
  - **Production Report:** *Includes day and shoot summaries, scenes shot, and overall notes.*
  - **Editor's Log:** *Lists the setups recorded in the order they were shot.*
  - **Facing Pages:** *Like the Editor's Log, it includes more detailed notes and is organized by set-up according to the corresponding page in the lined script.*
  - **Lined Script:** *Script pages with annotations denoting which takes cover which lines on and off camera.*
- Dailies Lab Report
  - *From the dailies lab*
  - *Details of footage that was received and associated technical information (file size, etc.)*

- Avid bins and ALE files
  - *From the dailies lab*
  - *I consider these "paperwork" because they are "digital documents."*
  - *ALE resupplies should **only** contain the affected clip(s) and affected column(s).*

As you can see from above, paperwork comes in via a few channels: The script supervisor sends their notes directly to editorial, the production office sends documents independently, and the dailies lab sends a collection of everything. This can lead to duplicates; I prioritize saving the documents that come directly from the departments. I organize the documents into their respective folders on the Nexis "Documents" drive.

I tend to prepend a date to almost all my folders/files. I use the format "YYMMDD" (as opposed to "*YY*YYMMDD" because the "20" is redundant to me. We will not be leaving the 21st century while working on the film). I also use "year/month/day" because it sorts chronologically. I stick to 2-3 number padding on most things for ease of eyesight and flexibility down the line should anything

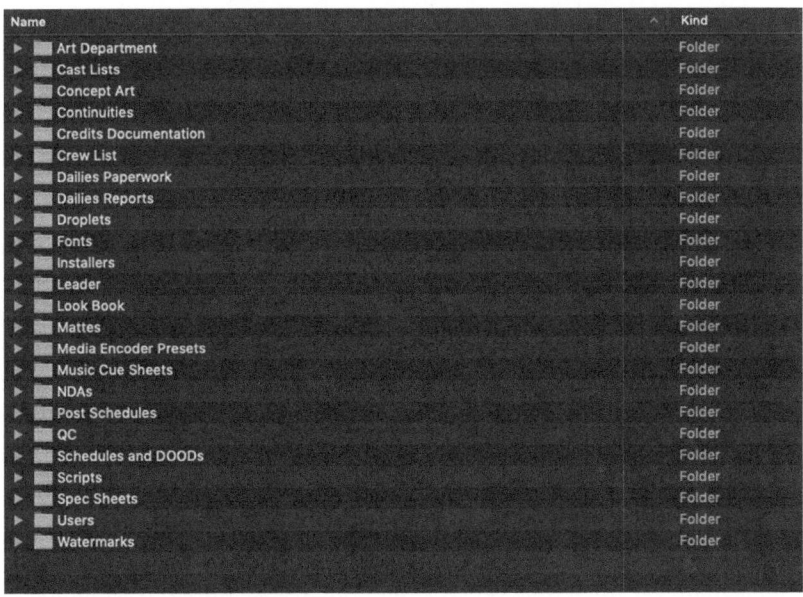

Figure 5.1 Finder-level organization of the "Documents" Avid Nexis workspace.

grow past double digits. I find it easier to read "DAY023" than "DAY23."

The call sheet comes in before anything else, usually a day earlier. I look at the advance schedule on the call sheet and anticipate getting pickups before we leave a location. The production office might send revisions to the script while shooting. I store these in a "Scripts" folder and print the revised pages only. According to the WGA West, the standard script revision color sets are (in order): White (unrevised), Blue, Pink, Yellow, Green, Goldenrod, Buff, Salmon, Cherry, Second Blue Revision, Second Pink Revision, and so on.

When the dailies media comes in, I reference the editor's log and facing pages. I highlight the director's favorites along with any sound and VFX notes. I'll look at these later when doing a final pass on the bin layout and add any additional notes to the clip names and note frames as needed (this will be outlined shortly).

Transferring Media

- Transfer the media
  - Aspera Drive automatically downloads the media. Copy to Media01, "Transfers" folder.
  - Copy production sound rolls to "Production Audio" on the ADR_SND drive.
  - **Move** MXF media into new MediaFiles folder(s) to scan.
    - *If picture and sound are delivered separately:* Move picture MXF media into one MediaFiles folder to scan, then move sound MXF media into a second MediaFiles folder to scan.
  - Copy Dailies bin(s) into the Avid project within the *Dailies by SHOOT DAY* folder.

I make sure to set up a transfer station with automatic downloading enabled. For dailies file syncing, my preference is Aspera Drive (p. 19), which can be set up to auto-refresh every 15 minutes. I request that the dailies tech use the same passphrase for all Dailies Aspera transfers; that way, the auto-download can decrypt upon download. I'll also ask the post facility if they can increase our bandwidth limit for the duration of dailies (p. 27).

MediaFile Folder Names

I copy the dailies to a transfer folder on the active Nexis media drive (I lock them off once they reach capacity—for example, if Media01 is full [2 TB] after 13 days, we move to Media02.) The media is **moved** from the transfer folder into zJared.2 and zJared.3 on the same drive. I put picture media in .2 and sound media in .3 because if/when

I import wild lines, Media Composer automatically creates a zJared.1 folder. The .2 and .3 folders stay in the "Avid MediaFiles" directory (*next to* "MXF," not in it) while I move files into them, so Avid doesn't scan the folders prematurely. After I drop these folders into the MXF directory and switch to Avid to scan and create MDB and PMR files, I can rename the .2 and .3 folders to reflect more useful information. I use a chronological naming scheme that includes media identifiers, like the camera or sound roll span it contains. For example, a folder could be named:

> ### 250810 DAY001 A001-A008 B004-B005 C001
> *[YYMMDD] [Shoot Day] [A Cam Span] [B Cam Span], etc.*

I will dispel a myth about changing the folder names: You can do it without issue once the .MDB and .PMR files have been created. Be aware that if the folder's name is anything other than an integer (or your computer name followed by an integer in a shared environment), then Avid **will not** rescan and update the enclosed .MDB and .PMR files. This can lead to an instance where if media gets deleted from the folder; another networked Avid station tries to look for it, and despite still being listed in the database files, the media does not exist. Surprise, surprise: Avid throws an error saying that the file doesn't exist (instead of throwing up the "media offline" image and turning the clips red). So... what can we do to avoid this? Quickly rename the folder to something scannable (zJared.23 [in this case, I picked a random number]), **or** you can use a naming convention that is *integer exclusive*, such as "**zJared.1001,**" where the 1000s series is your dailies and the 1s place increases to reflect the shoot day number.

Resupplied Media

Occasionally, we get resupplied media (for example, if a color change is made to a whole scene.) For this, I separate the old media (in this example, picture files *only*) from the MediaFiles folder and copy the folder name to my clipboard. I then move the new, resupplied media into the folder and name it "zJared.1" to let Avid scan it and register the new media before pasting the folder name back. If I have to relink, I can do so without reverting the folder name. **Note: Make certain no one is actively editing these files while doing any of this media management.** Regardless, they sometimes may need to relink on their machines (if only to refresh their .PMR files.) In these cases, it might be best to simply restart the Media Composer application.

Importing Wild Lines and Variable Speed Clip Audio

- Bring in variable speed clip audio and/or playback music.
  - Check paperwork for any wild tracks or off-speed takes recorded with sync sound and import them to a new folder on the active media drive.
  - Dupe Start TC into SoundTC and add Soundroll (same as folder and bin name.)
  - Copy "Music Masters - Playback" media (if it exists) to the MX drive and import it into an Avid bin.
  - Set to 5.1, stereo group ch.1-2 for playback music.

I refer to any production audio I import into Avid at this stage as a "wild line," even though that's not the exact definition. The reason for this is that I want to separate the audio generated by the dailies technician from the audio I import on my own. Generally, the files I import are wild lines and occasionally sound from off-speed takes. I make a bin named with the shoot date, day, and sound roll, then import audio into it. I use a bin view named "Dailies Audio," which has Tape, Soundroll, Start, and SoundTC columns (in that order) so I can dupe the Start TC into the Sound TC column and add the Soundroll into the Soundroll column. This is important for sound turnovers down the road. These clips need to be set as 5.1 "sequence" clips, but we'll handle that in a bit.

Wild lines, wild tracks, and sync audio recorded during high frame rate takes need to be brought in separately from the media that comes in from the dailies lab. In some cases, the lab will marry the associated audio with the conformed high frame rate take, but it won't be in sync. This is something to talk about on the workflow call, and my preference is for them to do it because it means I don't have to spend time importing more files (more on rectifying sync later [p. 102]). A common event if you have a music-centric scene, is receiving a new Music Master file used for playback. More details on multichannel audio (p. 98) and audio timecode data (p. 99) embedded in these files can be found in their respective sections.

Checking Metadata and Exporting to the Codebook

- Open the Shoot Day bin in Avid and check that metadata and clips match the paperwork.
  - Switch into the Codebook bin view and make sure all clips are online. Check metadata.
  - Rename the MediaFiles folders to reflect the proper info:
    - Picture: **250810 DAY001 A001-A008 B004-B005 C001**

- Sound: **250810 DAY001 SR001-SR002**
- Production Sound: **250810 DAY001 WildTracks**
- Dupe the Name column into the Slate column.
- Physically highlight the clips on the editor's log while confirming the clips exist in the dailies bin. Check slate name, clip name, and all notes that may exist. Verify the information is consistent across all department documents. Coloring the clips in the bin *only while checking* helps. The quick search box helps, too.
- If the clip is off-speed, append the fps it was shot in to the end of the clip name (for example, **D66A-4(A)* 120fps**) in both the master clip and subclip. These will need to be conformed if a sync sound was recorded for them. This process is outlined below and should happen before subclips are made.
- Select all master clips and set all clips to "5.1 Sequence" (enable this feature in AudioExtras). This will ensure the production audio plays out of the center speaker instead of the left and right speakers. Do this for any imported wild tracks as well.
- Export the dailies bin in Codebook view to a tab-delimited file and import it into FileMaker.
- Create stills using codebook ALE and import them back into FileMaker. Delete the stills subclips.
- If working with multiple aspect ratios, add source colors to the clips accordingly.

Everything stems from the metadata. After our workflow call and before production begins, I send the dailies lab a template bin in a codebook bin view ("Dailies Codebook Bin (downloadable)" found on www.routledge.com/9781032843285). I use a Codebook bin view because the order of the columns is important to me for two reasons: One is of relevance to my cross-checking duties, and the other is so that the files I export for the codebook stay consistent. The information displayed in a bin view is what gets exported when saving out an ALE or tab-delimited file. I run a pipeline test and make sure the metadata is flowing through correctly when setting up the show.

Tape Name

The tape name is used as the unique ID in most digital cinema workflows. I use it in the database extensively. An example tape name (using ARRI's formatting) would be **A031C009_241215_Z39B**. To break this down into information that we can easily parse:

A	Camera Designator	Which camera it is
031	Reel Number	Number of reels (cards) recorded (with three number padding.) This is incremented each time a new camera card has been inserted.
C009	Clip Number	Number of takes recorded on the camera card. Each press of "record" increments the clip number. Resets to 001 with each new reel (card).
_	Separator	n/a
241215	Date	Formatted YYMMDD
_	Separator	n/a
Z39B	Unique ID	Randomly generated ID per camera. It prevents duplicate tape names in the event there is accidentally more than one camera with the same designation.

So, the clip with a tape name **A031C009_241215_Z39B** is the ninth clip recorded on the 31st "A" camera reel, which was shot on December 15, 2024. If there were a second A camera recording at the same time on the same card number, we'd be able to differentiate it from this one because the Unique ID would be different. While footage from RED and Sony cameras might be named in a slightly different format, the same concepts apply, and you should be able to parse it at a glance now that you're primed on what to look for.

Custom Columns and Requests

I duplicate the Name column into a custom column named "Slate" so that if/when the master *or* subclip names change, the original name still lives somewhere. I do this because the clip names change when we add notes, and it becomes cumbersome when using a burn-in to reference the name column. Instead, my burn-ins reference the Slate column (p. 209).

I ask for AuxTC1 to contain a Sound Timecode, which is fairly common. If there's playback with an audio timecode, I'll ask for that data to be dumped into AuxTC2. A "Good Take" or "Circle" column can be used for Circled Takes. I've seen this shown in binary form (using 1 and 0 for circled and non-circled, respectively) and in another form wherein circle takes were marked as "Y" (for "Yes"), and non-circle takes simply left this field empty. I prefer the latter.

If metadata is incorrect or missing (p. 95), I'll request that the dailies technician look into it. If they make a correction, I'll ask them to send us an updated ALE file containing **only** the affected clip(s) and column(s). I can then select the clips in question, import the revised ALE, and expose the shoot day bin to the scene bin so the updated metadata propagates through to the subclips. I won't stop processing dailies to wait for the updated ALE, which is why I need to expose the bins to each other. Sometimes, I get the ALE a few hours later; sometimes, it takes a day or more to get to the bottom of it.

Metadata and FileMaker Pro

As detailed throughout this chapter, dailies metadata passes through the Avid bins and into FileMaker Pro. FileMaker Pro can use this data to summarize, sort, and create new documents such as dailies reports, ALEs, and, down the line, even EDLs for VFX pulls (the latter two via script steps). Custom calculations transform the data for use in various circumstances—like adding handles to start/end timecode, modifying the number of subclip audio tracks, and merging script supervisor descriptions with Avid data. As long as the integrity of the metadata is maintained, there's a lot that can be automated and presented cleanly.

I export a **tab-delimited file of the dailies bin** (p. 97) from Avid and import it into the codebook table. I then run two scripts that generate different ALE files: One for still images (to be used in the codebook) and another that creates subclips, which are used in the scene bins and the digital lined script—more about these ALEs and what I'm modifying in the FileMaker Pro chapter (p. 70).

We return to the database two more times after this, first to import the stills and camera data (p. 120) and another to add shot descriptions and kick out a dailies report (p. 122). Of course, depending on your workflow (and sometimes mine), some of these database steps happen at different points. I might create the dailies report now, or at least ask the PA to start working on it. Otherwise, let's keep chugging along.

Accounting for Footage and Handling Discrepancies

In my own personal and humble opinion, everything in this book is important. This part is perhaps the *most* important and the most understated. To understand the weight of its importance, think about the time, effort, and resources that are poured into production. Millions of dollars and hundreds, if not thousands of hours, were spent making sure everyone and everything on set was available for the shoot. The actors have rehearsed, the equipment has been rented and schlepped, and every single second costs money—even (*especially*) when they're not shooting.

It's important to have reverence for every single person who came together to make sure that every frame got recorded. **Every frame counts**. It is absolutely imperative to account for what was recorded. I account for the footage in the dailies bin by cross-referencing the paperwork before ever importing the data into the codebook; I also account for the footage once the subclips are put into their scene bins. I cross-reference the master clips against the editor's log and the subclips against the facing pages, which is also a great way to add any notes from the facing pages into the clip names.

Sync Maps

One easy way to get an overview of a complete shoot day is to build a sync map of all dailies shot that day. It's a great way to get a sense of how the day went, as you can see how much time passed between takes and how much overlapping footage there is; it can help spot discrepancies or find footage in linearity. Select all master clips, right-click, and select "AutoSequence." This will lay every clip into a timeline based on its source timecode. One issue with this is that for multi-camera setups, overlapping clips will get cut off (instead of stacking angles on higher video tracks like a group clip). An alternative to this is to select "MultiGroup" instead of "AutoSequence." While this function **does not** map out the day like the previous method, it will give you a better sense of overlapping footage.

Discrepancies

When dealing with a discrepancy, I check three documents in this order: The editor's log, the camera report, and the sound report. First, I'll be in a bin and crossing off what's in the editor's log. Generally, I don't look at the data report (or telecine report, as it used to be called) because what's in the bin often matches it word for word, so I'll only check it as a last resort. If something from the editor's log is missing from the bin, I'll double-check that I'm looking at the right scene and take. If it's a series, I'll be more forgiving because that's usually a splinter unit, and they're just letting it roll. I'll also be forgiving if there's one more take in the bin than on the editor's log—more is typically ok, and less is almost always a problem. I just need to be sure that there aren't any notes associated with the extra clip, so I'll ask the script supervisor about it just to cover my bases.

When something is missing from the bin, though, I'll check the camera report to ensure they actually rolled and it's not just a typo from the script supervisor. If the camera report says they rolled, and the script supervisor says they rolled, then I check the sound report (assuming it's not an MOS shot). Nine times out of ten, if it's on the sound report, they definitely shot it. Sometimes, the discrepancy stems from shooting multicam—one camera rolls, but the other doesn't, so it's marked accidentally. I need to be able to answer these questions with authority.

All of this is just to gather as much information as possible because, at this point, I'll have to email the script supervisor and dailies technician/DIT. I usually wait until I've gone through all the day's footage to consolidate all my questions into one email. I give them as much information as I have for each instance and ask for clarification. I **never** assign blame. There's a huge difference between these two sentences, wherein 93D-1 has no audio, and I think it might be a mistake:

🚫 *"You sent 93D-1 without audio."* (Implies the dailies tech messed up)
✅ *"93D-1 appears to have no audio."* (Factually details the issue without assuming cause)

Most of the time, it's just a typo on one or more of the reports, but I need to get it in writing and confirm that we're not missing anything. Leave no stone unturned. Hurt no feelings, you dig?

Detour 1: ALE vs Tab-Delimited Files

Let's take a breather from the dailies workflow so I can opine on a few relevant things, starting with ALE files (see "240103 EFC DAY003. ALE" and "240103 EFC DAY003.txt" on www.routledge.com/ 9781032843285). I'll return to subclips, but I think this is a worthwhile detour.

It's possible to export a bin in two formats: An ALE and a tab-delimited file. I use both but at different times. The information in these files is generally the same, but there are some differences worth noting. Both files represent the bin, which is effectively a spreadsheet. Each clip is a record, and each column is a field. Exporting a tab-delimited file saves *just* that data in a text file with tabs separating the fields.

Exporting an ALE will export the same data with the same formatting—but it will add a header. The header allows Avid to identify the information in the file as an Avid bin, with information about the project, like the video, audio, film format, and fps. One other difference: Tracks. A video clip with four audio tracks looks different in an ALE than in a tab-delimited file. An ALE will display it as "**VA1A2A3A4**," whereas a tab-delimited file displays it as "**V1 A1-4**." The only time you need to account for this is if you're importing tab-delimited files into FileMaker and need to use that data to create an ALE. You might be me.

The tab-delimited file is cleaner to bring into FileMaker because we don't have to account for the header. The modifications we make to the data within FileMaker (like renaming clips, removing tracks, adding script supervisor descriptions, or setting in and out points) will be reflected in subclips when we reformat the data into an ALE using FileMaker and import that back into the same Media Composer bin. Sometimes, an ALE import will fail. If this ever happens, I adjust the bin view to show only the columns I'm importing in an order that matches the ALE. I have a bin view specifically for ALE importing, which usually works.

Detour 2: A Few Words on Multichannel Audio

Now let's discuss multichannel audio as it pertains to our dailies clips. Assuming we're working in a 5.1 project, there are some considerations to make—more on audio and 5.1 surround workflow later in the Audio chapter (p. 152).

Mix Format

What can be confusing from the previously mentioned terminology is that there's a difference between a clip with 5.1 multichannel audio and a clip with 5.1 mix format (sequence setting). The former can be set as expected by right-clicking a clip (or selection of clips), choosing *modify > modify clip > set multichannel audio*, and changing the grouping of tracks from mono to stereo or 5.1, which naturally remaps the audio tracks to discrete channels. For example, a dual mono clip would be two channels, center-panned. Modifying it to be stereo would pan A1 left and A2 right. The same would go for a 5.1 surround clip—the mono channels would be center-panned until modified when they would be remapped in the order selected (SMPTE, ProTools, or EXT).

Sequence Setting

The setting I change during dailies is the "**sequence setting**." This is different in that it doesn't change the mapping of the channels, just the space they're in. It must be set one clip at a time in the audio mixer *or* by using an "unsupported" feature (enabled via the console by typing in "AudioExtras" and checking the box "Modify Clip can batch change mix format"), which allows me to change this setting on batches of master clips.

By default, clip audio tracks are center-panned and considered a "stereo sequence," meaning you can pan the channel left or right. When played back in 5.1 space, the "stereo sequence" audio is split between the front left and front right speakers, **not the center speaker.** This is because, in a stereo sequence, *there is no center channel.* By changing the mix format of the clip from "stereo sequence" to "5.1 sequence," the clip tracks stay center-panned and in 5.1 space— displaying the square panners in the audio mixer instead of the knobs. The sound now comes out of the center channel.

Typically, you keep clips in stereo format unless you need to route the audio to a specific channel. A stereo clip cut into a 5.1 sequence will automatically be panned to the front left and front right in 5.1 space. Music, as I mention later (p. 66), I throw into 5.1 space on the clip level and pan -40% into the rears. This way, whenever that clip gets cut into a sequence, it will bleed into the surrounds. I also change a mono clip (like dailies or ADR) to 5.1 so it comes out of the center speaker as described above.

Clip Type Considerations

Besides the dailies footage itself, other multichannel audio that might need to be considered during dailies is any playback music masters, depending on the stems provided. On one project, when a new Music Master came in, it usually had the mix on tracks 1-2 and stems on lower polyphonic tracks. Some stems were stereo (like backing vocals), and some were mono (like a solo instrument or a lead vocal). I'd modify the multichannel audio and group the stereo pairs, leaving the mono stems alone. This allowed us to carry a fuller mix, as we could pan the vocals to the center speakers and to the left and right into the rears.

Detour 3: A Few Words on Timecode Audio Data Tracks

We're used to seeing timecode represented as a number and trans- mitted via text. It can also be encoded as an audio signal and carried as an audio track; it sounds like a modem trying to connect to the internet in the early 2000s. The data in this audio signal can be extracted by pointing Avid towards the audio track containing it and using the "Read Audio Timecode" command from the Clip menu to dump the data into an AuxTC field (I use AuxTC2). This data ripples through to subclips, and this function can also be performed on subclips. The most common use case for a timecode audio data track is during music playback.

In theory, it's good. In practice, it has been tricky for me to work with—*especially* when the timecode is intermittent (for example, multiple playback elements within one take, or if it's paused and resumed). I still find myself syncing via waveform, using AuxTC2 data generated by a Timecode Audio Data track *as a starting point*. Just make sure to **mute the data audio track** so when you or your editor match back, you're not blasted with that modem-esque sound.

Creating and Working with Subclips

- Create subclips, clean up names, and set audio for all.
  - Subclip all master clips, using only A1. Add four frame handles on heads and tails.
    - *Some Editors might want you to maintain all audio tracks on subclips.*
  - Mute any audio timecode or click tracks. Usually done in conjunction with the previous step.
  - **Optional***: Solo the first audio track (the mix) on all clips, so that's all the editors will hear. Usually done in conjunction with the previous step.
  - **Optional***: Deselect all tracks but V1 and A1. This is so the source tracks don't auto-enable when the editor wants to cut them into an assembly sequence with fewer audio tracks than production tracks.

  *Optional Steps: *Only* performed if working with all production tracks instead of just the mix track.

Why make subclips at all? For one, it helps further organize footage by allowing us to keep master clips from one shoot day in the same bin while the subclips from different scenes shot on the same day live in their scene bins.

Why not clone or copy the **master clips** into their appropriate scene bins? Cloning would mean that what happens to the clip in one bin happens to the same clip in the other bin. Renaming could get messy, and the worst part is that matchback gets absolutely wrecked. Depending on which bin was last exposed to the sequence you're working in, that's where the matchback will take you. It doesn't matter if you wanted the scene bin; you're taking a trip to the shoot day bin. Terrible. Copying (or "duplicating") the master clip leads to a secondary instance completely disconnected from the shoot day bin. Any added metadata won't be reflected in the original master clip; you can't perf slip, and you'd have to unlink and relink to pare down the tracks. It's not destructive, but it's also convoluted and time-consuming. Also, with all the above, you run the risk of someone accidentally deleting media unless you select all your master clips and "Lock bin selection." But that's an impossible mistake to make when working with subclips. So, yeah, I like subclips and their parent-child relationship with master clips.

Subclip Creation Methods

There are currently a few ways of creating subclips manually: Via ALE, and via Batch Create Subclips. To **create subclips manually**: Load a master clip into the source monitor, select the tracks to include (and a range—leaving no marks takes the entirety of the clip), then drag from the source monitor into a bin (or use "make subclip"). A more clever way of creating subclips is to use the data to create a **modified ALE**. An ALE can be simply exported and re-imported, that's totally viable. The ALE can be modified to include fewer audio tracks (like **only** the mix track) or a shorter range, which then allows room for perf slipping. The timecode calculations required to do this are best left to something like a FileMaker database. When creating subclips via ALE, ensure your Shot Log Import Setting is set to "Merge events with known sources and automatically create subclips." **Batch Create Subclips** (p. 46) is a great feature that is remarkably simple and intuitive. It even lets you add handles, and you can batch-create subclips from a sequence (which is great for VFX).

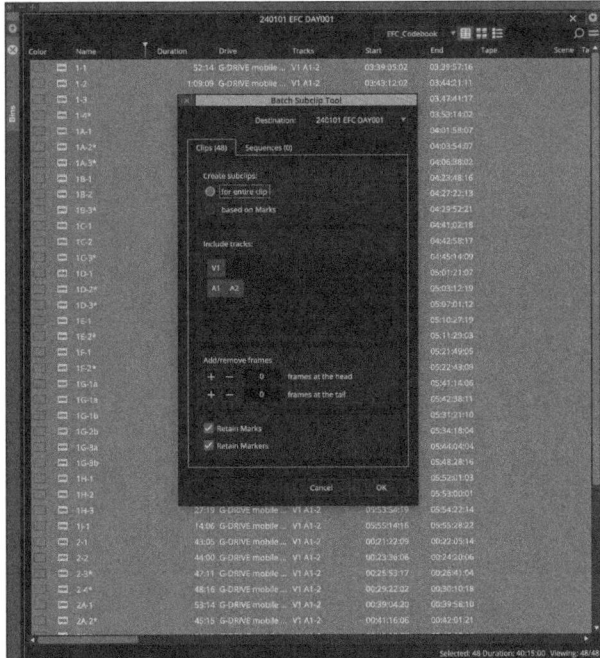

Figure 5.2 "Batch Create Subclips" dialog in Avid Media Composer.

However, I'll probably continue using ALEs since I'm already exporting that data to the codebook. It's also used for the dailies report (p. 71), and I need to create those still images somehow.

Film Setting Implications

A lot of people know to check the "Film" setting box when creating a new project, but they might not know why. As it pertains to subclips, perf slipping is one reason. Another is that subclips created in a "Film" Avid project are bound by their in and out points upon creation. You can't extend them past the beginning and end without matching back to the master clip it came from when cutting a segment from that clip in. Conversely, when the "Film" option is unchecked, the subclips that are created can be extended at the head and tail for as long a duration as exists in the original master clip. The subclip itself won't even show its duration in the bin—it will show the duration of the master clip, which is the easiest way to tell whether you are looking at a subclip made in a "Film" project or not.

Matching Back on Manually Synced Clips

When syncing clips manually, whether to rectify a sync issue or conform to a high frame rate shot, be aware that matchback may be a little wonky. If matching back from video, it will point to the original clip (either MOS or with bad sync). Matching back from audio will point to the imported audio file. This is especially important if the clips are being manually synced and then subclipped to reduce the number of tracks (i.e., mix track only). A subclip of a subclip does **not** leave a trail through subclips to the master clip. It leads **directly** to the master clip. Matching back from a subclip of a group (which is a relatively new feature as of this writing), however, will take you to the full group; then again, it will take you to the chosen angle, which, if it's a subclip, will then take you to the master clip.

Syncing Off-Speed Footage

- Sync off-speed footage or MOS takes (OPTIONAL—only if anything was shot off-speed).
  - Delete/move subclips of takes that must be re-sped if anything was created for them. New subclips will replace them.
  - Cut the video of the master clip into a timeline named to match the clip name.

- Using the timewarp effect, re-speed the clip to play at "real" speed.
  - For example, 48 fps will require 200% speed.
- Select a small in-out range around the clap and use "replace edit" to cut the audio in.
- Extend and edit both sides of the audio to maximize available media.
- **IMPORTANT:** Trim the sequence to the last frame of movement before the timewarp freezes it. If this is not done, the editor will most likely receive an underrun error during playback because the timecode (or lack thereof) from the frozen remains of the timewarped clip will confuse Media Composer.
- Autosync the sequence to turn it into a subclip. **Note: This cannot be undone.** It will cut off the clip at the nearest edit points and will lop off either the audio or picture if one is longer than the other.
- Append the new synced subclip name with the percentage it was sped up (for example, **D66A-4(A)* 120 fps 500%**).
- If the original master clip has associated audio married to it, relabel the clip and include "bad sync" to indicate that the audio is not in sync with the picture.
- Ensure the new subclips are set to "5.1 Sequence" in the audio mixer (if audio is present).

"Off-speed" refers to anything that isn't shot at the project frame rate. On feature films, we generally work at 24 fps (*not 23.976*), so anything that isn't shot at 24 fps needs a motion effect. It's common to shoot slow motion in frame rates that are multiples of the base frame rate: 48, 72, and 96. Also common are half steps of the base frame rate, like 36, 60, and 84. These all lend themselves well to conforming to the base frame rate without leading to artifacting. Regardless, applying a timewarp to a clip shot at any frame rate will have it running at the correct speed, and you can sync it with sound if needed.

Timewarp effects are set to "both fields" by default when generated, but when they're cut into the timeline, you can change it to Fluidmotion and render; this is especially useful for frame rates that are not multiples of 24, where using both fields will result in media that stutters. This can also occasionally lead to artifacting, which can be reduced with Fluidmotion Edit (p. 177) but will ultimately need to be sent to a VFX vendor or the DI. Often, DI kicks the event back because there's too much noticeable stutter in the motion estimation. These dailies clips are at a constant speed by default, but you can change that once it's cut into the timeline to add keyframes, etc. Variable speed timewarps almost always get sent to VFX—more on this in the VFX Chapter (p. 193).

When to Respeed Clips

Generally speaking, a clip only needs to be resped if there's a sync sound associated with it. In the past, I've encountered footage shot on a Phantom camera, which produced ultra slow-motion (up to 768 fps on that particular show), in which case, sync sound wasn't even recorded. That's an example of a shot I didn't respeed (*or group*, for that matter).

What I do respeed (and group, if the situation calls for it) are setups with one camera running at 24 fps and another running at another speed, like 36 fps (which is more common). I take that second camera, speed it up, group that with the first camera, and then leave a note (p. 113) to let the editor know they can match back on that angle to access the slow-motion footage.

Workflow to Respeed Clips

The workflow I use for respeeding clips is to take the master clip *from the beginning of the clip* and cut it into a new timeline. I usually copy the name of the clip (which should look something like this: **D66A-4(A)* 120 fps**) and rename the sequence to match, appending the respeed percentage (**D66A-4(A)* 120 fps 500%**). I then apply a timewarp to the clip.

The table here shows the different percentages I've used. I have timewarps with these settings saved in a bin, so I don't have to keep doing the math and punching in numbers.

fps	%
24	100%
36	150%
48	200%
96	400%
120	500%
200	833%
300	1350%

When you need to do the math, the equation is, $\dfrac{fpsshot}{projectfps} * 100 = x\%$

Avoiding Timecode Underrun Errors

When a timewarp effect runs out of frames, it holds the last frame for the remainder of the clip's duration. So, let's say you apply a 200% timewarp to a clip shot at 48 fps. This results in a segment that runs twice as fast, freezing halfway through; this means that the timecode also stops running halfway through. This can lead to a timecode underrun error because when this "frozen" material is trapped in a subclip and played in a timeline, Media Composer throws an error basically saying, "This clip plays for 10 seconds, but the source timecode doesn't go past 5 seconds, **I can't play this**."

To avoid this error, trim any frozen frames out of the sequence *before* autosyncing the sequence into a subclip.

Syncing Sound with Resped Clips

Once the clip is resped appropriately, I find the slate and park on the clap. If the clip has sound married to it by the dailies tech, I adjust the timing of the audio and add "bad sync" to the original master clip name. This is because the audio will, by default, be recorded at 24 fps, whereas the picture will be at another speed, hence, out of sync. If I must import the production audio, I'll cut that in and append "MOS" to the original picture master clip name.

When I load the audio, I park on the clap in the source timeline and then use "Replace Edit" to cut it into the resped picture in the record timeline. Sometimes, there's not enough audio to fill the record timeline, so I'll make a small in-out region around the clap in the timeline, replace-edit the audio in, and then extend-edit the head and tail of the audio to its full extent. I then extract any overhang of audio or video (unless there's something useful in there, then I'd subclip that out, but that's rare) and autosync the sequence.

Autosync

Autosync is a feature meant to synchronize audio with picture. It can only be performed on a clip-by-clip basis, not in bulk. It was built to select one audio clip and one video clip. Executing it would sync the two together (based on specified criteria, e.g., timecode) in a new subclip.

What's kind of neat about autosync is that it has a special functionality when performed on a sequence. Autosyncing a sequence turns the sequence into a subclip. As noted above, **this action cannot be undone**. When performing autosync, the shortest piece of media will become the basis for the duration of the new subclip (and video is prioritized over audio).

Where do I Put My New Subclip?

This subclip gets promoted to the scene bin, and it can be matched back to get to the original slo-mo footage. It can be included in group clips but will need to be done based on audio timecode (which might be found in AuxTC1) or in points or audio waveforms, as the video timecode will not match.

Grouping Clips

- Group clips (OPTIONAL—only if more than one camera is recording during a take)
  - If there is more than one camera rolling during a take, group all cameras for that take.
  - If the action in the two angles are unrelated or don't benefit from being grouped, do not group them.
  - Make sure A cam is above B cam in List View when grouping.
  - Use Source TC (or AuxTC1, it's the sound timecode that the dailies tech duped into that column) to sync. For off-speed clips, use FilmTC/SoundTC. When all else fails, manually mark in on each clip at a sync point.
  - Audio should **not** follow video (this is the default setting.)
  - Remove the camera designation, decimals, and generated numbers from group clips (example: "53A-1(A)*.Grp.01" becomes "53A-1* Grp").
  - These new group clips will need to be set to "5.1 Sequence" in the audio mixer.

Once all the subclips have been created, I sort by name and then select the clips from different cameras that need to be grouped. The obvious use of group clips is for takes shot with multiple cameras. The only time I won't group multi-camera clips is when there's no sync sound— there's not much to sync to and no apparent benefit. What follows is scalable regardless of any atypical grouping scenario.

Group Clips and Off-Speed Footage

Group clipping only works well when the frame rate matches; if all clips are at 24 fps, then group clipping will work when editing. If an off-speed clip is used in a group clip, changing to that camera in the timeline will result in an out-of-sequence shot; a properly re-sped take would work just fine.

Typical Multicam Grouping

Typically, there will be an A and B cam and, sometimes, a C cam. We could keep counting all day. In this use case, syncing by source or sound timecode should do the trick. The bin order in which clips are sorted determines their order within the group. Using "Edit Group" will allow for retroactive re-ordering but be aware that this does not affect clips that have already been cut into sequences. It's possible to refresh the sequence "group edits," but I'd advise doing this in a subsequence first, as it doesn't duplicate the sequence like committing multicam edits does.

You should be able to group clips based on Sound TC, if not Aux TC. This won't work for re-sped clips that don't have associated audio because there's no Sound TC metadata! In most instances where this comes up, the actions in the angles are unrelated and don't benefit from being grouped. For example, they might be a bunch of unrelated angles from an action scene. Therefore, you should not group them. If you do, put the groups at the bottom of the scene bin as described below in the bin layout section (p. 116). Of course, say it with me: Ask your editor about their preferences.

A faster way to group a whole bin of clips in bulk is to select all the subclips in your scene bin (ensuring the order of the clips matches the order in which you want them to be synced—A cam above B cam, etc.), and execute the "MultiGroup" command from the Clip menu. You have all the same options within the "Group Clips" dialog box but with an added checkbox at the bottom: "Multiple Groups." It will automatically group all overlapping subclips instead of making you

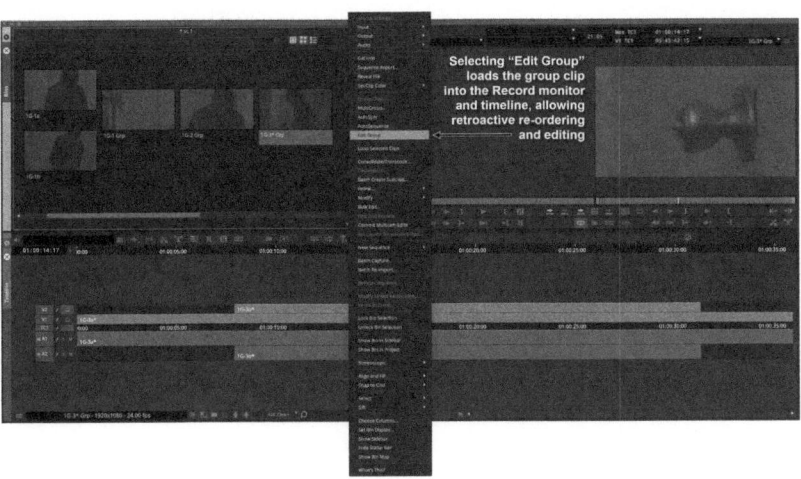

Figure 5.3 The "Edit Group" feature, showing multiple angles represented in the timeline.

do them one by one. It's not bulletproof and will need to be double-checked, but this can save a lot of time and manual labor.

All group clips will need to be tended to independently regarding multichannel audio, setting the solos on the first track (if that's part of your workflow), and changing the sequence mix format from stereo to 5.1.

Grouping Playback Performances

Another use for group clips is when multijple performances are synced to playback (p. 167). In this scenario, only one camera might roll many times, and the clips should be synced by playback timecode (or waveform) instead of source or sound timecode.

One important feature to highlight is "Audio Follow Video" (AFV)—a setting that's off by default and located in the group clip menu in the upper left-hand corner of the source monitor when a group clip is loaded.

In a scenario where A and B cam share the same source audio, keeping AFV off prevents the audio track(s) from changing when toggling through the group clip video angles. AFV **should** be enabled in scenarios involving a live performance—it's desirable to hear the sync sound of the live performance when switching angles.

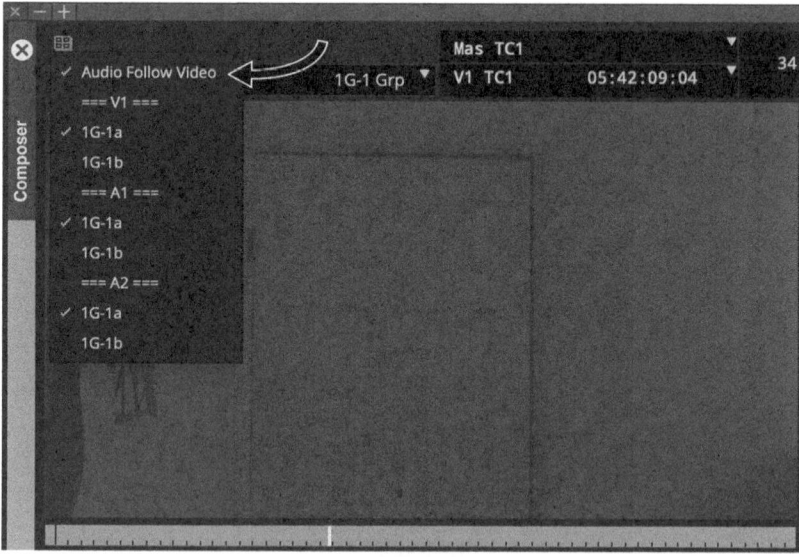

Figure 5.4 Group clip menu in the source side Composer window, showing the "Audio Follow Video" option.

Super Groups (Big, Big Groups with Many Angles)

When there are many cameras and many takes, it might be preferable to group the clips in KEM roll order (all takes from A cam, then B cam, etc.). This allows the editor to shuttle through all takes of one angle before switching to another. Otherwise, they'll end up pingponging between different camera angles, which can be jarring and distracting when choosing the right take.

When there are resets within a take, and all resets need to be grouped, subclip the resets into individual "takes" before grouping. If this isn't done, it will throw off AFV (if enabled), and the duplicate audio tracks will disappear after editing the group.

When modifying (editing) group clips, use the "Link Selection Toggle" to move all audio/video elements. I like to use an additional temporary set of tracks to either replace-edit playback (p. 167) or move clips around to adjust sync based on waveform. Also, if markers are placed on tracks *other* than V1 within a group clip while modifying it, know that once the group is saved, all markers will be moved to V1. If two markers exist at the same point in time, only the one on the lowest track is kept. I specify the angle in the marker text when notating large group clips. If a large scene group with multiple angles is grouped before markers have been added to the individual clips, edit the scene group, reverse match frame to clips with markers, cut it in temporarily, and drop the markers down to V1. Make sure no markers are on the same frame.

Group Clip Performance

Depending on your drive speed/network bandwidth, there may be performance issues viewing the quad or nine split. If you're dual-ethernet connected, there likely won't be an issue. If you experience lag when viewing a nine split, especially if more than one editor tries to access the footage at once, the solution might be to transcode *just those* setups to a lower bitrate. You can change the split view order by Command-clicking angles while in quad or nine splits and selecting a different angle (and the option to restore the default order is at the bottom of that menu.) But that's not a good solution because it involves a lot of thinking and resetting every time the group clip is accessed. After dailies (or before a screening), you can always relink everything to the higher resolution dailies media.

Creating Scene Bins and Note Frames

- Create scene bins and add symbols.
  - Check script report for scenes shot (partial or completed) and any owed footage.
  - Create scene bins based on the facing pages.
  - Restructure the scene number for sorting purposes. Example: **A43** becomes **43A**
  - Add bin symbols (in hierarchal order, shown here: "•$P sc 57A").
    - *Symbols*: • new scene (or footage), $ needs scripting, and **P** owed footage (Partial).
  - The editor will add a description to the bin name and remove • after watching the footage.
- Move subclips into scene bins, cross-check the scene bins with facing pages, and add notes.
  - Move subclips from the dailies bin into their appropriate scene bins.
  - Cross-check the bin with the facing pages to make sure everything on the page is in the bin.
  - Add notes from the editor's log: How many resets are in the clip, if it's ng, circled, etc.
  - Remove anything the lab labeled as a "Series" (SER) and replace it with resets. If the number of resets is unknown, append "**x??**" to the end of the clip name. This, along with the notes from the editor's log, are guides for later when placing action markers, a sort of "heads up."
  - Remove camera designations for anything not shot multicam if it's not done by the lab.
  - Remove false takes that aren't useful to the editor (e.g., slate only, crew in shot, misfire).
  - Note any VFX balls and color grids, they will go at the bottom of the bin with the KEM roll clips (as described later).

I create scene bins based on the progress report and facing pages in anticipation of the subclips I will eventually move into them. I look at what scenes were shot and assess what is complete, partial, or otherwise. The names of the scene bins are based on the facing pages because sometimes production will film two or three scenes covered by one number, like 42 and **A42**. The facing pages may reflect that they might both be part of the same scene, whereas the progress report may show they were shot separately. This is an example of when multiple scenes could (and should) be combined into one scene bin. Any bin containing multiple scenes should be labeled to reflect that. A contiguous span is shown with a dash (sc 18-22), and intermittent scenes are listed with or without commas (sc 18, 20, 22).

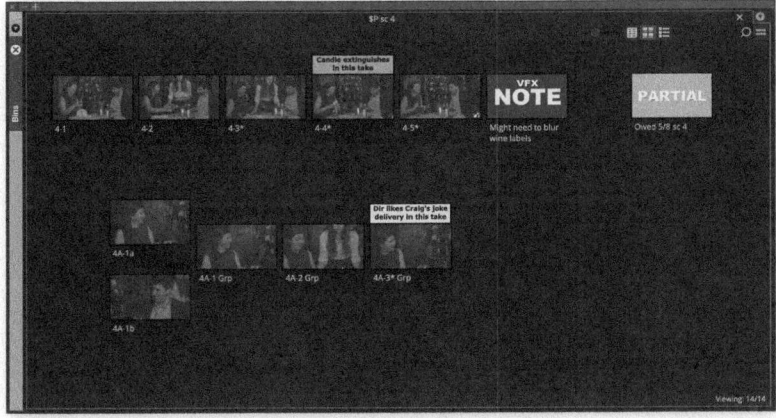

Figure 5.5 Scene bin reflecting a new, partial scene.

For a New Scene (Shot to Completion)

Move all scene subclips into the bin, add any necessary note frames (p. 114), and perform bin layout (p. 116).

For a Partial Scene (New, Nothing Else from it Shot Yet)

Move all scene subclips into the bin, add a note frame, and rename it to communicate when the owed footage is expected to arrive.

For a Partial Scene (Already Binned, now Completed)

Create a temporary bin to move the new subclips into and add a "New Footage" note frame with the date it was *added to the bin* and the setups that were added. Perform bin layout (p. 116), move these subclips into the already existing scene bin, remove the corresponding "Partial" note frame, and then go ahead and trash the temporary bin.

Labeling Bins and Leaving Notes

I add a scripting note frame with the assistant's name who needs to do the scripting to the new bins. I try to put the setups they need to script in the name of the note frame clip, especially if it's new footage added to an already scripted bin. Once all the dailies have been added to the scene bin, the note frames are in, and the layout is done, I add symbols to the beginning of the bin name to denote the status.

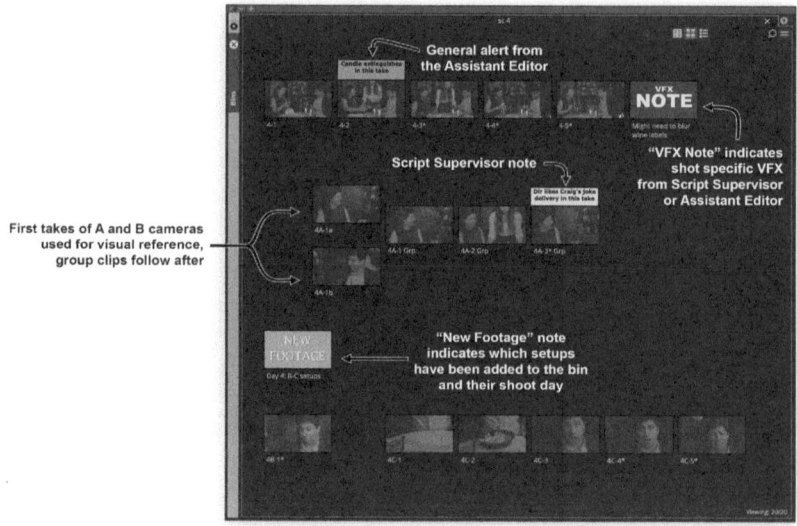

Figure 5.6 Updated scene bin reflecting completion of photography for the scene.
Note the 4A setup, which is multicam.

Status	Symbol
•	New scene
$	Needs scripting
P	Partial (owed footage)
Sc 42 **pt1**	"pt#" appended to a large scene broken into multiple bins

Note: The bullet point and dollar symbols are considered "illegal characters" and might cause issues in a Windows environment or older versions of Media Composer.

One idea you might consider is using the bin background color to reflect the scene's status. One color could denote a completely shot scene, while another means there's footage yet to come. This is a feature I don't see used all too often, and any opportunity to further organize and color code is worth thinking about.

Clip Names

Media Composer allows viewing two rows of clip name text while in Frame View within a bin. Adding a bunch of spaces can push a note to the second line. This has worked well for my team's purposes, where we like to add comments to the clip names. The problem downstream becomes burn-ins requiring the scene and take. Typically, the clip name would be used in this scenario. One workaround for this is to take up two display tracks in the timecode generator effect, one reading from the "scene" source metadata column and the other from the "take" metadata column. A simpler approach is duplicating the clip name into a custom column (I use the "slate" column) when the dailies first come in. This lets us preserve the original naming and scene-take concatenation for burn-ins and other uses.

Dailies Macros

When processing dailies, I find there's a lot of text clean-up that needs to be done between all the ".sub.01" and ".grp.01" generated, along with removing camera designations from group clips. In newer versions of Media Composer, you can use "Find and Replace" within the bin or bulk edit to batch-rename clips. Some people prefer programs like Keyboard Maestro or QuicKeys and peripherals like Keychron Q0 or StreamDeck. As of this writing, I've been mapping simple keystrokes to my keyboard (p. 42) because it's convenient.

Duplicated Banner Note Frames

In addition to clip-level notes, I like to use banner frames as scene-wide notes. These are imported still images with bold words on a solid background. The master clips are stored in a "project locked" bin to be easily duplicated (*not cloned*). They get placed in scene bins with their clip names changed to communicate information such as: "New Footage," "Partial," "**Note**," "Music Note," "Sound Note," VFX Note, or someone's name (to draw their attention). The clip name can be changed to add clarity; hence, duplicating instead of cloning. The assistant note clips should be deleted once the work is complete (clip only, not the media).

Sequence Note Frames

These function as a sort of Post-It Note in Frame View (see figure 5.7). They're a bit hacky, but they work for complicated clip-level notes that won't fit in the clip name. It also lets you see immediately what the nature of the note is based on the color. These sequences have title media with a color effect applied and a SubCap effect on Track 2. Dupe the sequence, give it a period or underscore as a name (so it doesn't distract), change the color/text as needed, advance it one frame in bin view (updates the thumbnail cache), and drag it to the top in Script View.

Frame View prominence is based on Script View, *loaded from the bottom up*. Items at the bottom of Script View will be in the foreground of items in Frame View that are higher in Script View. When

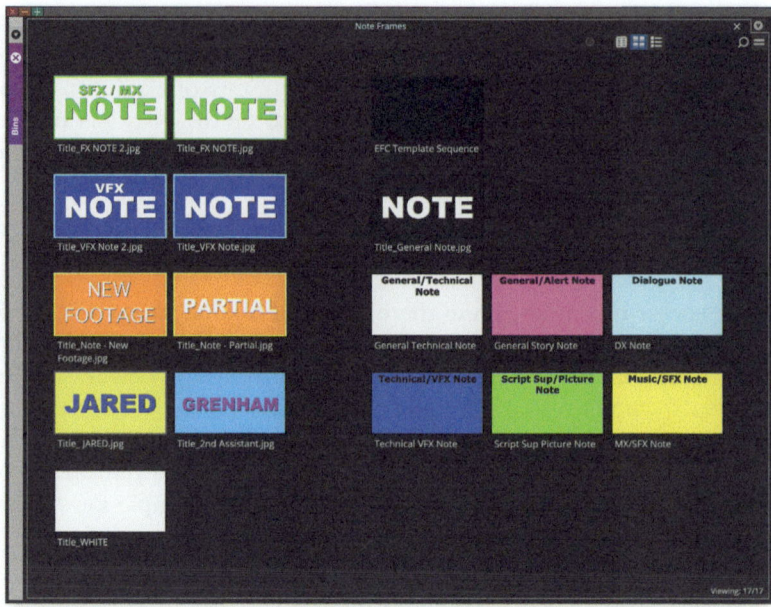

Figure 5.7 Note Frame Bin.

duplicating multiple note frame sequences, the representative frame might have to be reset; otherwise, they might all say the same note (since their representative frames are cached). This sometimes happens after closing and re-opening a bin—in that case, just select all clips and nudge them forward by a frame.

Note Color	Type	What it Could Mean
White	General Technical	x number of audio tracks, mis-slate, surrounding clip DNE
	General Story / Alert	from the assistant, heads up
	Dialogue	alt dialogue, mic info (if a character isn't lav'd)
	Technical / VFX	shot specific VFX, like a tattoo removal or paint out in BG
	Script Sup / Picture	from the script supervisor, sometimes blocking/ action-related
	Music / SFX	if a sound occurs in a take, or if something's different about music playback

Bin Layout

- Perform bin layout
  - Add note frames to communicate dailies inf as needed. The clip name is the note; the frame is the kind of note. This might include any of the following: "Partial - owed 2/8 per prog rpt day 12", "note - no A cam takes 1-3", "script 16 16A 16B 16C," "new footage - 5/20 16A 16B 16C", VFX, playback MX (and add the associated music clips).
  - In List View, sort by name and then by clip type. This will put all groups together at the bottom. Switch to Frame View, enlarge as much as you can, and Fill Sorted.
  - Layout bin in alphabetical setup order (or editor's preference). Use "align selected" to align clips without disturbing other ones. You can't undo bin actions.
  - For group clips, stack the first takes from each camera vertically, then line up all groups horizontally. Don't stack the first two takes too close together; allow room to see the clip text.
  - Keep subsequent takes from group angles (Takes 2, etc.) at the bottom of the bin in KEM roll order, separating the cameras and setups. Include useful false takes and VFX clips as well.

This is usually done in conjunction with creating the note frames outlined previously. Typically, I'll move the subclips for a scene into the scene bin and add any notes I find as I cross-check the paperwork (all in List View). Then, I'll let it hang out until I've organized all the subclips for the day of dailies into their respective bins. Once I circle back to the bins to flip them into Frame View, bin layout begins, and I refine/clarify the notes.

Facing Page Notes

Checking the facing pages while moving subclips into the scene bins is a good opportunity for one last cross-check. This step allows the opportunity to add any notes from the script supervisor to the clip names, like "ng" for not-good takes and "x#" for a take with any number of resets.

Usually, circle takes are denoted with an asterisk; the script supervisor on your show might use something else (like a "FAV" tag for anything that is the director's favorite, for example). There might come a time when you have seven takes, three of which are circled, and the second to last one has "FAV" appended. That FAV-tagged clip? It's like a super circled take.

I only include false takes in the scene bin if they could be useful to the editor—for example, if it's three seconds long and has crew members in it, then I disregard it. However, if it's a full minute and has the director talking to the cast, or it's a possible establishing shot, I'll keep it in the bin because it could inform the editor's work.

Frame View and Layout

Working in Frame View is a visual way of interacting with the media. It's akin to having a desktop scattered with photographs, where you organize the photos in a way that's meaningful to you—freeform. The editor will always prefer bins laid out the way they're used to working. Some prefer alphabetical order, while others prefer script order (which is not always alphabetical). As an example of script order, if the F setup happens to be solely a transitional element meant to open the scene, then I'll place that near the top of the bin as opposed to near the E/G setups.

A quality-of-life tip is to temporarily enable "snap to grid" when performing bin layout. This can be found in the bin fast menu. I otherwise prefer the freeform nature of working in Frame View, and it's necessary when using note frames that are meticulously positioned.

I lay the clips out left to right in the desired order, and for group clips, I like to keep the first takes of all angles stacked vertically with all groups trailing horizontally (see figure 5.6). The angles that comprise the groups get organized either at the bottom of the bin and out of sight or in a separate scene bin within a subfolder titled "Multicam Subclips," which I keep at the bottom of the "Dailies by Scene" folder. Regardless of where the subclips live, they're put in KEM roll order (p. 116), meaning that all takes for each setup are separated by camera—for example, A cam takes 1-5, followed by B cam takes 1-5.

KEM rolls

The editor might like to construct their own KEM roll after watching dailies. This is to organize all scene footage and consolidate (thereby creating a backup of) all dailies markers. It's also a great way for the editor to scan through and look at all the footage for a given scene.

If you are tasked with creating a KEM roll, clear the in and out points on all clips in the bin first. Then, you can Option-drag a selection of clips into the record monitor, which will insert them sequentially into a new sequence (or a sequence that's already open.) Note: Avid will add them according to the order they are listed in List View, so be certain this order is correct before Option-dragging into the record monitor. Insert the clips in the order previously specified and rename the sequence to the scene number and "KEM roll" ("**sc 9 KEM roll**").

Checking Sync and Marking Clips

- Check sync and mark clips
  - Check slate claps on all groups and single camera clips, and then check consonants in speech downstream in all clips. *Fix sync or update group clips if needed.* Similar to the process of off-speed

audio syncing (p. 102), do the same for clips that are out of sync. Delete the old, out-of-sync subclip and replace it with the new one. Make sure to use the master clip to fix sync, not the subclip in question.
– Mark action/resets with **red**, flubs with **yellow**, pickups with **yellow and red**, and flaws with **blue**. Other markers will be added when scripting or watching footage. For additional action calls and resets, append the clip name with this information (example: "**x5.2**" means there are five resets [from top of scene] and two pickups).
– Mark in on poster frames while doing this.
– Set poster frames for all clips ("Go to in"), including the KEM roll clips, then clear marks.
– Export a still of the scene for continuity (if it's a new scene).
– Run "Read Audio Timecode," if applicable.
– Set the bin background color to reflect the scene's status, if applicable.
– Move the bin to the top of the project.

Checking Sync

Everything that has gotten us to this point has relied upon and assumed that the timecode has been jam-synced and is correct. Sync issues can be found on a clip-by-clip basis after bin layout while marking clips. I like to display waveforms when checking sync. To a trained eye, the waveforms show things quickly that might take a lot of time to find by playing the take, like second sticks. Watch out for those—that's when the audio was rolling before the cameras, and they needed to clap again once the camera started rolling. Another scenario is that you might confuse one camera's slate clap with the others when checking sync. It's easy to mistake the wrong clap for the one you're looking for. Sync issues are extremely important (as are all other discrepancies with dailies, including metadata) and need to be addressed as soon as possible during dailies because everything flows downstream.

If a group clip is out of sync, I check the subclips it was created from. If those are fine, I'll edit the group clip to compensate. Otherwise, I'll fix the subclips themselves. This can be done the same way off-speed footage is conformed (p. 74): Cutting the master clip into a sequence, adjusting the audio, and then autosyncing the sequence.

Sometimes, the synced audio from the lab is incorrect, or it doesn't run for the duration of the take. If so, import the sound file from the original sound roll and cut that into the sequence. In any case, match back to the master clip and append the clip name to reflect that the sync is bad (**ng sync or bad sync**). If you need to create two subclips for a take because of a break in recording mid-take, add "Pt 1, Pt 2," etc., to the end of the clip names (or create a Multi-Group).

Perf Slipping

Perforation refers to a strip of film, wherein a 35 mm strip of film contains four perforations per frame. Slipping refers to changing the timing of a clip. Therefore, **Perf Slipping** is when you adjust the timing of the audio by one perforation (in this case, 1/4 of a frame) for better accuracy.

When checking sync, look for the clapper blur and where the transient is positioned within the frame. If the clapper is blurry, the transient should be closer to the head of the frame. If it's crisp and clear, the transient should be closer to the middle of the frame. This can be adjusted on the subclip level by perf slipping, which is only available in a film project, and if you created subclips with handles (as mentioned earlier [p. 101]).

Marking Clips

Here we go again; everyone in the back, just shout it out: **Ask your editor what their preference is!** Adding markers to clips is another editor-specific preference. Almost every editor will want a marker when the director calls "Action." When there's playback involved, I mark action twice; once on "action," and again on the first pop of the click track of playback. I like to mark more than just action, though. When watching clips, I check sync (if I haven't already done so), mark action/resets/flubs/pickups, and **mark an in-point as a representative frame**. When group clips are present, markers are placed there instead of in the individual angle subclips.

As a reminder for me (I always get flubs and pickups mixed up), a **flub** is when a line is unusable. Place a yellow marker where the line is re-done. A **pickup** is when the line is unusable, *and* they back it up a line or a few lines. Place two markers (yellow and red) when they take it back a few lines (this is more of a visual thing—you should be able to see the red and yellow markers near each other in the composer window). A **reset** is when they do more than one take without cutting. Place another red marker after "action" is called. These events should all be logged in the clip name, x[resets].[pickups] or "33C-1 **x1.4**" (that's no resets, four pickups.)

If the camera bumps noticeably, the focus jitters, or the boom is in frame, or there's a shadow, I place a blue marker on the event. If you're in a group clip, you may want to put the camera designation ("A Cam," etc.) in the marker comment. The editor will place all other markers (like improvisation, notable moments, or different actions) when they watch the footage. These marker colors are just what I've used in the past—more on markers in the Markers Section (p. 127).

Poster Frames and Scene Still Images

After going through the clips, make sure you're in Frame or Script View, select all the clips in the bin, and hit "go to in," then "clear marks." This will set the poster frames and remove the in-points.

As previously outlined, I use the continuity to track the shoot progress during production. Once I've set the poster frames, I'll choose a representative frame and export a still image for the continuity. After I've added the still to the database, I'll change the scene status to "BIN" to reflect that the scene is entirely in the bin (see figures 4.5 and 4.6).

Moving Bins to the Top of the Project

These scene bins are hidden in a work folder while I prepare them. When they're ready, I move the bin(s) to the top of the project for the editor. When working with a larger team, this process can be split up; generally, the second assistant will add all these notations, and I will remove the "•" from the bin name once I get eyes on it. I then verify that all notes from the facing pages and editor's log are included. These are displayed in a couple of ways: In the clip name, using duplicated banner clips, and using sequences with verbose notes.

Scripting the Scene

- Script the scene
  - Import a placeholder script or open a script that has a relevant partial/connecting scene.
  - Open the scene bin. Line the script and drag resets or pickups onto the same slate, adjusting the take length accordingly. If these are not already marked in the bin, make a note so the markers can be added later (or by whoever has the bin open).
  - Color script lines and squiggle off-camera lines.
  - Add improvised lines to the script in <carrots>.
  - Name the script with the word "script" in it; that way, when it's tabbed with scenes, it's not confusing (example: "sc 53 script" instead of "sc 53").
  - Remove the $ symbol from the bin name (and the note frame if it exists) when complete.

Lining a digital script in Media Composer is more involved than a blurb in this chapter can contain—see the Digital Scripting section

(p. 51) within the Avid Media Composer chapter (p. 31) for everything script-related. Otherwise, this is generally done by a second assistant or apprentice editor after the scene bin is complete. There will be a $ symbol in the bin name and a note frame with someone's name. Both should be removed once the work is complete. I prefer a font for the Avid script: Courier Prime. It's free, and it looks great in the Avid-lined script.

Backup the Media, Update the Database (again)

- Back up the media, update the codebook, and release the cards.
  - Run a ChronoSync backup of all partitions, or at least the dailies drive. Consider doing this while the editor isn't working to avoid hogging Nexis bandwidth.
  - Import any remaining data into FileMaker. This may include codebook stills, camera data, or the Avid bin data itself (depending on your workflow).
  - Send a reply email to the dailies thread for that day (the same one that the ALE and bins were sent in), which confirms that editorial has received all expected dailies for the shooting day and that the camera cards can be released. This might need to be drafted and sat on **until LTO archive verification is received**.

Backing Up Dailies

ChronoSync is my tool of choice. There's more on ChronoSync in a later section (p. 46), but for the purpose of backing up dailies, I'll only run one or two of the synchronizer documents instead of the container (which backs up every partition on the Nexis)—it's whichever partitions I most recently loaded new media onto. While the backup runs, I typically return to the database to deal with the camera data.

Manual Data Entry

If I'm lucky enough to have digital camera reports delivered via CSV and/or digital script supervisor notes via CSV or XML, I simply import those into my database, give it all a once-over, and move on. If these documents are handwritten and scanned, we have to take additional steps to manually enter them via transcription.

For the camera data, I export an Excel file of the shoot day from the codebook and hand it off to the production assistant. It's mostly blank, and I ask them to fill in the empty columns with information from the camera reports, like lens info, f-stop, and filter. It's extremely useful to have all this data in the system for VFX later down the road.

When they're finished, I import their spreadsheet back into the database, which merges with existing records based on the tape name.

I'll also ask them to add the script supervisor description from the editor's log (which may have been started earlier when preparing the dailies report). Both steps are unnecessary if the information is coming in digitally, but when it needs to be transcribed, this is the last stop on the data entry train.

It's imperative that whoever is transcribing the data does not guess or enter incorrect information. If it can't be read clearly, it should be left empty. The only thing worse than no information is **wrong information**. In fact, it's called "Dirty Data." We work clean.

Releasing Cards

What does this mean? Production has a finite set of camera cards. Let's say they have 20 and they shoot enough footage in one day to fill five cards. Those cards remain spoken for until the footage on them is accounted for and backed up, so production now only has 15 cards to record new footage onto. This becomes an issue with more cameras rolling simultaneously and if discrepancies are holding up the release (erasure and return) of these drives to production.

Certainly, release cards when you're able, but *only* when you're absolutely sure you've accounted for all the footage. As mentioned, you might be requested to **wait until LTO archive verification is received before releasing the cards**. If you're waiting on one card because a discrepancy still hasn't been cleared up, release the cards you can and very clearly communicate that the card in question **should not** be released.

Distribute the Dailies Playlist, Report, and Screening Bin

- Distribute the Dailies playlist (review and approval [p. 21]), send Dailies Report and Bin.
  - **Dailies Report:**
    - Ensure the Script Supervisor's descriptions have been entered for all clips in FileMaker.
    - Create a cover page and include the show title, shoot day, shoot date, camera rolls, scenes, and total duration. Append to the top of the dailies report.
  - **PIX Distro:**
    - If you're distributing the playlist, create it and match the order to the dailies report.
    - If the lab is distributing the playlist, check the dailies playlist they sent against the dailies report.

- Dailies Screening Bin:
  - Create a bin with clones of all dailies clips.
  - Re-order them to match the PIX playlist order.
  - Create a sequence (option-drag clips from dailies clips bin into the Record monitor) and keep all production tracks.
  - Add a matte to the top track (if necessary).
  - Send an email to executives (designated individuals) with the dailies report and cover page, along with the Avid bin.

Dailies Screenings and Reports

The big picture here is that the dailies get distributed to all production members on PIX, and the executives may watch them together. They have someone at the studio who runs these screenings, but they just open a bin and hit play. Therefore, it's incumbent on you to create the sequence they'll be watching, along with the corresponding paperwork that allows them to follow along.

Sometimes, they'll want the script supervisor's facing pages, which takes some work off your plate. I, of course, prefer to use (drumroll please) *the database* to summarize a day of dailies data and kick out a sorted PDF of all clips (or conversely, **only** circle takes, if requested). That's the Dailies Report (see "Custom Dailies Report generated from FileMaker database [downloadable]" on www.routledge.com/9781032843285). Avid can do this natively by switching the dailies bin into Script View and going to *File > Print*, but it's not as aesthetically pleasing to look at and a little finicky to set up. Plus, Avid can't currently make a cover page with summaries. Information that benefits from summarization includes camera rolls shot, scenes shot, and the total running time of the dailies stringout.

It's important to ensure that the paperwork you generate matches the order of the stringout. Sometimes, it's not you who's distributing the PIX playlist; it's the lab. In this case, cross-reference the paperwork you're creating (and the Avid bin you're preparing) with the playlist you received.

As with every aspect of this book, no two productions are exactly the same. Some productions might not need or want a Dailies Report. I still like to save one away for posterity. I generate my Dailies Reports in FileMaker from the codebook, where a primary sort takes place based on Scene Number, Camera, and Take. This can be overridden as needed, usually while inputting script supervisor notes (assuming you've received handwritten notes).

Going Solo

Much of what's been outlined to this point has been largely linear, but when working as part of a team, there's a lot of overlap. There's data entry happening by the PA while the second assistant starts accounting for footage, and all the while, I'm preparing a scene bin—and then the second assistant pivots over to the Dailies Report and sends the PIX playlist. The point is these steps can be shuffled around as needed while you delegate and manage the room. But what happens if you're on your own?

When I'm working solo (boo!), I wait until the end of the process to import the stills generated earlier and start going through the codebook to add shot descriptions from the editor's log (in preparation for the dailies report). Also, now that the media is backed up and everything is accounted for, I can email the dailies tech confirming that all the media is received; they can clear the cards and cycle them back into production. I usually draft the email but then wait until receiving LTO confirmation to release the cards. I won't send this email if I'm still waiting for a discrepancy to be cleared up from earlier (regarding which an email should have already been sent). Finally, I find it best to "reply all" on the email thread where the dailies tech originally delivered the media.

Bonus Considerations

I keep a few things on my radar during dailies that help prepare me for requests that might come in down the line. I only start thinking about these things when we get closer to wrapping up a location or the whole show. There are also a few things to keep in mind during production, like collecting and editing outtakes for a gag reel and being prepared to replace media in the event of a re-grade.

When Production Wraps

- Export stills of all locations. Production may want set decoration stills, too. This might need to happen when wrapping a location instead of wrapping the show.
- If you've had time to edit a gag reel, that might be fun for the wrap party—just get approval (and potential watermarks [p. 210]) sorted out ahead of time. Figure out how to transfer the media and to whom in production it should be sent.
- Request the master sound drive from the sound recordist (if it exists) and send the production sound files to the sound team (if they're on payroll).
- Request the script supervisor's database or an export of the data from it. The script supervisor should also be able to provide a full-lined script.
- Ask for wrap gifts. *Always*.

- Notate the final camera and sound rolls. If additional photography is to happen, it's easier to collect all this information when production wraps rather than months down the line.

Additional Photography

If and when it's decided that additional photography is needed, another workflow call will take place, and you'll need to be prepared to share the last camera roll and sound roll shot so it can be picked up from there. Agree on a new way to label/slate shots (appending "AP" to the beginning usually does the trick: **AP8A-2**).

Many departments will ask for references—from costume and make-up—to production design, props, and assistant directors. Some may ask for stills; others may ask for a short sequence to reference. You'll likely have to provide a cut with slugs; see more about that in the Cutting chapter (p. 125). The dailies workflow stands; the only exception is that at this point, you might be required to send some shots from the new footage to marketing pretty quickly, and you'll want to flag any potential VFX to let the head of the department know about them as soon as possible.

Regraded Media

At any point during the dailies process, the director or director of photography (DP) might want to change the color grade and resupply media files. In this event, two things need to happen: The original media files need to be replaced, and the metadata needs to be updated to reflect the dailies color data.

First, the media files will be resent, and they can completely replace the old files. Make sure no one is actively working with any footage from the affected day. In Finder, keep the .MDB and .PMR files, move the old media files into a quarantine folder, and move the new ones into the MediaFiles folder alongside the database files.

In Media Composer, the master clips should now point to the new media files. Bins in Frame View will need to be nudged a frame to reflect the new color, as the thumbnail images will have been cached. In the dailies master clip bin, import the supplied ALE with updated CDL data and **merge events with known master clips**.

Ideally, the new ALE will *only* contain the affected columns; otherwise, you risk overwriting any data you may have entered manually. This data should also be fed into the codebook by either re-importing the Avid bin, or performing a FileMaker import, updating matching on tape, start, and end timecodes.

6 Cutting

This chapter covers everything we do as assistants while the editor is, well, *editing*. This includes our interactions with Avid and the workflow I lean on, which utilizes markers and clip colors. All of this is to work collaboratively and thoughtfully.

An editor doesn't just put clips in a sequence—they're watching and marking footage and creating multiple versions of any given scene. Developing methods to keep track of all these thoughts and ideas is vital, and the faster these can be recalled, the more efficient the cutting room and overall editorial process will be.

Here's a general overview of the editing workflow:

- Dailies are assembled into a sequence.
- Once a version of the scene is complete, a dialogue pass is done, and temp sound effects and backgrounds are added. Sometimes, music will be included at the scene level, but often, I've seen music bridge scenes when they're first stitched together or added to a reel.
- Scene assemblies, alt sequences, and side edits can be stored in their respective scene bins (or "Experiment"/"Side Edits" bins).
- The scenes are inserted into reel sequences when they're ready. The reel sequences have head and tail leader in them.
- Further side and alternate edits are performed in subsequences and stored in "Experiment" bins separated by version. These alts can be cut into the reel depending on the notes. Asymmetrical trimming is performed within the reel to address other notes.
- The show gets built from the reels by extracting the head and tail leader using the FFOA/LFOA markers (First Frame and Last Frame of Action, respectively).
- Markers are left in the notes track to communicate work that needs to be done, something that is outstanding or needs attention, or needs to be shown to a director or producer.
- This notes process continues through multiple screenings until the picture is locked.

DOI: 10.4324/9781003516491-7

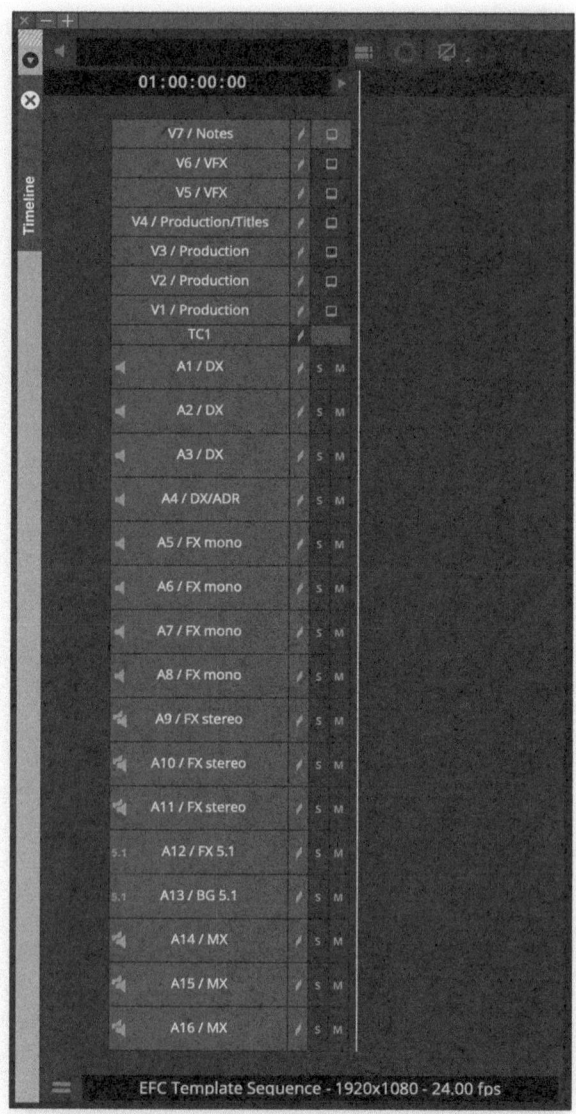

Figure 6.1 Avid timeline with named tracks.

Track Layout

A track layout that's worked for me includes seven video tracks and 16 audio tracks.

The video tracks are mostly dailies on V1-2, with VFX on designated tracks and the topmost track being strictly for notes. Some editors like to carry dedicated video tracks for titles, VFX banners, or on-screen ADR slugs, and sometimes, VFX needs more than two tracks. Regarding VFX banners, I opt for clip comments, which can be burned into the picture when applying a generator effect to a top track (only when needed). This saves on tracks but might not be a viable solution for assistants who rely on a SubCap track for VFX tracking purposes.

As far as audio goes, there are eight mono tracks (half of which are for production audio and the other half for effects) plus three more stereo tracks for effects. I have two 5.1 tracks for effects and backgrounds (great for when you receive patches from the sound department), followed by three more stereo tracks for music. After a temp mix, I add three 5.1 tracks at the bottom of the sequence: DX SM, FX SM, and MX SM (SM stands for "Stem"). Additionally, I'll carry as many stereo tracks as needed below for music to be reviewed (deleted upon review).

The track layout is incredibly personal and specific to the editor you're working with. The only thing I feel strongly about is keeping the tracks consistent across reels, *especially* if you're using RTAS effects. Otherwise, you risk your mix sounding different when stitching the show together if you're not paying close attention. But this track layout might be a good starting place for you to discuss with your editor.

Markers

The marker system outlined in this book has been adopted from working with John Axelrad. It utilizes the eight main marker colors available in Media Composer and their context changes depending on where they arc. As of this writing, Avid has introduced an additional eight colors that match the Pro Tools marker color set, which is yet another move toward increasing the compatibility and interplay between the two applications. The new colors are purple, violet, pink, denim, forest, orange, gold, and grey. What's great is that under the hood, these new colors get remapped to the original eight for backward compatibility. Also added is a "Marker Name" field, which is conveniently displayed in the composer window when you park on a marker.

Markers can be utilized within source clips, clips in the timeline, or even within filler. They can appear in AAF, EDL, and Pro Tools Session file exports. They can be exported as a TXT or XML file, and there are at least three fields to enter data: Name, User, and Comment. I use markers largely in the context of a team, and I'll detail how a team can use markers to communicate with each other. There's no one consistent way to use markers, and you might need to abandon or switch a color depending on various factors. Keep in mind that this system is from before the introduction of the expanded marker colors, so even I am looking forward to fully taking advantage of those!

Color	Source Clip	Timeline Clip	Notes Track	Mapped Expansion
Red	Action, reset (**x2**.1)	Problem area; needs smoothing	Sound note	**Orange**
Green	Ad-libs, improv	DI shot, (optical): tag=DI=**shot code= description/specific info**=end	Picture note	**Forest**
Blue	Technical problem (glitch, focus)	VFX shot: tag=VFX=**shot code**=elType=el#= **description**=end	VFX note	**Purple**
				Violet
Cyan	Director's favorite, select	ADR line: tag=ADR=**character= "line"=reason=note=** cue code=end	ADR note	**Denim**
Magenta	Very different action within take - multicam	Editor or assistant change to review	Assistant note	**Pink**
Black	Good moment	Director change reviewed (completed white)	Changed	**Grey**
Yellow	Flub, redelivery	FX on MX track or vice versa	Music note	**Gold**
White	Very different action within take - single cam	Director changes to review	Show to director	--

Multiple Use of Marker Colors

To illustrate how flexible using marker colors can be, I want to share a few additional ways we used white and black markers outside of what's described in the above table. Now that the marker's colors have been expanded, this kind of reuse might be less of a need. But even within an established system, you and your team can agree on what the same colors might mean in different contexts.

We originally used black and white markers to track changes in the cut via the notes track. When a change was made without the director in the room, a white marker was added to the notes track with details added. Once reviewed with the director, the marker would be switched to black. It served as a guide for areas that changed since the previous cut. These markers were cleared when versioning up.

We also used white FFOA/LFOA markers, with the name and comment reflecting the reel and the frame ("**LFOA R1**" is an example of Reel 1's LFOA marker name *and* comment). These were always on video track 1, at the head or tail of whatever clip began or ended the reel.

Within Scene Group clips (large groups that contained multiple takes across a full scene—a musical performance, for example), we used black markers for anything that needed sync, white for anything that didn't (reactions), and magenta for POV setups. The comment "**rxn**" meant "Reaction." In these large Scene Groups, I put the clip name (112A-3A) in the comment.

Timeline Clip Markers

The main function of a timeline clip marker is to associate a note with a specific timecode and/or clip, the timing of which changes every time an edit is changed. Placing markers in timeline clips allows us to maintain our notes as the timecode continues to change. The marker "formulas" allow me to pass information through a text parsing program, which in my case is FileMaker Pro. Two different contexts exist: a marker list and an EDL. In either instance, refer to the FileMaker Section to understand how the marker comment with equal signs gets parsed (p. 76).

With a marker list, the markers are exported from the Marker window within Media Composer, and that text document is imported into FileMaker. The text document is interpreted as tab-delimited upon import, so the timecode, marker name, and comments all come in as separate fields. A script then runs which goes through the comments field of every imported record. It delimits by the equal sign, putting the information between each instance of "=" into a predefined field within that record.

The second context I mentioned was within an EDL. In this case, the timecode of the marker itself is less important, but the EDL event that *contains* the marker (the actual nomenclature here is "locator") gets identified and associated with all the information within the marker as well. The import process for this is a little different because, unlike the marker list, the EDL is not tab-delimited. This means that before the marker string is parsed, the EDL needs to be parsed. All timecode and source information is collected and stored within one record and associated with the marker, which was placed within the body of the clip.

Timeline Notes Track Markers—Reels

If we are watching back a reel and are given notes, the kind of note determines the color of the marker, and then the note is left in the marker's comment. It might be something like "trim this part down" or "add some sound effects here." We leave markers in the Filler of the notes track as a "to-do list." If a VFX shot needs a temp, a blue marker is placed on the notes track with the description of what to do. If it's an ADR note, a cyan marker is left in the notes track. When the task is complete, we delete the marker. In the case of VFX or ADR, a timeline clip marker is also created for that event.

Occasionally, instead of deleting the notes track marker, I change the color. I tend to change the color from whatever it was to magenta and prepend the note with "JS DONE." This way, the editor can review the sequence, delete the marker themself, and know their note has been addressed. I drop magenta markers with thoughts, ideas, or warnings as needed. These exist at the editor's discretion, and I establish with them that they can delete these markers whenever they want. Magenta markers are a one-way road from me to them.

The only markers that don't get deleted are the black and white markers described earlier—this is so we can track the changes made within the cut. Only when versioning up do those markers get deleted.

Maintaining notes track marker sync when trimming is vital. The markers must both reflect the changes made and stay in sync. There's a trim setting called "Sync Rollers at Position in Filler," which makes this less of an issue if enabled, but sometimes you'll need to add an edit in filler to avoid a marker being rolled out of existence while trimming. In earlier versions of Media Composer, if a trim was made with sync locks on, there was no edit naturally within the filler of the notes track to tell what was downstream to trim accordingly. This meant that when trimming, you needed to add an edit to all tracks with filler before you trimmed (if you wanted the filler itself to stay in sync—which we did if we had markers in the filler!). This is still easily accomplished by holding down the Option key while executing an "add edit" before trimming.

Clip Colors

As far as I'm concerned, there are two main types of clip colors: Local and source. Other options are enabled by default, which help identify mixed frame rate footage, proxy footage, and offline footage (the last of which is arguably the most important and oft-encountered). Those are all applied automatically, whereas local and source colors are set manually by you, the user.

Source colors are set in bins, and local colors are set in the timeline by selecting clips, right-clicking, and setting a local clip color. Local colors override source colors in the timeline. All clip color display options can be found in the timeline fast menu and are saved as part of your timeline view.

If you apply clip colors consistently, you can select a clip in the time-line, right-click, and choose "Select > Select Clips with Same Source Color," which can be helpful when reorganizing sequences or creating new ones based on the selection. Custom colors are a good way to ensure that you're assigning the same unique colors consistently.

As outlined in the chart below, I primarily use source clip colors. I do use local clip colors when the situation calls for it. Like with marker colors, the context of the clip and track changes the meaning of a color: A yellow clip on the VFX track means something different from a yellow clip on a music track.

Color	Scene Bin	VFX	Music	Production Audio / SFX
	Scene Assembly	Could Be Better	From Music Editor	-
	Alt Sequence	Offline Temp	Temp Score	Temp ADR
	Aspect Ratio ID 1	In Revision	Source	Temp SFX
	-	Avid Review	From Composer	-
	Note Frame Accent	-	-	Recorded ADR
	Aspect Ratio ID 2	-	Playback	Temp Foley
	-	DI Review	-	From Sound Designer
	Alt/Sequence	Final	-	-
	Leader			
	Mixdown			
	I don't use bright red! To me (and *many* others), it's indicative of offline media or a serious issue.			

Scene Bins

Production clips are uncolored, except for multiple aspect ratio identi-fication. Note frames have accented border colors. Sequences are given a color so they are highlighted with border colors in frame view (this can be toggled on or off in the user's Bin settings).

VFX

Outside of music, VFX is where color coding clips is most important to me. I color offline editorial temps (anything round-tripped through third-party compositing software and re-imported) yellow.

For VFX editing (versions received from a vendor), there's an expanded set of colors to reflect the status of the shot. See the chart of these colors in the VFX editing section (p. 186) for more, but I also included the relevant ones in the chart above. These change during VFX reviews (p. 205).

Music

I leave music clips uncolored until they're used in a sequence. It's a good idea to differentiate between source and score cues so they're easy to separate when needed.

SFX

Most SFX colors are a grab bag, but I color my Foley collection ice blue. I think there's something to be said about using colors to identify different subsets of clips, but I haven't been able to implement it quite yet. It makes me think of how Final Cut Pro uses Roles, though.

Other

I assign both Audio and Video Mixdowns brown because it's a color that reminds me that the associated media is not good to use and should be removed before turnover (albeit left in any QuickTime and guide track files for creative reference). The head and tail leader are white. I don't like using bright red; it's reserved for offline media, and I associate it with the word "**problem**."

Watching Dailies and Assembling a Scene

As an assistant, you don't always get to cut. Cutting is a luxury not always afforded to you on every show, in schedule, your position, the editor's preference, and the amount of footage. I always ask the editor what would be most helpful. Perhaps there's a scene they'll want to see an alt of or a particularly large scene they could use your help with. Conversely, a small scene might be easier for you to knock out while they focus on a larger sequence. Whatever the scenario, if you're fortunate enough to be able to practice editing by assembling scenes, what follows is how I've taken advantage of this incredible opportunity.

1: Approaching the Footage

My approach thus far has been to watch *all* the footage for a scene before putting anything in a timeline. Being familiar with all the footage informs my roadmap and allows me to answer any questions down the line about why one take was used over another. I find that by watching everything, I'm able to start putting the scene together in my head and keep in tune with the performances. I can see how the direction progresses and what the intention on set was.

Being able to watch everything linearly is my preference, but if I have to compromise, I'll prioritize watching favorite/circle takes first, and then I'll explore other takes. Again, as an assistant, this is your way of learning how to form a relationship with footage as an editor.

2: Responding Emotionally

Whenever I see anything that feels raw, honest, true, or just jumps out at me, I place a marker on it. When I'm done watching everything, I like to step away for a minute and think. Usually, this works out because I can pivot to a different task that's equally productive.

3: Assembling a Scene

I start assembling the scene by casually placing one clip after another—emphasis on casually. I tend to stick with the circle takes, but I use the lined script to see if there are any alts I can use. I check to see if any line readings have one of my markers near it—that means my gut had an initial, visceral reaction.

When cutting a scene, I go from moment to moment, reacting to the footage. I think about what I feel and what I want to see. I look at eyes and fall into the rhythm of dialogue—a lesson I learned from cutting films in foreign languages that I didn't (and still don't) speak. I find that those attributes can motivate a cut over a dialogue. Sometimes, the blocking motivates a cut.

I **do not** remove any dialogue in the first pass. The first cut of a scene should have everything, even if it's not working. I make it the best it can be, knowing full well that the scene will have to be trimmed. It's important to show the editor (and, by proxy, the director) what coverage we have to work with. I create alt sequences when I can; that way, I can be prepared to show a version that fixes an issue or showcases another performance that stands out to me. My primary sequence always has what resonated with me originally—I go with my gut and what feels honest.

4: Trimming a Scene Assembly

Once the scene is assembled, I go through the sequence to smooth out audio edits. I'll make any J or L cuts (pre- and post-laps) and ensure the production sound is consistent across takes and edits. I'll lip-sync any lines that need more clarity or a tone shift. Then, I'll take a trim pass and finesse the timing. I'll also add some sound effects (and possibly music—although, at this early stage, the music isn't necessarily a priority).

Most times if I add any effect at this stage, it's to mask something that's distracting from the scene. This could be a split screen or a paint out (p. 175), but it could be an audio bump that needs to be removed or noise that needs to be reduced. Anywhere I use any effect, I drop a marker (ADR, DI, VFX) with a brief description. They'll be re-assessed later on, but it's easier to mark them and add specific information while it's fresh rather than going back and trying to remember what I did and why when it's time to turnover a cut. A lot of times, these markers can be sparked by the note frames in the scene bin, which originate from the script supervisor.

Select Media Relatives

This is a tiny little feature that, when used at this stage in this context, can help give you a look at the coverage you used. Right-click on your sequence and select "Select Media Relatives." Media Composer will select all items used in the sequence. Neat! John Axelrad used to do this after I showed him a scene I assembled so he could see how much I explored the footage. This isn't an advocation to use every single recorded take—the best takes are still the best takes, and continuity can play a big role in what is selected. It's more of a statistical curiosity that might lead to further exploration!

Reel Breaks (Changeovers)

Once the scenes are all assembled, the show gets built and then broken into chunks we call reels. Where we choose to break the reels depends on a few factors: music presence, scene conclusions/ambiance, and length. I've been taught to avoid having music cross a reel break and find an organic hard transition to break a reel at. An example of an ideal reel break would be at the end of a scene where there's no pre- or post-lapped audio and no music.

Reel Length Limitations

When we start building the show, I'll ask the post supervisor if there's a limitation on reel length. Some projects—even entirely digital ones—still archive on film. A limitation could exist depending on the available film stock and the amount of film that can physically fit on a reel. Reels are typically between 1300–2100 ft., which works out to about 15–24 minutes (there are 16 frames in a foot of 35 mm 4-perf film).

If it's a purely digital show; the only real consideration regarding reel length is its "busyness." I've worked with longer reels that are fairly dialogue-driven and shorter reels that have more action or VFX sequences. All this depends on the editor and their conversations with other departments.

Identifying Phenomenal Reel Breaks

To find the ideal reel break, I start with the longplay. I navigate 15 minutes from the film's beginning and scrub around to try and find a good transition point, keeping the previously mentioned traits in mind (no music, a change in ambiance). I'll find a few potential points, mark them, and then advance another 20 minutes in the film to find the next reel break. I do this because sometimes, as I go through the film, it becomes harder to find a good reel break, and I need to backtrack to make sure they're all evenly balanced.

It's a miracle if you can nail the reel breaks from the outset; it's like trying to predict the future. Of course, during editing, the reels will fluctuate in length. This leads to rebalancing the reels (p. 219). You don't want to rebalance more than once if you can avoid it. Why? Consider the other departments and how disruptive it can be. If a rebalance needs to happen, it'll happen—just check with other departments beforehand to make sure they're aware of changes, why it's happening, and whether or not it's a good moment to do so. Usually, if we're going to rebalance, it's done just before we lock picture (unless there's a good reason to do so beforehand: like if a new music cue now crosses a reel break.)

Each reel begins with the head leader and ends with the tail leader. There's a whole section on creating leaders in the Turnovers Chapter (p. 221).

Addressing Notes (Managing Alt Edits)

In terms of notes, there are small trims and big swings. Some stuff might be so small that it's just done in the reel, but other notes might be better enacted in sub-sequences before cutting them into the reel. How your editor chooses to organize themself is something you should adapt yourself to, and it's a great way to learn if you're allowed to help by addressing notes. Just like with dailies, ask your editor if there are any notes they would find helpful for you to work on specifically.

Noting Changed Areas

Every editor works differently; this is one way to keep track of notes. We leave white markers where changes are made that need to be shown to the director. These might be changes in the reel or a note pointing to a subsequence or two in another bin (experiments bin or scene bin). Once the note is reviewed, we change the color of the marker to black. When asked about changes, these markers can explain what was enacted (or not enacted, if a clarification was added to the marker comment). When versioning up, all black markers are removed from the notes track (since they've been accounted for).

Of course, there are other notes to address, and using the marker system outlined earlier helps keep track of those as well. These markers help communicate notes between editors, too. For example, when I address a note in a sub-sequence, I leave magenta markers in the notes track where I made changes (along with the details of my changes). Another example: When cutting in music, I leave a yellow marker in the notes track that has the date, whom the cue is from (composer, music editor, etc.), what track it's on, and if there's any playback information ("mute A11", or "play with source cue").

Comparing a Change to a Previous Version

After working on a scene, I've been trained to compare it to the old version, measure the time difference, and put that information in a marker comment as well as the bin comment column for the sequence. The fastest way I've found to measure this is:

1. Load the last version of the scene into the source monitor and select relevant tracks.
2. Reverse-match frame just before the changes start and mark in on both sides.
3. On the record side, go to just after the changes are done and reverse match frame again.
4. Mark out on both sides.
5. Subtract the record side duration from the source side.

After following those steps, you can determine how much shorter (or, if it's negative, longer) the scene is.

Organizing Alternate Edits

As notes accumulate, your editor will likely need somewhere to store different alts. Some editors prefer to use an "Experiments" bin, keeping one experiment bin per stage of the cut. The bin view displays the sequence name, scene number, and comments. It's important to put the scene number in there so you can sort them in scene order. Comments are vital so you can remember the context of what was being addressed in the alt (especially if it's a preferred alt). Other editors prefer to keep these in the reel bin and sort to the bottom, displaying all these columns.

Cutting Alternate Edits into the Current Cut

A best practice when cutting anything into a reel is to **deselect all tracks, restore the default patch, and check your track patches.** To keep track of which alts get cut in, we add "cut in" to the comments column and perhaps label the sequence with a color. I always put my initials and the date somewhere in there, too.

Presenting Alternate Edits

Your editor likely prefers how these alternate edits are presented, whether they are strung out into one sequence or presented as separate files in a playlist on PIX, and if they want to include the previous version of the scene for reference.

When naming these sequences, keep everything consistent, straightforward, and numbered. For example, if I have four sc 18 scene alts and it's a scene that is labeled in the continuity as "Rebecca's Car Ride," then I might label them as follows:

- 240728 R1 v8 wip sc 18 alt 1 - shortened car ride 1
- 240728 R1 v8 wip sc 18 alt 2 - shortened car ride 2
- 240728 R1 v8 wip sc 18 alt 3b - montage car ride "[mx 1]"
- 240728 R1 v8 wip sc 18 alt 3b - montage car ride "[mx 2]"

Notice how I employ a standardized naming convention followed by numbers (p. 213), which sorts the files appropriately. After " -" I add name that identifies the alt. "Alt 3" is a good example of how I present two identical alts where the only difference is the music cue, whereas the first two alts are different edits entirely.

In the past, I had output a sequence with a four-second slate briefly describing the change (or scene) before playing the alt. Within the same sequence and after a second of black, I used a "Previous version:" on-screen title and included the edit that was currently in the cut. This helped the viewer see what effect the changes had.

Slugging Missing Scenes

A slug is a short segment of black video with text on the screen. At the very least, it says something as simple as "Scene Missing" or perhaps something more specific like "Sc 76 - To Be Shot". You might slug missing scenes during the assembly phase, but otherwise, you'll likely only have to slug missing scenes ahead of additional photography.

There's a chance that the director won't want to carry the slugs in the current cut, which necessitates carrying two versions of the cut: A screening version and a slugged version. I've found that the easiest way to manage this is to keep a longplay (or labeled subsequences!) with the slugs cut in exactly as the editor intends and then keep the slugs muted on the topmost track with white markers denoting whether or not there's a time change. When the time comes to output the slugged cut, you can go marker to marker and unmute the slugs or cut in the small section from the slugged longplay. This allows you to keep any pre/post-lapped audio edits and output the latest version of the cut without trying to keep two versions in sync.

Versioning Cuts

The editor dictates the version and when to version up. It's likely going to be after significant screenings or milestones. It might just be after a long period of time, and they want to clean out old and scarcely referenced notes and versions. Everyone versions differently, and their methods evolve—especially to fit the situation. Some directors make changes in a linear way where a simple versioning schema can be implemented. In contrast, other directors may want many alternate edits, thus creating a flurry of micro versions. Depending on how involved the studio is, you might end up tracking more than one version of the cut altogether. How you version depends largely on how your editor likes to work. Most editors have an "active cut" (sometimes referred to as "live reels") or just the last sequence they worked on. Regardless of how they like to work, I am a proponent of coloring the most up-to-date sequences bright green.

I've worked on projects where we duplicated and dated the current version of the reel every day we went to work on it. Sometimes, more than one duplicate in a day would exist, in which case a simple point increment was added to the sequence name. On other projects, the editor preferred to have only one version of the current cut (relying on daily backups to go back to any day-specific version). Regardless of how your editor chooses to version their work, there must be synergy with the other departments, namely Sound and DI. They don't care about how you version if it's clear what the current version is and

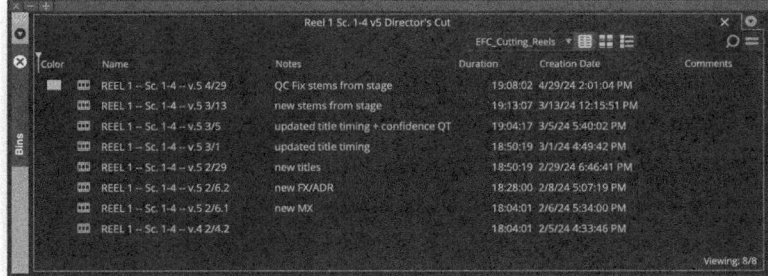

Figure 6.2 A reel bin with multiple versions.

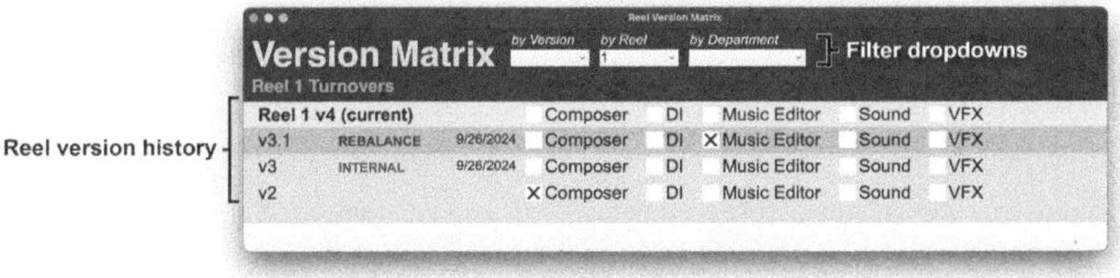

Figure 6.3 Reel Version Matrix in custom FileMaker database.

what changes to expect. The only hard and fast rule I feel strongly about following is **the version number always goes up**.

Sounds easy, right? Well, it can get complicated if your editor wants to version the cut based on the phase (Editor's Cut, Director's Cut, Preview Cut, Locked Cut, etc.). Imagine you work on Director's Cut 1, then Director's Cut 2, and then Preview Cut 1. It might make sense to you, but remember that other departments might be working on many projects at the same time, and they're likely to get confused when they've been working on vD2 (Director's Cut 2) and suddenly vP1 (Preview Cut 1) comes in. If they don't know what the letters denote, it would look like you went from Version 2 to Version 1. Confusing!

One solution is to maintain a version matrix where you can track which version went to which vendor. Then, when you turnover, you assign a version based on what last went out the door. The problem with *this,* however, is that the editor and the Sound team are now prone to confusion when communicating. The sound team will be talking about version 7 while the editor says, "I have no idea what 'Version 7' is; I'm talking about Version P1." The version the editor is referring to (the internal version they're used to seeing) doesn't match what the other department is working on (the version I assigned it upon turnover.) So, we're back to square one! Well, not quite.

The version matrix is good, no matter what. So, you keep that idea, and then you discuss with your editor when they like to version up and how often they like to reference old cuts. They tell you that they want every reel on the same version. Okay, no problem! Now, let's come up with a method of versioning that's easy to maintain, crystal clear to other departments, and aligns with the editor's preferences.

First, all reels must be on the same version, so we'll introduce the **major version**. This major version will change during those significant milestone screenings. Alright, now how will we handle small changes in between those screenings? We introduce a **minor version**. This gets incremented with each turnover. Let's also introduce an alpha appendage that indicates a non-sync change (like an updated VFX shot or a new ADR cue). Now, we have a version schema which looks like this:

v1 → v2 → v2.1 → v2.2 → v3 → v3.1 → v3.1a → v4

You can provide a version schema sheet to other departments that outlines how versioning will happen, or at the very least, have a phone call when you start turning over to them and discuss your plan. They'll appreciate your mindfulness.

Versions only need to be assigned when turning over to another department or screening the film. Outside of that, I usually use the current major version and append "wip" to denote that it's a work in progress, not a "complete" version. I do this especially if I have to turn over a small segment of a scene for a quick turnaround from, say, a music editor who's working down the hall.

The editor can now refer to "Version 2" without thinking about the point or alpha updates. The core of what I'm talking about revolves around taking a work-in-progress cut and assigning it a version when it goes out the door. Some editors don't mind all reels being on independent versions, and I've seen versioning that simply relies on using the date as the version. As with everything in this book, there's no right or wrong way to go about it. Whatever works for you and your team is best.

Building the Show

To build the show, I duplicate Reel 1 and rename it to match the screening or output name. I do this to ensure Reel 1 is first and that the start timecode of the longplay begins at the one-hour mark.

Next, I clear my marks, go to the end of the sequence, and load Reel 2 into the source monitor (making sure to clear marks if there are any).

Leader between reels
should be extracted

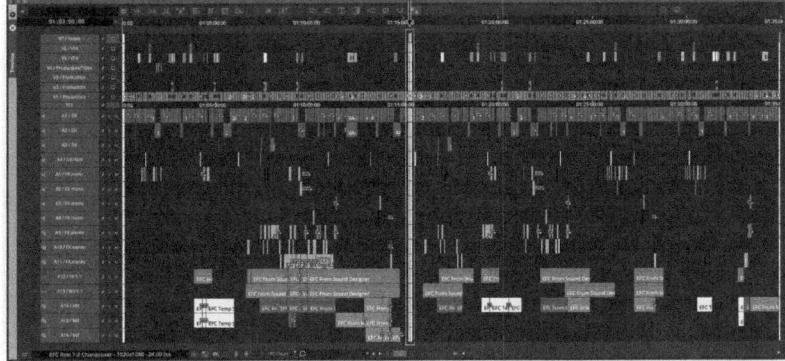

Figure 6.4 Changeover between two reels in a longplay timeline.

I select all tracks on both sides, restore the default patch, and append it to the end of the timeline of the longplay (insert or overwrite edits both work). I repeat as necessary for all remaining reels.

Once all reels are cut in, I navigate to the reel breaks (they're easy to find because they're colored brightly and stacked on all tracks. See the Head and Tail Leader Section [p. 221] for more). You can also search for "LFOA" in the Marker Tool. With the playhead positioned anywhere within the leader, I use "Mark Markers" to place an in and out point on the nearest markers: My FFOA/LFOA markers. I "go to in," scootch it out a frame, and "mark in." Then I "go to out," scootch it in a frame, and "mark out." I extract and check the changeover.

A sign of a successful extraction is hatch marks on the match frame edits. Again, I'll repeat for all reel breaks. The only time I'll remove the head leader from Reel 1 and the tail leader from the last reel is if I'm outputting to a review and approval platform (p. 21), like PIX. It's better to leave them on in other cases, especially if the sequence is being turned over to a DCP vendor.

Updating the Continuity

I build the continuity before we start shooting using both the script supervisor's breakdown and the assistant director's one-liner. The editor revises the descriptions as they see fit. Because the continuity is already built, it can be used to track shoot progress during production.

Each scene has a status, as seen in the table to the right. As we shoot, I'll flip the default "TBS" status of a scene in my database to either MTC ("More to Come") or BIN ("It's in the Avid Bin"), depending on whether it is partially or completely shot (respectively). I'll also add a still image once we get the footage in. When we wrap production, all shot scenes are marked as "In Cut," and the scenes that weren't shot are marked as "Omitted." At this point, I assign a reel number to each scene that is in the cut.

TBS	to be shot
MTC	partially shot (more to come)
BIN	complete
In Cut	active
Deleted	lifted
Combined	merged with another scene
Omitted	never shot

Throughout the editing process, the continuity gets updated before any major cut goes out. You'll want to make one available for any spotting sessions, studio screenings, or preview screenings. Updating the continuity consists of making sure the scenes on the continuity are in the cut, in order, and, in some cases, measured by the length of the scene. If the scene isn't in the cut, it's considered "Deleted," and the reel number should be removed from the scene. Therein lies the difference between deleted and omitted scenes. Deleted scenes are edited and lifted from the cut, and omitted scenes were never shot to begin with.

In my database (p. 72), scenes are put in order not by their scene number but by using a "Sort Order." This is useful because oftentimes, scenes will change in numerical order—but their scene number should remain the same. Also worth noting is that while I spend the remainder of this section discussing a picture continuity, some studios might want a "Music Continuity" document (p. 167). It's a document that's formatted similarly to the picture continuity, but instead of scene descriptions, it lists per-scene music cues.

Split or Combined Scenes

Sometimes, scenes are split into parts or combined with other scenes. For split scenes, duplicate the scene and append both with "pt. 1" and "pt. 2", etc. Break the description across the parts and update the still images. For combined scenes, pick one scene to be the hero, change the scene number to reflect the range (such as 128-129), and combine/condense the descriptions. In the other (dare I say "cannibalized") scene(s), note in the secondary description that it was combined, add the date, and then remove the reel number and change the status to "Omitted." Of course, I've written a FileMaker script that performs all those changes at the click of a button.

Scene Timing and Total Run Time

Once all the scenes are verified as in the cut and order, you can measure the duration using frames to round to the nearest second. The TRT will be derived from the reel durations in a separate table, so the manual scene timing doesn't have to be frame-accurate. This is different from a format sheet in a TV environment, where frame accuracy is essential. One important note about timing: Ask the editor if they even want to include it. It's possible that if a continuity goes out with scene timing and there's a scene that's, say, five minutes long; someone might look at the scene timing and, on sight, give a note that it must be two and a half minutes without even watching the cut.

If you do have to measure scene timings and you're going to do it manually, here's the method I've used: I duplicate a sequence of the longplay, strip it of markers and audio tracks, then place markers in the top track for the scene starts. I use "Mark Markers" to calculate the minutes seconds, ganging an old cut with the new cut to reverse-match frame when needed.

Wall Cards

The continuity can also be represented as individual cards taped to a wall or whiteboard. Each scene gets a card—sometimes 3"x5", 4"x6", or 5"x8", and potentially with representative images. These cards are initially based on the continuity but might be altered for brevity. Keep in mind that they'll be looked at from a distance and need to be legible in low light.

The cards can be hung up so that we can see the overall continuity of the film visually and manually rearrange or annotate scenes. We'll use sticky notes on top of the wall cards to mark things, such as recurring themes or flashbacks. Whiteboards are preferable for me because they allow us to annotate *outside* of the cards, which is helpful for scene-spanning events, perhaps music cues that cross multiple scenes.

Spotting Sessions

These are long screenings where you gather with the director and the members of another department to watch the film and discuss the scope of work. They happen early on during the Director's Cut phase. Typically, there is a lot of stopping and starting while going through the cut together, but hopefully, the participants will have received and viewed a cut before the session.

The director will communicate their intentions and expectations. Be prepared by sending a continuity ahead of time for notetaking—the other departments will find it helpful. They may even want it in Excel format. Below are the primary spotting sessions you'll likely have and the things discussed. Oh, and if this is on-premises, make sure you have enough parking validation for all the attendees.

VFX

Attendees: VFX Supervisor, VFX Vendor, and any Members of Their Team

This is likely going to happen before shot codes are assigned (p. 190), but markers will have been placed based on VFX notes from the script supervisor and any temps that have been created thus far. Prepare by using the markers to generate title overlays that display the work description on screen (or at least a green dot in frame to indicate that the shot is a VFX shot). SubCap will do the trick, and the process can be automated by using something like a database.

If there's a virtual component to this spotting session, make sure something like cineSync is set up ahead of time and that the reels (or a longplay) have been sent to the appropriate recipients.

During the session, point out any temp VFX you had difficulty achieving and voice any concerns like significant roto or a poorly lit green screen. It's a good idea to get the ball rolling on cosmetic work as well; ask the director if there is anyone you should be looking out for in the footage (maybe an actor had a pimple on one day of shooting). Then, after the session, go through and mark any potential cosmetic shots.

Confirm the schedule and delivery specs previously discussed on the workflow call (p. 12). Determine a schedule for deliveries that works best for review and feedback: I like to suggest deliveries by the end of the day on Mondays. That way, we can cut shots in and review on Tuesdays. It's frustrating when shots come in on a Friday at 6 pm, and the director doesn't always want to start with VFX on Monday mornings anyway. So, this is the time to have that conversation!

Sound

Attendees: Supervising Sound Editor and Anyone From Their Team

This is mostly to discuss the sound design and ambiance in the film. You'll talk about where music will be more dominant over sound design. Point out any problematic production audio and lip-syncing that was done, as well as any potential ADR. This is a good time for you to meet the first assistant sound editor to discuss workflow, but you shouldn't do that during the spotting session itself—better done in person afterward or in a follow-up email.

Music

Attendees: Music Editor, Composer, Composer's Assistant

Themes and motifs will be the crux of the conversation. Instrumentation, transitions, and where specifically in the film music will be placed. What do we want the music to do for the film? This is a good time to talk about workflow with the music editor (or composer's assistant—perhaps both). Similar to the other spotting sessions, it is best to follow up with this conversation.

Titles

Attendees: Titles Designer and Anyone from Their Team

This is not normally a spotting session, but I think it fits in here in terms of reviewing the cut and having other creatives weigh in. The biggest thing you can do to prepare is provide texted and textless versions of the sections of the film that contain titles. When applying the watermark, ensure that its placement doesn't conflict with the work that the title house needs to do.

Stock Footage

Attendees: N/A

This is not a spotting session, but I don't spend much time discussing stock footage in this book, and this feels like the most appropriate place to mention it. If your project contains stock footage, you'll need to keep track of it and "spot" it with your post supervisor. Do not assume that any stock footage downloaded from YouTube or the like is licensable. In fact, assume all stock is temp until proven otherwise. Keep track of where stock footage came from so you can track the source back down. I like using a custom bin column for this purpose and clip colors (like dark red) to indicate unlicensed stock.

Backing Up

Keeping a backup of your work is **critical**. A daily project backup is paramount; just below that is a backup of the Avid media and Nexis files. I like to keep a backup of the entire Nexis and update it daily during production, then weekly for the duration of the post. This allows for the flexibility to:

• Let the editor work with local media on the mix stage.
• Send a clone of the Nexis to an additional editor without missing a beat.

- In a worst-case scenario, rebuild the Nexis completely if it implodes and catches fire.

That last one has never happened to me before (as Avid's hardware is excellent), but the point is to be prepared for anything.

Autosave

As mentioned previously, the Avid Attic (p. 37) is where bins get auto-saved. This should be thought of as a temporary buffer throughout the day, and your daily backup is for retrieving work from past days. If you need to restore a bin from the attic, copy it to your desktop, append ".avb" (that's the file extension for an Avid bin file), and then double-click it. Because it's a copy of the bin that it's a backup of, you won't be able to open it if the current version of that bin is already open. Close the current version, open the attic backup, and copy the contents into a temporary work bin; then, you can close the backup bin and re-open the project bin.

Daily Backup

The most important backup is your daily backup: The project. It is not just the reel bins or the new bins but the **backup of the whole project every single day**. I run an Automator script that copies the project folder to a folder on my desktop (and the database, for that matter) and then zips that folder (bins compress very well), renames it to include the date and copies it to my encrypted flash drive. I do this at the end of every day and bring the flash drive home with me. *No exceptions.* The project is every little bit of editorial work. None of the added metadata, organization, or **the edit itself** exists outside of the project. As mentioned earlier, the media can be regenerated (sure, it would be a headache, but it's not *impossible*), but it's all for nothing if there's no cut to relink to.

Weekly Nexis Backup

For this task, I choose ChronoSync. I know very little about Rsync, but this seems to be a robust and friendly GUI for that. The overview is this: You pick a source and a destination, and ChronoSync analyzes them to see what the differences are. It only copies over anything new. There are quite a few settings to look at, but the main one I use is "archive deletions" (except for the Project drive—bins and attic files balloon like crazy). This way, nothing ever gets lost.

I like to set it up so that there's one folder on the backup drive for each Nexis partition. Using folders instead of partitions allows for greater flexibility, especially if you have to resize a Nexis workspace down the road. A workaround that lets you use this drive locally is to create Sparse Bundles for each partition with SymLinks within them.

ChronoSync is built for repetitive synchronizations. It saves source and destination paths with their associated settings as "Task" documents. You can bundle multiple task documents into a "Container" document so that when you run the container synchronization, it performs all the tasks within it sequentially.

When I'm moving a lot of files around, and I'm not using ChronoSync or Carbon Copy Cloner, I choose Forklift or Transmit. I like these tools because they give a more detailed account of the transfer progress than Finder. I've run into issues using Finder for large copies; sometimes, not everything will complete, or a file will be missing/corrupt, and I won't receive an error.

When setting up your backup drive, make sure it's encrypted and physically locked down. Choose a size that is large enough to fit all the Nexis media (or a reasonable projection of what it could be) yet physically small enough that the editor can travel with it easily. The studio might ask for this drive (but unencrypted) upon wrap. As of this writing, a 16 TB drive has worked well for me.

Sparse Bundles

A sparse bundle is a type of disk image that was created to support Apple's Time Machine backup protocol. It's faster to use than a sparse disk image due to the internal architecture of how it was designed. For our purposes here, we're not using it to back anything up but more so to redirect the filepaths from folders to disk images that Media Composer will see as individual, locally connected hard drives.

I create one sparse bundle for each folder on the backup drive that I want to mount as its own drive. This reflects the mounted Nexis drives 1:1. I then create an Avid MediaFiles folder on the root of each sparse bundle and run a terminal command to create a SymLink of the corresponding MXF folder within each one:

```
ln -s (source) (destination)
```

In this case, the source is the *backup drive MXF folder,* and the destination is the *sparse bundle Avid MediaFiles folder*. You can drag and drop the folders into the terminal window. Note that it's important to respect the space between source and destination.

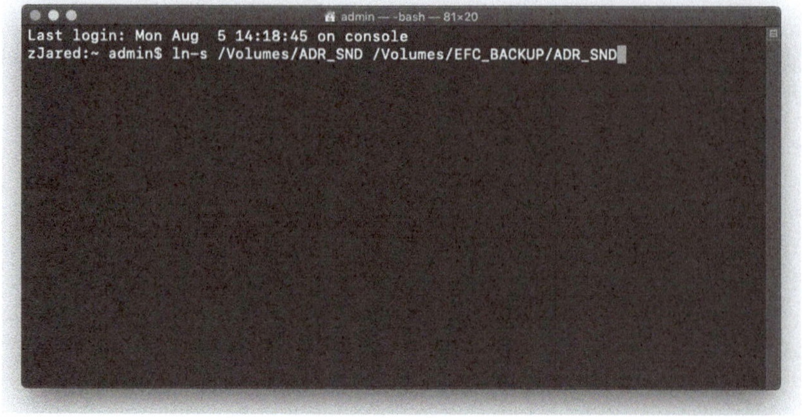

Figure 6.5 Terminal window displaying SymLink command.

As mentioned, these SymLinks will "re-route" Media Composer to the appropriate directories when the sparse bundles are mounted. Sparse bundles allow the folders on the backup drive to function similarly to the Nexis/a partitioned drive but will leave the drive space flexible as opposed to partitioning it.

Always. Keep. A. Backup.

7 Audio

We all know the importance of audio. I was once told that an audience is more accepting of lower image quality if the audio is clear and consistent. Hearing pops, clicks, and abrupt transitions within dialogue scenes can distract the viewer, take them out of the story, and remind them that they're watching something. I often think about how far audio technology has evolved in non-linear editing systems, having expanded the abilities of the film editor. While the film editor's expectations might be higher regarding having a more fully fleshed-out temp mix, our tools make creating and maintaining a rich sound mix easier. I believe having these tools allows us to better lay a foundation by establishing creative intention. The work we're able to do also acclimates the director by allowing them to review the film in a state that more closely resembles the final product.

We have the added flexibility to change and experiment in the cutting room rather than in a more expensive and time-sensitive environment, like the mix stage. Not every project demands third-party plug-ins like iZotope RX or working in anything more than stereo. Whether you need to go the extra mile or not, I believe it's good to at least know what's possible.

My work entails meticulous gain adjustments, volume and pan automation, and dialogue clean-up work. It includes switching out line readings, matching ambient sound (room tone), finding the right temp sound effects and music—and editing music; all these are complete jobs in and of themselves. We try to keep a full temp mix with as clean a dialogue track as possible before the "big guns" come in (the sound team).

Production Sound

It all starts with what was captured during production by the production sound mixer. Most productions use a mix of boom and lavaliere (lav) microphones, and the tracks are laid out such that the mix track is first, followed by the boom(s), and then however many lavs there are. I've seen Schoeps CMIT 5U booms and Sanken COS 11D lavs show up pretty frequently. You'll want to know what equipment is

DOI: 10.4324/9781003516491-8

used during production so you can use the same mics later during ADR. Production sound mixers will add names to the tracks that come through as metadata in the Avid bin. This is all great stuff to talk about on the dailies workflow call (p. 12).

Working in 5.1

5.1 surround sound can be thought of as an expansion of stereo. Mono is one channel, stereo is two (left and right), and 5.1 is "surround" (Left, Right, Center, LFE, Left Rear, Right Rear [that's in SMPTE order, by the way]). 3.1 is like 5.1, but without the rear speakers. Dialogue, hard effects, and foley tend to go to the center speaker. Sometimes, I'll pan those and automate them to place a sound in the space. Dialogue rarely leaves the center channel, but it can be useful to pan it in certain cases, like if someone is off-screen and you want to make a point of it. Be gentle; it can get distracting.

So, where do the rear speakers come in? Many ambiances often just play in the front left and right, but I will "toe it in" a little on the panner to get some bleed into the rears (and sometimes the center channel), which helps fill in some empty production track moments. You can link and mirror the left and right channels of a stereo clip, so they match and sound even across channels. Most of the time, the surrounds are more for atmospheric sounds and the occasional

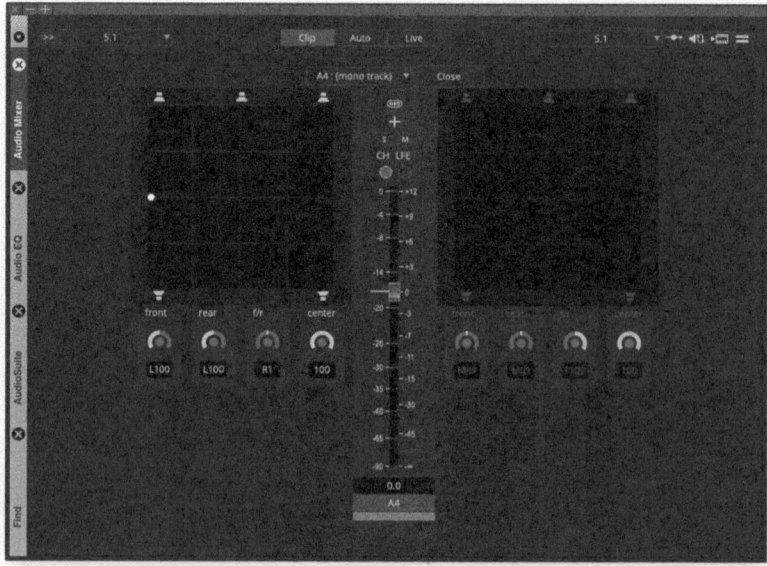

Figure 7.1 Avid Audio Mixer big panner.

specific sound effect, especially when something is coming on or off the screen. The sound designer might provide some nice, designed ambiance. When called for, I create surround ambiances from stereo tracks, wherein I pan a stereo file into the rears (or a mono clip to the exact center of the big panner). I'll kick in the LFE occasionally, but only for specific things like a hit in combat that I want to punch up, or a low and ominous rumble you can feel in your gut.

Sequence vs Monitoring Settings

On the technical end, there are two main things to be aware of when working with 5.1 in Media Composer: The "output monitoring" audio setting and the "sequence" audio setting.

As I expressed in a previous chapter, the sequence audio setting applies to clips and sequences and is representative of **how the audio is being routed within the program**. The output monitoring setting tells Media Composer **how you want to listen to that routing**. For example, you can have a stereo clip (or sequence) and monitor it using 5.1 output settings, but you'll only hear it populate the front left and right channels. Conversely, if you take a 5.1 sequence (or clip) and

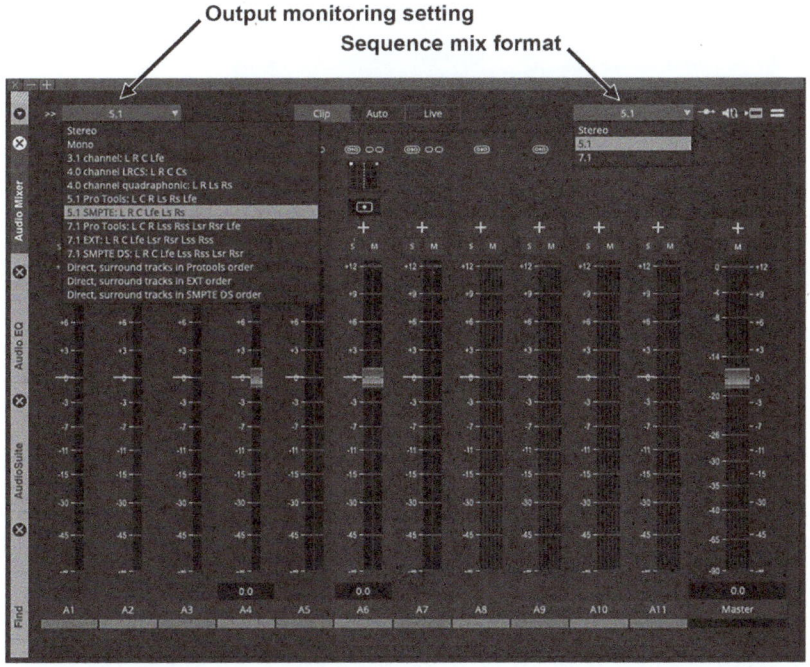

Figure 7.2 Avid Audio Mixer delineating "output monitoring" and "sequence" audio settings.

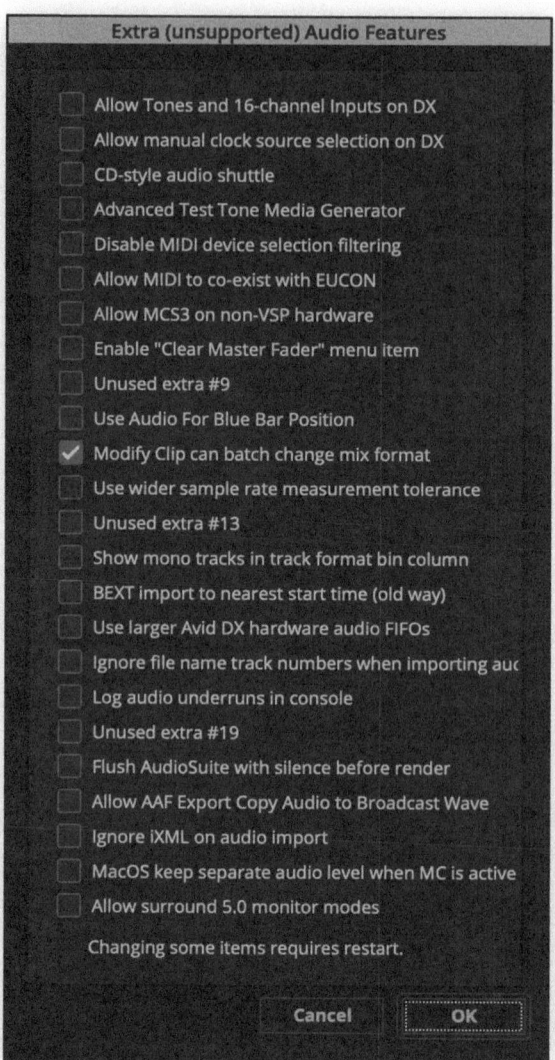

Figure 7.3 "Audio Extras" dialog.

choose to monitor it using stereo output settings, you'll hear that 5.1 routing mixed down to the left and right speakers (rears will be folded down, and the center channel will be split).

I create a template sequence that is already set to 5.1, so every subsequent sequence created by duplicating it has the same settings. For an apprentice editor with an LCR or stereo setup, Avid does the appropriate down-mix—folding the rear channels into the front left and right and lowering by 3 dB. Note that not all machines in your cutting rooms need to have the same audio configuration. You may choose only to have your room and the editor's be 5.1 while VFX and second assistants monitor in stereo.

I think that working in 3.1 is a good compromise because you can carry a full surround mix and contribute to it but not necessarily need the bulk of extra speakers or a bigger room. Full surround is lovely, though, and it's super fun.

As mentioned in the Dailies chapter subsection (p. 98), dailies should be treated specially for 5.1 space. Production footage is inherently treated as center-panned, stereo-formatted clips. This splits the signal between the front left and right speakers when viewing in the source monitor. Once cut into a 5.1 timeline, the center panning respects the 5.1 space—because the *sequence setting* is 5.1 surround. This is why the "sequence setting" of the master clips needs to be set to 5.1 as well for a more accurate audio experience when viewing dailies.

There's a list of special audio settings that aren't supported. However, typing "audioextras" in the Media Composer console provides access for users.

One setting I like is "Modify clip can batch change mix format." This allows me to take a bin full of master clips of dailies and switch them all from stereo to "5.1 sequence," which mitigates the above issue of going between source and record monitors while viewing dailies.

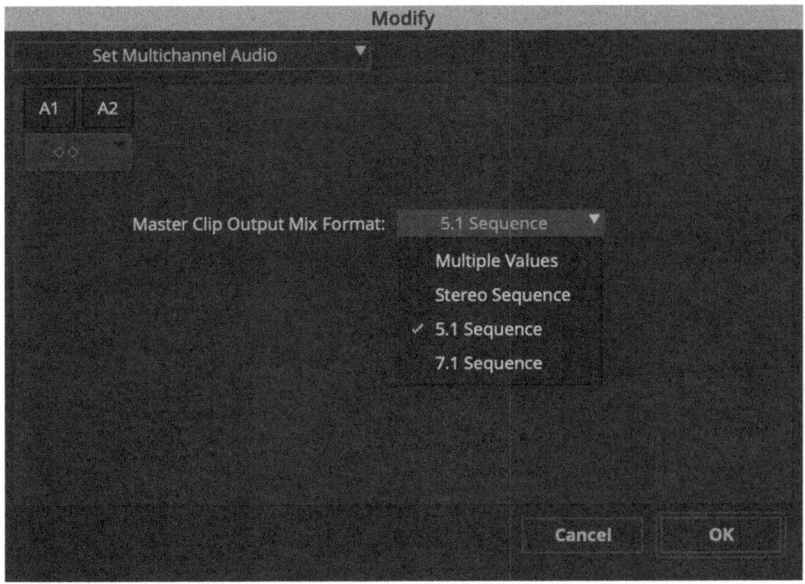

Figure 7.4 "Modify Clip" dialog, displaying 5.1 and 7.1 sequence options.

Importing Audio Files

By default, all clips have a "sequence setting" of "stereo." All imported sound files, especially ADR (and, if time permits, stereo music), should be reassigned from stereo to 5.1. It's preferable to pan them on the clip level to avoid being inconsistent later if matched back to and re-cut in.

Whenever I import files from the music editor, I toe the panning into the rears by -40 (on the left channel, with both channels linked and mirrored). Check with your music editor (especially when the composer is on board) because you may **not** want to do this in order to preserve the integrity of the composer's work.

Subframe Automation

As of Media Composer 24.6, we can now control audio keyframes on a sub-frame level. This is awesome, and believe it or not, it makes Media Composer *more* compatible with Pro Tools despite the added perceived complications.

It's very simple; the same way you could normally add an audio keyframe (**Command-Shift-click** on an audio clip while volume audio data is displayed) now allows you to add a keyframe in the middle of a frame by adding the **Option** modifier key. If you want to move any audio keyframe on a subframe level, **Command-Option-click** and drag it.

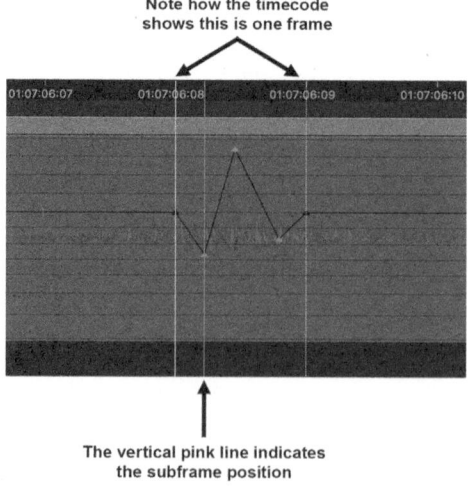

Figure 7.5 A clip with subframe keyframes, displaying a vertical pink line.

5.1 Turnover

In terms of turnover, all departments I've worked with still expect traditional deliverables: Mono and stereo guide tracks for turnover. They might benefit from a 5.1 FX guide track—ask them. This is detailed later in the Turnover chapter (p. 224).

Speaker Calibration

Regardless of whether you're cutting in stereo, 5.1, or using digital or direct out, you can calibrate your speakers using pink noise set to -20 dB in the system (as monitored in the audio tool):

1. Set your physical volume controller to 50%. I use a piece of tape to mark this for future reference.
2. Place your calibration tool (in my case, an iPhone running an app called DecibelProX) where the director will primarily sit or wherever is best for the editor.
3. Pan the pink noise to one speaker using the Media Composer audio mixer. I start with the left channel and work my way around the room clockwise.
4. Adjust the speaker level physically (the knob on the back of the speaker), so your calibration tool reads 85 dB (and a little less for the LFE).
   • When calibrating the LFE, you'll want to center pan the pink noise, raise the LFE to 0 dB in the big panner, and then **physically disable the center channel speaker**.
5. Keep the calibration tool in the same physical spot for the duration of calibration. Repeat for all speakers.

Audio Editing

Best Practices and Audio Editing Tips

• Keep the tracks organized by dialogue, sound effects, backgrounds, and music (usually in that order).
• ADR should go on its own track whenever possible. This isolation will help down the line when turning over for sound or ADR.
• Consider using multiple timeline views. I have one each for dialogue, effects, music, and stems. Each one makes the specified tracks taller, zooms the waveforms, and displays relevant clip and audio data (volume, clip gain, and waveform).
   – Displaying waveforms can slow down the system. For that reason, I have one timeline view which **does not** display waveforms.

- I opt for the waveform display to be saved within timeline views over using the toggle in the track control panel. The track control panel can be more granular, but it takes a more precise click for me to activate.
- That said, **Option-clicking** the waveform icon in the track control panel will toggle waveforms for **all tracks**, not just the selected one. This functionality extends through all track control panel selections.

• Use the mix track when possible; otherwise, favor the boom. Only go to the lavs when necessary. The boom usually contains a good atmosphere.

- The EQ between the boom and lav is different, and the lavs (while sometimes more clear) have less ambiance and potentially more rustle and low end than the boom. If using them in tandem, be wary of phasing.

• When editing dialogue, try to keep similar ambiances on their own tracks. Use keyframes to feather new ones in. A dissolve can be used between two similar ambiances. Pre-lapping dialogue should also pre-lap any associated ambiance on other tracks.

• I tend to apply AudioSuite effects before applying an EQ, as the former will need to be rendered, and the latter will play in real time. Avid will always process a real-time EQ after an AudioSuite effect, anyway.

• It's possible to apply audio effects in bulk by selecting the clips using the segment tool and then **Option-double-clicking** the effect (either in the effect palette or a preset saved in a bin).

• Real-Time AudioSuite (RTAS) effects are enchanting. You can use them to apply reverb to everything on a given audio track, for example. I generally don't use them because I find that they can slow down a system, introduce an unwanted variable into my workflow, and need to be consistent across all reels. I prefer to render effects clip by clip, and I know that when I play back a timeline, there's nothing left to chance. I don't want to have to remember to apply RTAS effects and wonder why a timeline sounds "weird."

- Some editors like to have one dedicated "ringout" track that has a reverb RTAS effect on it. Its sole use is to drop the end piece of a music cue onto the track and allow the cue to end less abruptly. This is in opposition to creating a mixdown that includes filler at the end, then cutting that back into the timeline and applying (*and rendering*) a reverb effect.

• I use both clip gain and volume audio data in my timeline view when working with audio.

- The most common thing I'll do is **Command-Shift-click** the volume automation line (not to be confused with the clip gain line) to create and adjust a keyframe simultaneously.
- Another quick thing I do for a fade (I favor keyframes over dissolves for more control in some situations) is create two keyframes, one each for the beginning and end of the fade. I'll lower one end, create a new keyframe between the two, and then Option-drag it left or right. This changes the "curve of the fade," so to speak.
- One tip/trick when using gain: **Option-Shift-up/down** will adjust the clip gain of any segment on an active track the playhead is parked on.

Dissolves: Linear vs Equal Power

There are a handful of different types of crossfades that a ProTools system can create which start involving S-curves and more formulas that I'm not privy to. Within Media Composer, though, there have historically only been two options, and the **default** option is tucked away in the *"Audio Project > Effects"* settings tab. This setting only dictates the default fade type when creating audio dissolves, and it has no bearing over real-time playback if it were to be toggled. For example, if the current setting is "Linear," then all dissolves added to the timeline will be "Linear," and will remain so even when the audio project setting is changed to "Equal Power." The type of crossfade can be changed individually by entering Effects mode, selecting the dissolve, and changing it in the Effects editor.

Ok, but what's the difference between Linear and Equal Power? A linear crossfade increases and decreases the volume of the incoming and outgoing clips at a constant rate. An Equal Power crossfade has a steeper curve than a Linear one. Normally, Equal Power sounds pretty good, but as outlined above, it's just a starting point. If you hear a slight rise in volume after applying an audio transition, it's because the two clips are in phase. If you hear a click or a pop, try shifting the dissolve a frame or two forward or backward or roll the edit itself. All this information is carried over to exported ProTools sessions and AAFs.

Channel Selection—AAFs vs EDLs

When editing audio, we use the mix track most often. In an EDL turnover, this points to the source file and timecode range to use, but it doesn't specify a channel to use. This is fine when it's the mix track. If you make a deliberate choice to cut in a boom or a lav, that decision will not be reflected in an EDL. This is not good!

The sound department will likely want both an EDL and either a ProTools Session or AAF export. The EDL allows them to rebuild using source files, while the ProTools Session or AAF export is a better representation of the editorial timeline (rich with metadata, effects, volume and panning automation, and **channel selection**.)

It's important to stress that the sound team defers to the AAF when reconstructing from the EDL. The person importing an AAF file will know, for example, that you used channel 3 (the boom) instead of channel 1 (the mix) or channel 6 (the lav). The person rebuilding from an EDL only knows the source file and timecode in/out—**not the channel**. You or your editor will likely make very explicit decisions when it comes to selecting audio channels, and you must maintain the integrity of your choices.

Lip-syncing

We frequently choose to lip-sync certain vocal performances from takes that are not being used on screen. In these instances, the best practice is to keep the original line in the cut (but muted). Keeping muted production clips in the cut is helpful for the sound department when they're building their sessions; it allows them to easily reference the on-screen sync waveform. Muted clips come through in an exported ProTools Session/AAF but not in an EDL. Usually, I'll create the ProTools Session or AAF, duplicate the sequence, and then unmute all clips (removing any temp ADR or mixdowns.)

This is all well and good, but what happens when you cut in stems from a temp mix? See how to work with stems from the stage in the Mix Stage Section (p. 171). It deals with handling muted clips and how they are represented in turnovers.

ADR (Automated Dialog Replacement)

Temp ADR: Recording Audio

I used to use a USB microphone hooked up to my computer (or an XLR mic plugged into a Blackmagic UltraStudio 4K Mini *with an SDI loopback*) so I could use Media Composer's Audio Punch-In Tool if needed. That's a quick way to get temp lines into the system. Another fast way to get temp ADR into the Avid is to use the Voice Memo app on my phone and then AirDrop it to my computer (provided that security allows Wi-Fi to be enabled). This way, we can record temp ADR anywhere—not just in my room. The latter is my preference.

I label Temp ADR using the following formatting: temp ADR [character] - "[line]." After importing it into a catch-all "temp ADR" bin,

I enter character names, scene, sound TC, and Soundroll (tempADR) in bin columns. It's not necessary to do all this for temp, but it's a good habit to get into.

ADR Markers

Here's what an ADR marker looks like:

> **PnewB=ADR=Brian="I'm training for a marathon, so we can't get burgers."=production line muffled=remove temp on A4 and unmute production on A1 before looping, sc 81==end**

Like DI effects and VFX shots, I leave a marker whenever I do anything as a temp. For an ADR line, I use a cyan marker with the name "ADR." The comments of the marker are formatted to include a tag, the character name, the ADR line, reason, note, and cue code. An example of a reason is "muffled production audio" or "added dialogue." A note could be "per director" or "remove temp on A4 and unmute production on A3 before looping." I also add the scene number in the note field. Check out the marker section of the FileMaker chapter for more in-depth marker formatting information (p. 76).

ADR Tags and Notes

Tags and notes I commonly use are:

- "**P**" tag (priority line)
    - "P" is added to the tag of an ADR marker that we want to prioritize the recording of.
    - My database searches all tags, and anything with a "P" is saved into a PDF for a recording session of priority lines.
- "**√**" tag (recorded line)
    - "√" is added to the tag of an ADR marker that has been professionally recorded in an ADR session.
    - My database searches all tags, and anything with a "√" can be omitted from any generated paperwork (else the line is labeled bright green to indicate its status).
    - A cue code is generally also inserted into the appropriate marker field upon entering a checkmark in the tag.
- "**OMIT**" tag (omitted line)
    - OMIT replaces the tag if anything is there.
    - These ADR markers are deleted after a turnover, which reflects omitted lines.

- **Scene Number** in the Notes field (should match scene number on continuity)
  - Starting with TBW (To Be Written) lines, I add the scene number to the notes field.
  - This is so that I can share PDFs with creatives of all lines that still need to be written or re-written.
  - Allows someone to cross-reference the line with the continuity for context.

I use a system that came from John Axelrad's cutting room. After the first turnover, we start adding a tag to indicate anything new or changed. That tag looks like this: **newA**. During the next turnover, I can search for all newA lines and provide a list of *only those lines*. Then—you'll never believe this—any subsequently added or changed lines get tagged as **newB** (and so on).

Adding the other tags, like P or √, just adds detail (which can lead to a tag that looks like this: **√PnewC**). This system is what I'm using for now, and yes, you're correct that there will be a problem when we get to **newP**. Hopefully, we don't have to do 16 full ADR turnovers, though. This overall method is used for DI and VFX markers as well to help actively track what we're changing.

ADR Cue Codes

Cue codes are typically assigned by the ADR editor and are usually formatted with a letter character ID followed by four-number padding, with the first number denoting the reel. An example of Brian's fifth ADR line in Reel 2 would be **B2005**. The only time *I* assign a cue code is if we need to generate paperwork ahead of a session and the sound department isn't on payroll yet.

I only update the marker with a cue code once we record a line. I add a "√" to the head of the Tag field, specifically when the line is cut into the timeline. This line will then appear as "RECORDED" on any ADR cue sheets generated from our system.

Putting it all Together

Knowing all about ADR markers now, let's break down the previous example:

- **PnewB**: Priority line added after the second ADR turnover.
- **ADR**: Identifies this as an ADR marker.
- **Brian**: Character name.

- **"I'm training for a marathon, so we can't get burgers."**: Line of dialogue to be recorded.
- **Production line muffled**: Reason for recording the line.
- **Remove temp on A4 and unmute production on A1 before looping, sc 81**:
- **[Empty]**: *No cue code has been entered here because it has not yet been recorded.*
- **End**: Ensures the entirety of the marker has been parsed.

Preparing for an ADR session

Before an ADR session, I prepare the cue sheets and prep sequences for the ADR stage. Creating ADR cue sheets is as simple as exporting the ADR markers from Media Composer and importing them into FileMaker Pro. I generate the following documents:

- All ADR lines by timecode
- All ADR lines by timecode (tag ONLY)
- All ADR lines by Character (separate PDFs)

I spell-check the documents (it's easy enough to re-output the PDFs if needed, which is why I tend not to proofread first), and I follow the notes—for example, removing or unmuting lines before creating a turnover for an ADR session. I print out three copies of the "All Lines by Character" documents: One each for the director, editor, and myself.

ADR Turnover Assets

You should consult the ADR section in the Turnovers chapter first (p. 226), but this is part of the process where I have to turn over ADR. I first generate a set of reels that have general burn-ins for ADR. These are all silent (MOS) video files, and while different vendors have varying specs, all the ones I've worked with have been amiable and accepting of MOS files with guide tracks.

For each vendor, I run the necessary reels through Media Encoder. Sometimes, I only send a reel or two if the character doesn't have lines in other reels. For each reel, I update an **additional, specific** watermark (p. 209), which displays the vendor name and date. This is because the general watermark only has "Property of" and "ADR" included. I've found this method of using a general and additional watermark to be more flexible.

Sometimes, the director might request that only a section be sent, not a full reel. It could be for any reason, but a common one might be that they don't want the performer to see the whole performance, just enough to set the tone. If I ever send a segment, as opposed to a full reel, I make sure the handles are lengthy enough, and there is a 2-pop at the head and tail. The way I do this is by marking an out point, then going to where I want the segment to start and rolling back eight seconds to mark in. I pull the subsequence this way so I can **overwrite** the head leader without affecting the timecode, and then I tack on the tail leader as well.

During the ADR Session

During the session, I take notes on the cue sheets by marking a take with a number. Rolling takes (when they don't cut after a line reading) are denoted using letters in superscript. I circle a number or letter if it's good and add one to three stars depending on everyone else's reaction (say, if the director or editor makes a positive remark.) If I have a thought, I'll text the editor or quietly jot a little note for them to read and act on if they agree.

The noted cue sheets get scanned into the system and saved with the session files, with the hard copies stored in a manilla folder in my office. (see "ADR cue sheet generated from custom FileMaker database, noted by hand after ADR session [downloadable]" at www.routledge.com/9781032843285)

ADR Session Wrap

I bring a hard drive to the stage so I can copy the files when the session is finished—unless they plan on sending us media using Aspera. Usually, they supply a ProTools session and associated audio files. I import the audio (adding any notes from cue sheets, if the editor wishes) and send all files to the sound department if they don't already have it. If we're working with ISDN or Source Connect, I make sure to request the session files from the remote vendor (even if I have to go through the sound department.) Otherwise, what the ADR tech might kick out is a scratch audio recording, not the split tracks of each microphone. What you want is one clip per take, which has a channel for each microphone recorded (boom, lav).

When I get back to the cutting room, I copy the original ADR files to the SND_ADR Nexis partition, organize them by session date, and then I'm ready to import them into Avid.

Importing Session Files

I import the session files into Avid bins organized by character. I give each character their bin, and I keep adding clips to it. Because I add metadata, it's easy to differentiate the session dates. As mentioned earlier regarding temp ADR, the metadata that should be added is:

- Character
- Date
- Sound TC (dupe Start TC)
- SoundRoll (Character ID + date [ex. **J0418**])

The reason for adding the metadata is so an EDL won't throw an error. One tip regarding Loop Group: It might be a good idea to create one bin per reel for Loop Group. In one case, we had 12 loopers recording remotely, which generated more than 5000 files.

If you're working in surround, set all clips to 5.1 so they play out of the center speaker.

Once all the ADR session files have been imported into Media Composer, back up the source files immediately; if you back up the ADR partition after importing the lines into Media Composer, you'll catch the original files as well as the Avid-generated media.

Cutting Recorded ADR lines into the Sequence

Not all lines will necessarily get cut in by the Editorial; just the ones needed for clarity or story (or whatever the editor decides to cut in). The sound department will ultimately handle everything. Regardless, it's good to have them all in the system for future reference. We let the sound department know which cues we cut in and on what track (we typically already have a dedicated ADR track, and the recorded ADR replaces any temp ADR). I make sure to add a √ to the marker tags and the cue code as well.

Syncing ADR Video with Associated Cues

In some cases, you'll find that video will be recorded during an ADR session. It might be a witness cam (like a security camera), or it could be head-mounted (think "performance capture"). In any case, there's a good chance someone will need to reference that video at some point, which means that you now need to sync the video to the audio.

Considerations need to be made to achieve this, given that sequential ADR takes will all be embedded with overlapping session timecodes. This timecode corresponds to the point of time in the reel where the line occurs and resets with each new take. The video, on the other hand, runs linearly. Ask the ADR tech if it's possible to record both the **session timecode** and **time-of-day timecode**. I don't know if this is even possible, but I figure it's worth a shot because right now, I use a work-around that revolves around time-of-day timecode and on-camera scratch audio. If there's no scratch audio available, then just stop reading this part now because you'll have to handle this manually.

This is a lot like creating a sync map (p. 96). I take all the video footage and execute an "auto-sequence" command, which places all video clips in a timeline at their appropriate times. This accounts for breaks in video recording as well. Then, I place all the ADR lines on a lower track and manually sync the takes. Using "Waveform Sync" works, but it seems to be a bit sporadic. When I use it, I find that going one take at a time and adding an edit in the video clip after each synced line helps. After the lines are all synced, I subsequence each take, rename it according to the cue code and auto-sync it to turn it into a subclip that can be used in the reel.

Sound Effects

Either the second assistant editor or I import any sound effects we need into an "SFX Loaded on [project name]" bin. This is helpful for two reasons: All our temp effects are in one place and are specific to the show, which in turn makes future shows easier to find SFX for. Your library is only as good as you're able to find the right sounds. When you associate certain effects with a certain show, it makes it easier to find over time. Be sure to use a column like "Description" or "Note" to add the category of SFX, which can then be sorted, sifted, and searched.

Some editors prefer discrete bins per SFX type (ambiances, cars, fights, etc.), which is great for separating different types of SFX. If you choose to go this route, consider creating an "SFX Loaded on [project name]" when wrapping the show by Option-dragging clips from all categorized bins into that one catch-all bin.

Other sound effects are sometimes provided by the sound designer. When we receive stems of full reels or patches after a turnover, we cut them into the reel, remove any of our muted clips, and mute all remaining SFX. We mix these stems as needed and unmute any sound effects from our temp if we feel they're missing or not emphasized enough.

Music

You're probably already familiar with the difference between source and score cues. If not, "Source" music is anything being played on screen, like a radio or concert performance. A character singing (or even humming, for that matter) is considered source music. "Score" is anything non-diegetic, typically written and supplied by the composer.

Subcategories of Music

I like to assign different colors for different kinds of music (p. 131): temp score, temp source, music editor, temp score and source edits, on-screen playback source, music supervisor source, and composer cues. This is a bit fluid, though; sometimes we don't need all that detail, and it's reduced to just differentiating the score from the source.

The thing I've found tricky is labeling music edits from the music editor since I'm inclined to color all those the same since they're all coming from the same person. All of this is food for thought, but the distinctions are helpful if it's ever requested to provide split music tracks.

Types of Music Cues

- **Temp** is score that we get from anywhere. Not used in the final product.
- **Demo** is temp score sent by the composer.
- **Score** is an elevated form of a demo, usually more fleshed out but not recorded for the final.
- **Final** is a score cue from the composer that has been signed off on and has been recorded on a scoring stage.
- **Source** is anything that's not a score cue. The types of usage are:
  - **BI**: Background Instrumental (instruments only)
  - **BV**: Background Vocal (anything with a choir or singing)
  - **VI**: Visual Instrumental (we can see someone *playing* the instrument we hear)
  - **VV**: Visual Vocal (we can see someone *singing* the song we hear)
  - **Logo**: Music that accompanies a production logo.

Working with a Music Editor

All things music go through the music editor. We work closely with them, especially on sync notes (p. 168), and ideally, they'll be there in the cutting room alongside you. The music editors I've worked with have all communicated with the director, composer, and music supervisor. Sometimes, you'll have a temp music editor who is different from the composer's music editor.

Typically, the music editor will deliver stereo WAV files to Editorial that have the date, reel number, version, cue number, and/or name, as well as start footage (or timecode) **in the filename**. Their files should also have an embedded timecode that matches the reel timecode from the turnover they are working with.

Importing New Music Cues

When new music comes in, I import the cues into a bin with the day's date and then copy the turnover sequence it corresponds to into the same bin. Typically, the music editor's files need no attenuation, and you should ensure they're not baking in any automation—you can copy the keyframes from the last version of the cue and paste them (**Command-Shift-V**) onto the new cue. Demos from the composer might have to be brought down a bit in volume; sometimes, they're delivered at full volume.

The new cues get cut into the duped turnover sequences and then conformed into the current cut from there. It's best to also take a dupe of the current corresponding reel into the music bin and perform the conform and mix there. This bin can function as both a music review bin and as an archive if it's ever desired to go back to an older version (p. 169).

After cutting new music into the reel, I assign a clip comment for my database to use later on, and then I mute the new clip and place a marker in the notes track. This marker contains the date and cue information; "**2/27 new MX from music editor on A15 (muted previous temp on A14)**," for example.

Conforming Music Cues

I typically turn over a version of the reel for the music editor to work on while the editor continues working with the director. This means that when we receive music cues back, they need to be conformed to the current cut. Conforming happens *after* any sync notes and *before* a music review (if there's time).

Let's say the music editor has Version 1 of the reel, and we're working on Version 2 wip. I'll import a new music cue, duplicate the turnover sequence from Version 1 into the bin where the new music cue has been imported, and then cut in the cue. It lines up 100% (unless there are sync notes that are needed).

Then, I take a duplicate of the current reel (in this case, "Version 2 wip") and dupe it into the same bin. Version 1 is loaded into the source monitor, and Version 2 wip is loaded into the record monitor. I go to the first frame of the music cue in the source monitor and perform a reverse match frame. I gang the sequences together and cut in as much of the cue as I can until there's a change. Then, I reverse match frame from the record side into the source side to re-sync after the change.

Once all the cues have been cut in, there may be a bunch of gaps or bad edits. I roll the edits and add dissolves as needed to make the cues sound correct. Sometimes there'll be no conform needed since there haven't been any changes. **This is not an assumption that should be**

made. If there are too many changes and the music edits sound terrible, it's best to present the cue to the editor and/or director from the turnover version. Then, if the director wishes to move forward with the cue, re-turnover to the music editor so they can conform it so it will sound correct.

Music Cue Sheets

Cues have names and numbers; the naming structure looks like this: **1m04**. As I have been told, this is derived from the days when the first number denoted the reel, and the letter denoted the type of sound (d for dialogue, e for effects, and m for music). The number is sequential in the reel. The above cue number is the fourth music cue in Reel 1. When we put all the cues into a list and make a document out of it, it's called a music cue sheet.

Typically, Editorial is not asked to supply cue names or numbers, and the music editor manages their cue sheet. If Editorial is asked to provide something like a cue sheet (sometimes called a "Music Continuity"), the only identifying information people expect to see on it are the scene number, type of cue, and cue length. Of course, using my database (p. 77), I'm able to provide more information, like the scene description and reel version, without lifting a finger.

The two layouts I use for sharing this information are a typical "Music Cue Sheet" and a "Music Continuity." The former is built to mirror what a music editor provides and looks more like what they would want to send. The latter I created from a specific studio request, and it looks very similar to the scene continuity.

Playback

Playback relies on having a music file to play on set, which the actors can listen to as they perform. It can be out loud, in their ear, or both. Usually, the take starts with a blast of the music out loud, and then it disappears **from the mix track** to prioritize the recording of dialogue.

If the playback music is a song that the actor is lip-syncing to, the odds are that you'll want to sync all takes together into a "supergroup" (p. 109). This is typically easy because there's consistency from take to take. You can see where the music starts in the waveform, and you can also probably make use of an audio timecode data track.

Live Performances

Live performances (no playback, no lip-syncing, live singing) add a layer of complexity to grouping because the nature of a live performance is that each take will be different enough that syncing them can

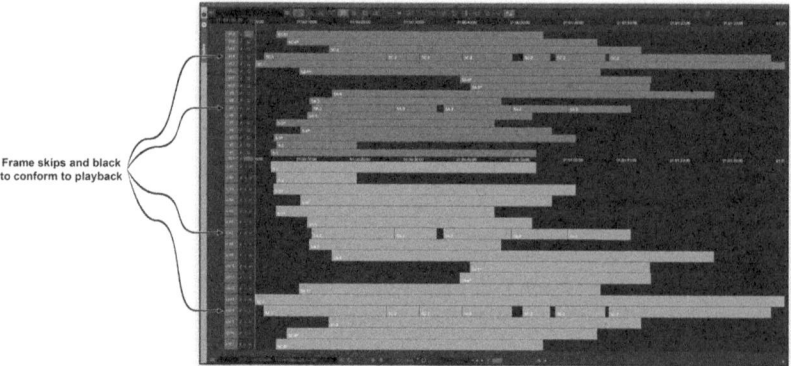

Frame skips and black
to conform to playback

Figure 7.6 "Super Group" clip, displaying multiple angles and setups. Note certain clips have frame skips or black to conform to playback.

become a fool's errand. What I do in instances of live performances that need to be synced together is to first ask, "Which performance is the hero take?" Subsequently, I'll hand-sync (really, it's more of a conform) all other takes to that hero take, adding edits or Filler as needed. This leads to frame-skips or black holes in a group clip for the conformed takes, but it allows us to quickly shuffle through different live performances in the timeline while keeping their respective live elements. When the editorial work is complete, you can then go in and clean up the edits, which I've found easier than trying to continually try and re-sync performances.

Sync Note Edits

On music-heavy shows, we sometimes make picture edits based on notes from the music editor for a cue to work. For example, on one show, we had turned over a version of a music-centric scene, knowing there might have been sync issues. The music editor took a look and cut the music accordingly but noted that to make the cue work, we would need to add one second at a certain timecode and then slip two shots by two frames each.

I cut the new cue from the music editor into a subsequence of the current cut and turned off the sync lock for that track. I addressed each note from the music editor **in sequential order** and left markers in the notes track everywhere I made a change (with details of the change).

This might be self-explanatory, but as a reminder to myself: **Advancing** an edit or a shot means moving it left, "towards breakfast," or earlier in the sequence. Conversely, **delaying** a shot means moving it right, "towards dinner," or later in the sequence. Rolls and slips might be interchangeable in this context, even though a roll usually refers to an edit, and a slip refers to a shot. Neither of those affect duration, whereas adding or subtracting frames does.

Frame additions/subtractions must be made **in order** so that the subsequent timecode notes make sense, like a traditional change list. If you skip one step, it throws all notes that come after it out of sync. There's usually a range within which the addition/subtraction can be taken, like in the example below. Let's look at a few sync note examples:

- The music editor requests "add 2 frames in [timecode range]."
  - This means you have to find an area or two in that range where you can add two frames—this changes duration.
- The music editor requests for the picture to be "rolled -2 frames."
  - This means you should **slip the shot left** (subtract from the head and add to the tail—no duration change).
- The music editor requests, "Delay this shot +5 frames."
  - This means you should **roll the edit right** (add to the tail of the outgoing shot, overwrite the subsequent shot, and come into it later—no duration change).

Music Reviews

A music review is like a VFX review in that you gather the troops and go through versions to give creative feedback. These sessions won't happen on every show, but in case you find yourself in the position of prepping and running a music review, here are some notes regarding them.

On certain shows, music reviews take place after the composer is on board and submits demos. We would receive new music just before the review, quickly cut the cues in, and review in person with them and the team. A music review can take place using the sequence that was duped into the bin alongside the imported cues. This sequence matches what the composer wrote the cue to and contains all the submitted alts. It's easy to toggle through different versions without messing with active reels. Once a version has been decided on, it's easy to cut into the current reel from here (conforming, if needed). My workflow on one show was to cut demos from the composer **directly into the active reels** on lower (muted) tracks beneath the stems. I'd add as many tracks as needed when there were multiple versions or alts. Once a cue was approved, I'd remove old versions and move the cue up and into the active music tracks. This replaced old temp cues both in the stereo tracks and in the 5.1 stem from the stage.

Otherwise, a music review consists of going through the submitted alts and playing them one at a time, with a little pre-roll. I like to keep the alts unmuted and selectively mute/unmute the audio tracks. Thanks to Avid's Live Timeline feature, you can do this on the fly.

Even so, remember to double-check which tracks are muted before hitting play. "Measure twice, cut once," as they say.

The Mix Stage

Once the show is at this stage of the process, depending on what's going on with the cut, you might be able to spend time on the stage, or you might be stuck in the cutting room sending out new turnovers, especially if the picture is being changed. What's more likely is that there will be VFX updates that need to be sent to the stage. The sound facility will need a separate turnover from the sound department (p. 225), and the watermarks (p. 210) can be adjusted to allow for more of the picture to be shown.

On-Stage Avid Reference

Whether you're there or not, the editor will be on the stage, and they'll likely want an Avid reference. I call this a "Stage Drive," and it can be as simple as using the Nexis backup (p. 147) if it's set up in a certain way. Just make sure to bring the drive back to the cutting rooms to sync it if the editor needs new material, and triple-check that the drive is secured with something like a Kensington lock when it's on the stage. If your show is already remote or hybrid, then I prefer using the remote connection when possible (like Jump Desktop [p. 16] on a laptop). The editor can use this to verify, on the fly, what take they used or if they had an alt muted on another track. They can share this information with the sound team so they can check their AAFs.

If the editor wants to make changes, they can do so and then send a bin back to the cutting rooms so it can be turned over to the sound department in a pinch.

Faders Up, Mix, and Playback

Generally, there will be pre-dub time for the mixers to get a head start on balancing individual elements (dialog, sound effects, music, etc.) before combining them into one session per reel, and everyone convenes at the mix stage. They slide their faders up and listen to the temp mix. Once we make it to the mix stage, the sound team goes through each reel, playing the whole reel back and making one more note pass. It's typical to focus on dialogue first, followed by effects, and then music. The next step is to watch the longplay and address notes that emanate from that viewing (and that viewing... that's "playback"). Finally, we watch the longplay with the executives and address their notes (along with small last-minute but important editorial notes).

If you're lucky enough to be on the stage and the environment is open enough for you to give notes, do so with tact. Time on the stage is valuable. It must be considered before giving a note on what the ramifications could be and if it's the right time to focus on any given thing. Pre-dubs are a great time to give detailed notes because they're a less time-sensitive environment. I like to wait until after the first notes pass in a reel before I speak up so as not to bog down the mixer while they're making their initial pass. As an assistant, I tend not to speak up when the executives are there. Even on days before they come in, I opt for passing my notes to the editor (via Post-it note or text message), and if they agree, then they'll share it... or encourage me to speak up.

Pro Tip: When taking notes on the mix stage, **use feet as a measurement rather than timecode** and try to categorize the note as either "dialogue" or "effect." A useful skill is to remember where scene delineations are, so you know how far to jump when skipping around sections. This usually happens automatically for me, as by this point, I am way too familiar with the show.

Working with Stems from the Stage

Before receiving stems from the stage, I talk with the mix tech to ensure they're sending me the files I need. I ask for 5.1 interleaved DX, FX, and MX (and sometimes BG) stems and a printmaster (PM). What I ask for changes depending on the context—if it's a temp dub, I'm less concerned with the PM and any stereo files. If the editor wants foley and design split out, or source and score music separated, then I request that.

When I get back to the cutting rooms, I import the stems in ProTools Order (that might be the default—check one reel before bringing them all in; they might need to be switched to SMPTE.), and the sequences need to be prepared. To do so, I add the necessary number of tracks to the bottom of the timeline and cut in the stems.

Next, I remove any muted SFX and MX clips that didn't make it into the mix. If they're not represented in the stems, they don't need to be in the timeline. This rule **does not** apply to the dialogue tracks. After I import the DX stem, I mute all clips on the production tracks. Now, anything **added** to the timeline will play **in addition** to the stem, and it's easy to see at a glance where new (or different) clips are. Moving forward, when turning over, I unmute all production tracks to create EDLs.

Here are three tips when editing 5.1 stems:

- Sometimes, you'll need to extract just the center channel or play only the left/right pair. To do this, take a subsequence of *just* the 5.1 track, open it, right-click on the track patch, and select "split track to mono." These mono tracks can be cut back in, or you can make a 5.1 mixdown and patch the 5.1 track itself.
- Consider making timeline views that move the stem tracks closer to the tracks they represent. For example, I've moved my DX Stem track (**Option-drag**) up towards the top near the dialogue tracks in some cases. I'll also increase the height of the track and zoom the waveform for greater visibility. It helps me compare the waveforms without scrolling.
- Ensure that when you're adjusting the timing of the 5.1 stems, **especially with dialogue, the muted clips on higher tracks are being adjusted accordingly.** There's no sync indicator for this, so add rollers or include them in your segment selection when futzing around with the stems. Oh my *god*, this is important! Please tell me you'll remember to do this.

Printmaster and Final Stems

Once we printmaster, that's delivered to us in 5.1 as well as to the finishing house that's making the DCP. I carry this alongside the final stems, as the stems are usually more helpful when turning over the locked cut with separated tracks. The music stems might not have 2-pops, especially if there's music crossing the changeover.

8 Visual Effects

Visual effects are a critical component of any modern film. They range in complexity from simple resizes, repositions, and retiming to paint outs, split screens, and set extensions. Then, there are fully CG characters and environments. On shows with many of the latter, there should be a dedicated VFX editor (p. 181) whose main job is to keep track of the various assets and versions for all the shots in the film. The following guide is for tracking and managing VFX shots without a dedicated VFX editor. This matches my experiences of tracking about 400 VFX shots with a small team of three (myself, a second assistant, and an apprentice). We'll get into the responsibilities of a VFX editor in a bit, but first, let's explore how to achieve some common temp visual effect requests. Here is a list of the temp work I regularly encounter:

- Removals and paint outs (p. 175)
- Split screens (p. 175)
- Chroma keying blue and green screens (p. 179)
- Stabilizations and screen replacements (p. 179)
- Stitching shots/custom wipes (AniMatte)

Why is it important to create good temp VFX? They help visualize the final product and nail the intended effect's timing. A poorly executed temp VFX shot can be jarring; this takes the viewer out of the story, thus the better a job we can do with the tools at our disposal, the easier it is for our collaborators to focus on the story and the intention behind *why* we need the visual effect at all.

Temp VFX: The Tools

I do as many temp VFX shots as possible on a show. I start during dailies and fine-tune during the director's cut. I tend to keep my work in Media Composer (as opposed to round-tripping into After Effects) because it's faster for me to swap out plates or backgrounds, and re-render with the director in the room. Plug-ins help accomplish this,

DOI: 10.4324/9781003516491-9

but sometimes I need to go into other applications (or "round-trip") to achieve an effect.

Avid Effects

I can get away with using three native Avid effects for most things: **3D Warp, AniMatte,** and **Paint.** Many basic effects can be promoted to a 3D Warp, such as a key pulled with Spectramatte. Using these effects, I can achieve a quick split screen, stabilization, paint out, or screen comp.

Some effects require the use of collapsing tracks (the submaster effect) to achieve the desired result, but it should be noted that *the contents of a submaster effect do not translate into an EDL.* The best practice is to always carry the plates below the effect in the timeline. This applies to Avid Effects and any import from After Effects or a VFX vendor.

AGAIN: *I always keep the plates accessible in the timeline,* even after cutting in the final VFX.

After Effects

I bring shots into After Effects if they need detailed graphic or compositing work, like a complex set extension or a lower-third graphics treatment. Something I've found useful in the past is creating static textless graphics in After Effects, exporting those with an alpha (transparency) channel, and then overlaying text on top of them in Media Composer. It's easier to edit the text in Avid than go back into After Effects and re-render.

After Effects exports that contain an alpha channel should use the alpha export setting "premultiplied." This allows Media Composer to import the clip with the alpha channel without inverting the key, as long as your import settings for alpha channels are set to "Do not invert on import."

Boris FX Plug-ins

Boris FX plug-ins are phenomenal in Media Composer. I typically work with all three suites of tools: Sapphire, Continuum, and Mocha Pro. **Sapphire** has great effects for beauty and light work; I've used it for glows, to simulate police lights on someone's face (utilizing Mocha, which is built into the Sapphire tools), and for muzzle flashes. It also has a "Builder" effect, which is dizzyingly powerful.

Boris Continuum Complete is like a Swiss army knife—a utility tool of sorts. It has many basic Avid Effect-type tools, but they're much more robust. The UI is more interactive thanks to a Heads-Up Display overlaid on the composer window, and most effects include Mocha built right in (which you can think of as a more refined AniMatte).

Mocha Pro is rather unassuming at first approach, as there's only one effect in this "suite," and the parameters are somewhat limited. You also might be led to believe you already *have* Mocha since it's "built-in" to the effects mentioned above. The part of Mocha integrated into the other suites allows you to leverage the tracking and masking engine, but only in the confines of the host effect. Mocha Pro is for advanced planar motion tracking, stabilization, rotoscoping, and screen replacements. I use it for paint outs and every screen and sign in a film.

Temp VFX: Tips, Tricks, and Examples

The following tips and tricks rely on using one or more of the above tools. Keep in mind that, as with all things technological, these specific methods will become outdated the further away we get from the time of publishing. The methodologies and approaches are worth consideration and can inform the way you choose to work with the tools that you possess.

Simple Removals and Paint Outs

Removals can be accomplished in many ways. The quickest way I do them is by using the Avid Paint Effect—for example, modern element removal (motion detectors and smoke alarms).

1. Apply the Paint effect and motion track the item to remove (if there's motion).
2. Draw a shape around it and feather it. The shape will be red by default. Don't worry.
3. Attach the tracking data to the shape.
4. Move the shape to the area you want to clone.
5. Switch the mode to "Clone."
6. Move the shape back to cover the item you wish to remove.

More complex removals and paint outs can benefit from more advanced tools like Mocha Pro to take advantage of clean plates.

Invisible Split Screens

When you think of a split screen, you might conjure in your mind's eye something out of a music video with thick black borders, a phone conversation showing both sides of the call simultaneously—or even something more stylistic like the brilliant sequence in the film 'Sideways' (edited by Kevin Tent, ACE). However, the split screens I'm commonly asked to pull off are invisible. It's usually to preserve continuity, say if we're cutting to a shot where a character's arm is down after it was previously raised, or to adjust the timing of a reaction or line of dialogue to hit more dramatically or comedically. There are several good reasons to employ an invisible split screen, so let's set the stage for an example.

In the case of a simple split screen, we'll have an actor speaking on the left side of the screen and an actor listening on the right. In this example, we'll pretend that the actor on the right begins to raise their arm at the end of the shot, and we need them to keep their arm down to preserve continuity going into the subsequent shot. Let's duplicate the clip onto video track 2 and slip the shot to remove the frames where his arm is moving (this adds frames to the head and subtracts from the tail). Now, the issue is that the actor on the left side of the screen is out of sync with their dialogue. We need to create an invisible split screen to maintain sync on the left side of the screen (track 1, "bg") and preserve the retimed arm movement on the right (track 2, "fg"). Let's say this shot is handheld to shake things up *even* more. That means there's now competing motion between these two clips due to the camera not being locked down. Ok, we're primed to begin temping this effect.

First, we need to negate the camera movement in the foreground clip by stabilizing it. Apply a 3D Warp, open the tracking window, select "**track foreground,**" and choose an area of high contrast: A lamp I just decided is in the middle of the screen and conveniently unobstructed throughout the shot. Now, in the Position parameter of the 3D Warp, select "Stabilize." Nice!

Next, we need to match the motion in the background clip. We'll nest another 3D Warp on top of the one we already applied by Option-dragging it onto the clip on track 2. We'll follow the same procedure as before, but this time we'll **track the background**. Before closing the tracking window, right-click in the track area within it and copy the enabled tracks. This copies the motion tracking data to your clipboard, which we'll use in just a moment. But first, under the Position parameter, instead of selecting "Stabilize," we'll just enable Position Tracking. Great!

Let's temporarily lower the opacity by setting the "Foreground" parameter to 50%. This lets us see the background clip, and we can adjust the placement of our foreground clip to align them. We'll use that convenient lamp as our convergence point. Once the clips are aligned, we can disable the "Foreground" parameter to restore full opacity.

The last step, I promise—it's time to finally split the screen. Nest an AniMatte effect on top of the two 3D Warps already applied by again

Option-dragging the effect onto the clip. Let's immediately open the tracker window, paste the motion-tracked data, and then close the window. We'll draw a shape that bisects the screen. The default matte option is to "key in" the shape, holding everything outside of the shape out. This shape should cover the right side of the screen with the actor whose arm remains down. Once the shape is completely drawn, the clip on video track 1 should be visible on the left side of the screen, and I'll bet you, they're back in sync now. Select the shape, and then in the Effect Editor, disclose the "Tracking" parameter set and point the first tracker towards your tracking data. This ensures your matte moves in tandem with the plate on video track 2, which is tracked to the motion of the clip on video track 1. Without this final step, your matte would be static and potentially more noticeable.

Feather the shape a touch just to eliminate any hard edges and you've got an invisible split screen!

3D Warp Tip: Update One Parameter

You can use a saved effect to bring in only one parameter set. For example, let's say you have a 3D Warp saved in a bin with values in both the Scaling and Position parameters. You have a clip in your timeline with a 3D Warp applied, and you want to use the Scaling parameters from your saved effect but not the Position parameters. *Click and drag the saved effect onto the Scaling parameter.* This works for most effects, not just 3D Warps. And it brings in keyframes.

Timewarps: FluidMotion Edit

This is a hidden effect, in my opinion. It's only available when a timewarp is rendered with the FluidMotion option. When this is done, motion estimation is applied to smooth out the pixels, which occasionally results in artifacts in the image due to the nature of generated pixels and motion. Sometimes, it's not the result of motion but instead a flickering light source like a candle or sparkler. The fluctuations in lighting confuse the algorithm, and the image jumps around. Regardless of why they appear, the artifacts need to be removed. If you're viewing in full quality (as opposed to draft), you can access **FluidMotion Edit**.

FluidMotion Edit behaves much like the AniMatte and Paint effects because it's an intraframe effect. You can draw a shape around the affected area, and it will remove the motion vectors from it, instead showing a blended frame. You can then drag and drop from a little (it is small, tiny, and possibly buggy) box onto an area where the motion vectors are more desirable. The on-screen colors will aid this. You can also manually adjust the sliders until the image comes into "focus." This is a helpful but tedious tool because you have to do one frame at

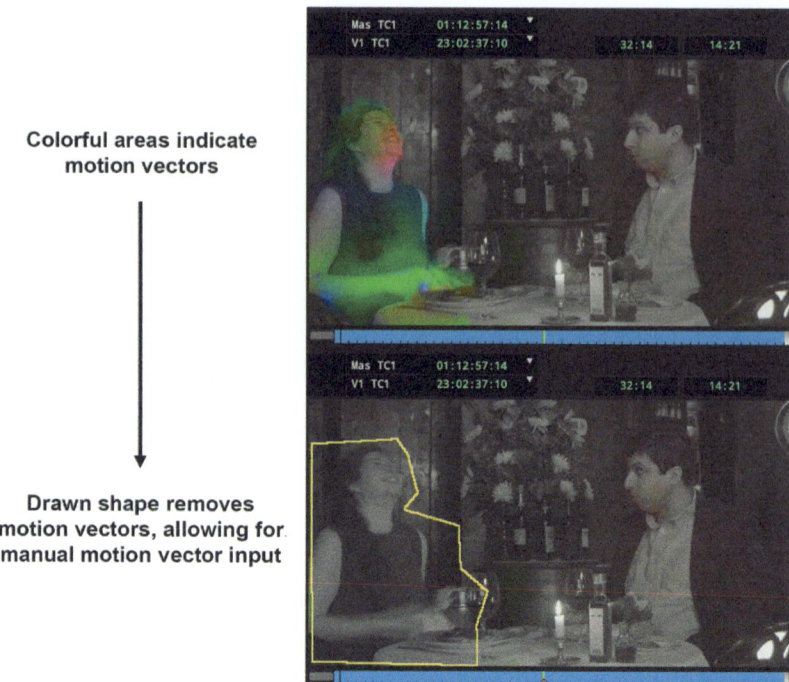

Colorful areas indicate
motion vectors

Drawn shape removes
motion vectors, allowing for
manual motion vector input

Figure 8.1 Before and after of Avid's FluidMotion editor.

a time. It's nice to know that it's possible to control artifacts, and it has been requested of me on several occasions.

Importing Still Images

For typical stills, my import settings are set to "Do not resize smaller images;" I bring everything in for a standard duration of 30 seconds. You can use a console command to set a custom import length in frames; otherwise, you're limited to full-second increments within the Import settings window. The console command is:

```
Cmd_setimportslidelength [number in frames]
```

Importing images means they will match the project resolution 1920x1080, which is fine in most circumstances. Larger images get scaled down to HD (pillarboxed/letterboxed), and smaller images are padded as needed.

When I'm working with much higher-resolution stills and anticipate significant resizing, I **link to** and transcode the stills. This retains the source resolution and applies a FrameFlex spatial adapter. You might run into alpha channel issues or the larger image size bogging down the timeline, but I haven't encountered either.

Chroma Keying and Motion Tracking

These are two common visual effects skills that are important to have because they can be used for any number of applications—keying out a background, stabilizing a shaky shot, creating a screen replacement, and creating complex split screens.

Chroma Keying

SpectraMatte is the name of Avid's built-in chroma keyer. It has its own effect, but it's also accessible within the 3D Warp Effect under "Foreground" (you can promote a Spectramate effect *to* a 3D Warp in the lower right-hand corner of the effect editor). I find that BCC's Primatte Studio has more parameters to fine-tune and masking options *built right into the effect* (as opposed to using AniMatte on a duplicated video layer in tandem with a Spectramatte key).

To pull a key using SpectraMatte, select a key color and fine-tune the chroma control parameters. I usually tick the "Show Alpha" checkbox and monitor the matte in black and white. The tolerance and key saturation line parameters have the most sway when quickly achieving a key. If I need a holdout matte in addition to my key, I duplicate the clip onto a higher video track and replace the SpectraMatte effect with an AniMatte effect. I'll then draw a shape around the area I don't want to be keyed (motion tracking it, if necessary).

All the above is if you're using the built-in Avid tools. Third-party plug-ins, such as Boris FX's Primatte, can accomplish all this and more.

Point Tracking

When looking at a shot that needs motion-tracking work, I first ask myself if I need a point or planar tracker. A point tracker uses one area of high contrast to track from frame to frame. It can only handle translation (x/y) unless paired with a second point tracker. When teamed up with three others, you have a four-corner pin track, which can be used for screen replacements. These point tracks can be done fairly well within Media Composer and are built into most effects by default. If the shot needs a split screen (p. 175) or a simple stabilization, I'll keep it in Media Composer instead of round-tripping it into another application. Avid's point tracker can lock two shots together or smooth out a bumpy shot with ease. If I see a screen with no major occlusion or perspective shift, I'll point to track the screen, copy the tracking data, and apply an AniMatte to the foreground. I then paste

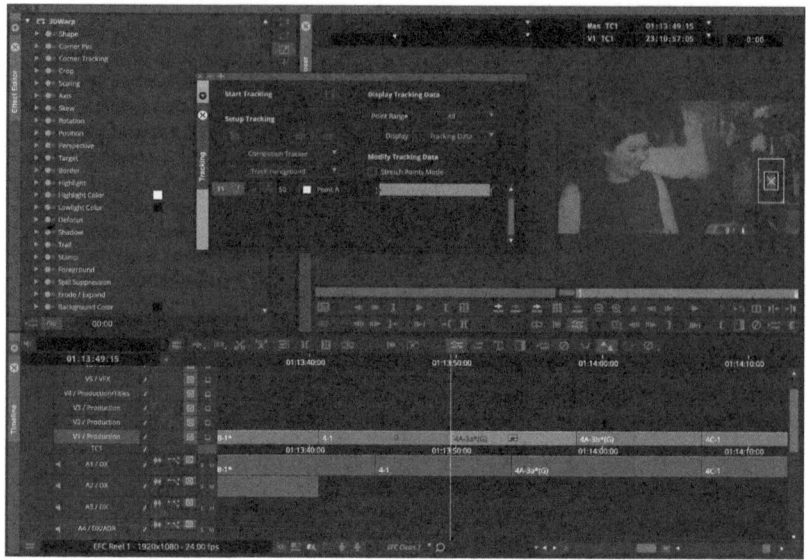

Figure 8.2 Avid Tracker Window with corresponding point tracker visible in Composer window.

the tracking data onto the background (fill) layer and give it a rough, un-animated four-corner pin distortion. This is crude and rough but fast and effective.

If there's a minor occlusion, I use offset tracking by right-clicking in the tracker window timeline and creating a new tracking region. When a range gets obstructed, I set in and out points and delete the tracking data—Avid interpolates. If I need to stabilize only a portion of a shot, I mark in-out in the tracker window, go to the in-point, and physically place my finger on the screen. Then, I go to the head of the clip and place the tracker where my finger is. It sounds silly, but it works.

Otherwise, if I see many moving parts or a huge shift in perspective, I take the shot into Mocha Pro.

Planar Tracking

This type of motion tracking doesn't look for one specific point. Instead, it looks at textures and patterns that reside on the same **plane**. Planar trackers can also track translation movement along with rotation, shear, and perspective. This makes corner pins much easier because, instead of trying to find those four corners, you find the plane of motion and perform one track. Then, you simply attach a shape to the tracking data. Media Composer does not have a native planar tracker built in, but third-party plug-ins (like Mocha Pro) bring this excellent functionality to the host application.

Approaching a Shot

When tracking in Mocha, I first scrub through the shot and see if and where there's an occlusion. I draw my spline and keyframe it around the occlusion, or, if it's severe enough, I first track the occlusion itself. That's right, I track the problem first. Mocha sees foreground to background, and when I track and matte out an object passing in front of the desired tracking area, Mocha will ignore that when tracking the background if the layers are organized properly. I keep the foreground layers at the top and the background layers at the bottom, like how the camera would see the objects in the shot. Now, I can track the background without keyframing the spline. Just remember to de-select the gear icon on the occlusion before tracking the background layer.

VFX Editing

VFX editing certainly involves creating the temp effects described previously, but that's not all. Until the publishing of the first edition of this book, VFX editors were classified in the eyes of the Motion Picture Editor's Guild as "assistant editors." Now, they have a classification of their own that stipulates their hiring on projects with a large volume of VFX shots.

A studio will try to anticipate the number of VFX shots there will be in any given film before going into production. Based on the script, this breakdown determines whether they feel it's necessary to hire a dedicated VFX editor or simply assign the VFX duties to the assistants on the show. Whatever the breakdown number is, double it! That's where you'll likely end up. Sometimes, the hiring of a VFX editor will be left until after production, when it becomes more clear just how much VFX work there is to do.

Overview

The general responsibilities surrounding VFX are as follows:

- Identifying VFX shots
- Creating temp VFX shots
- Communicating with the vendor and getting the footage to them
- Receiving and noting versions from the vendor
  - *Flagging any issues before showing the editor*
- Reviewing multiple versions with the crew
- Reviewing proposed final shots in the DI at full resolution
- Tracking the status of all shots throughout the show
- Dates are the most important pieces of information, such as when the shot was received and noted, when a new version is expected,

and the drop-dead delivery date for a preview. More on this in just a couple of paragraphs.

A lot of how I keep track of VFX, and what is outlined later in this chapter, is based on using a custom database with scripts and calculations written specifically for these purposes. Using a purpose-built relational database allows me to pull related information from the codebook to generate documents like Line-Up Sheets (also called "Count Sheets"). By pulling data from the related reels table, documentation can also have the reel and cut version displayed alongside the codebook metadata, all with minimal effort on my part.

Tracking VFX Shots

Throw out the idea of "motion tracking" because from here on out, it's in a new context when I refer to tracking shots. Here's the overview: Flag shots that need VFX work, keep track of the changes in shot duration and scope of work, note the dates when the full resolution frames ("scans") are pulled for vendors, provide vendors with references and all applicable plates and data (line-up sheets), and finally, keep track of every single version and note. Dates seem to be the most important topic to me. Here are a few of the questions I hear regularly, all of which revolve around dates:

- When did the shot get flagged?
- When was the shot pulled?
- When was the change made, and can we use what's in the handles?
  - **Hold up!** *What are handles?* They're extra frames beyond the bounds of the clip being used in the cut. They allow for wiggle room should the shot need to be extended at the head or tail.
- When did this version come in?
- When did we give them the notes for this shot?
- When was the last time we received a version of this shot?
- When is the next version coming in?
- When was this approved (and by whom?)
- When do we review this in DI?

With this list of questions in mind, there are ways to be proactive every step of the way. The system I've used involves breaking each shot down into several elements. A basic split screen, for example, has two elements. Each element in the timeline is given a marker **and** clip comment with the shot code (shot codes are assigned before the first VFX spotting session. Before then, we just carry blue VFX markers with work order descriptions).

VFX Markers and EDLs

Here is an example VFX marker:

```
newD=VFX=EFC_005_020=MP=1=Remove production equipment and stabilize=end
```

We'll get more into markers later in The Lifespan of a VFX Shot section (p. 187), and there's more detail on markers (p. 127) and parsing them in the FileMaker chapter (p. 76), but to break this down here and now:

- **newD**: This shot was added after the fourth VFX turnover.
- **VFX**: Identifies this as a VFX shot.
- **EFC_005_020**: This is shot 2 in scene 5 of the project "Every Frame Counts."
- **MP**: Identifies this as the Main Plate.
- **1**: This will determine the order in which this element is sorted.
- **Remove production equipment and stabilize**: Description of VFX work.
- **end**: Confirms that the complete marker text made it through.

Each part of the marker is used to identify what's changed in the shot and the shot itself (the shot code). The marker indicates that the segment in the timeline is being used for a specific duration at a specific point in the timeline. This comes across in the EDL as a tape name as well as "source" and "record" timecode pairs, in and out (clip and timeline, respectively), and a marker (p. 215). Let's look at how this VFX marker appears in an EDL:

```
000001 A122C020_241215_ROW4 V C 17:40:21:05 17:40:25:19 04:03:23:12 04:03:28:02
*LOC: 04:03:26:12 BLUE =VFX=EFC_005_020=MP=1=REMOVE PRODUCTION EQUIPMENT AND
STABILIZE=END
*SOURCE FILE: A122C020_241215_ROW4
```

In parsing this text, the record and source timecodes for the in and out points, the clip's source (tape), and the marker text are all consolidated into one record. The marker itself is then parsed from a text string into a value list (not too dissimilar from how I broke it down in list form above) and ultimately into individual fields (see figure 4.8 and p. 76). By identifying these elements, I can continuously run EDLs into the database and automate checking the status of shots as they exist in the timeline.

Two quick EDL tidbits:

- VFX marker descriptions **should not be longer than 230 characters**. This is because the EDL will truncate the marker description to 256 characters, and with *LOC 00:00:00:00 BLUE* and identifying information, the entire marker comment text won't make it into the EDL.
- EDL timecode is **inclusive**. This seems to be a remnant of the digitization of film, per Michael Phillips on an Avid blog: "This is because it follows EDL type designation of IN and OUT with the OUT being +1 frame. While the *film* world likes INSIDE/INSIDE counts, the *video* world likes INSIDE/OUTSIDE" (Phillips, 2009). The implication is that while the data in the EDL will be correct, when displayed on a PDF it will be one frame off. I account for this in my database by having a separate calculation field for "timecode display."

Checking the Cut (Updating the VFX Tracker)

Using markers in EDLs to automate the process of checking the cut highlights changes such as:

- Whether the shot has been lengthened or shortened at the head or tail.
  - *This is four questions asked and answered when you think about it.*
- If the classification or description changed.
- If a new element has been added and needs to be pulled.
- Where the shot is within the context of the cut.

We'll go into greater detail regarding updating the VFX tracker (p. 199) in a later section, but briefly, here's how I **update** my VFX tracker (*not* bring shots in for the first time):

- Check marker formatting.
  - Flag any new shots as "new[X]" in the tag. Do this in the active reel.
- Commit multicam edits and bring duplicate sequences into a separate bin.
  - Remove dissolves and clean up as needed.
  - Export EDL from Avid.

- Import EDL into the database.
- Check every shot in the reel. The database will only flag shots that have changed.
  - If it's inactive, investigate why.
  - Note the changes.
  - Flag pulls/repulls and check handles.
  - Send Pull EDL, Line Up Sheets, and updated QuickTime reference.

When a Shot Disappears

If a shot is removed from the timeline, it shows as "Inactive" in my database and must be investigated. A "Cut Status" of "Inactive" usually leads to one of two conclusions: Either the shot has been omitted, or the VFX marker has been deleted by accident (perhaps *too much* of a head or tail trim such that the marker disappears).

After digging through the last few versions of the cut, if I still don't have a clear answer, then I will check with the editor to make sure the shot is omitted. Sometimes, they are just trying something out, and I don't want to omit a shot that might come back.

If it's truly an omitted shot, I update the status in the tracker. If it has already been pulled, **I let the vendor know immediately**.

If the shot is omitted for VFX, but the clip is still in the cut, **I keep the marker in the sequence and change the tag to "OMIT"** (for a version or two, then I delete it).

If the marker is missing, incorrect, or too long, I grab the marker's text from an old cut and recreate the marker in the active reel, updating it with any new details.

Version Tracking and Statuses

Cutting in New Versions

After importing the new versions, you can go one by one and cut them into the reel. Most of the time, all shots have the same amount of head handles, something I take advantage of. This allows me to do the following: Throw the bin into script view, select all, and advance the frames by however long the head handles are. I mark in and then switch back to List View. This lets me mark the in-point on all clips at the same time, expediting cutting in the new shots.

Everyone has a different way of updating reels and cutting in shots. I've seen methods that involve relinking based on shot code, ignoring all instances of an underscore after the third one (to separate the shot code from any versioning or other naming conventions).

Avid VFX Reviews

For Avid VFX Reviews, we go through all new versions and keep notes in the database, marking any reviewed shots for a Revision Note so we can send them out when we're finished. Ideally, you can have a second assistant run the review, while your apprentice takes notes, or you can have any combination of a two-person team to run the session. If one doesn't already exist, I like to establish a system with the VFX vendor wherein they can submit a shot with a submission status. This allows them to submit a shot "for review," "for final," or anything in between (perhaps "final pending tech check" or "slap comp"), and that lets me know what kind of feedback they're anticipating as well as what I'll show to the director. The director and editor aren't always involved—this depends on the show and the scope of VFX. I try to review everything beforehand so I can show them the highlights and get feedback in as little time as possible. I might not bother showing the director strictly technical revisions, but I'll need them to weigh in on something creative in nature.

It's during these reviews that the status of a shot changes:

Clip Color	Shot Status	What That Means
(no color)	n/a	Received but not reviewed or cut into a timeline
	Scan Check	ALE generated a subclip representing the scanned element
	Avid Review	Needs creative feedback or approval for DI review
	In Revision	Creative or technical feedback was given to the vendor, expecting a revision
	CBB	Could be used as final, but if time allows, then there could be another revision
	DI Review	Approved to review in the DI suite, the vendor sends the version in high resolution to the DI
	Final	Version is approved as **final** at the DI suite in high-resolution

I keep shots on the "VFX Reviewed" track after sending them as drop-ins (as opposed to dropping them down to the lowest available track). This is helpful for change lists because I can run a change list on the "VFX Reviewed" track **only** and share changes regarding the VFX versions to, say, the sound department. This is especially important in films that are more dependent on VFX for sync.

VFX Color

Color seems to be an evergreen hurdle between the lab, editorial, and VFX vendors. It can be common at the beginning of the show to see a discrepancy between the dailies footage and a version received from the VFX vendor, which is one reason version 0s are requested (at least for the first few shots). In theory, the color pipeline should look like this (p. 242): *On Set Colorist/DIT with original footage > CDL applied > LUT applied > Dailies media rendered and delivered to editorial.* When the lab pulls plates (remember, plates are from the camera originals, which **do not** have a CDL or LUT applied), the VFX vendor can apply the CDL and LUT in the same order when they monitor their work and render for editorial but send non-color-affected EXR files to DI. This color pipeline must **always** be non-destructive. Typically, a color mismatch is noticeable in Avid, but the EXRs are fine (because the pipeline is—say it with me—non-destructive). However, this presents a problem for editorial screenings and previews, as color should be consistent.

There's no one reason why the color pipeline might be inconsistent between originators due to the number of variables involved, but it's worth discussing. I start by talking with the VFX vendor about their pipeline and asking how their editorial files are being rendered. Are they exporting EXR files and then transcoding them to HD? If they're not, is the downscaling in resolution affecting anything? Sometimes, VFX vendors employ custom FFMPEG scripts, which could have a flag improperly set, and that trips up the Media Composer import. In other cases, a transformation in color space happens improperly. If you feel it's beyond the scope of your knowledge (it happens to me *all the time*), ask the lab if they're comfortable speaking with the VFX vendor and then loop the two departments into an email thread. They'll hammer it out quickly.

The Lifespan of a VFX Shot

Now that we know how to create temp VFX shots and what to keep on our radar while tracking them let's take a step back. We'll walk through every stage of the VFX pipeline, from flagging to finalizing. Please note that this section is specific to my workflow involving my FileMaker database (p. 63), naming conventions, and scripts I developed. This should be used as a reference to create a system that works best for you.

Here's the VFX shot we're going to follow: EFC_005_020

This might look familiar from the previous section, where we discussed what a VFX marker looks like. It's the second shot in scene

5, and the work order is to paint out production equipment and stabilize the shot. We'll come back to this shot a few times throughout this section.

Flagging and Preliminary List

As mentioned previously, potential VFX shots get flagged during dailies. Near the end of production, I send a preliminary list of shots to the studio's head of VFX. Thanks to how we format markers, while there are no assigned shot codes currently, it's easy to export marker lists per reel and send a document with a breakdown of how many shots per reel there are, along with their scopes of work.

```
=VFX====remove production equipment, stabilize=end
```

Because a healthy amount of VFX get flagged during dailies, the scope of work is already in the marker and can be further clarified during a spotting session (it can also be displayed on-screen during the spotting session; more on that below). Each shot has a scope of work and falls into one or more categories, including set extensions, split screens, stabilizations, paint outs, wire removals, screen replacements, etc.

Often, a shot will contain more than one of the work orders previously outlined. Our shot is both a paint out and stabilization, and it will be flagged as such later. Perhaps if there was no need to paint out the production equipment, this would be a DI event instead of a VFX shot. Alas, since it's already going to be a visual effect, we'll include the stabilization as part of the work order. Now, just for kicks, consider that you have two vendors, one that exclusively does paint outs, and another that does stabilizations. These might happen in stages, so the stabilization will have to be approved before the paint out work starts. This is an example of something to consider before or during a spotting session.

VFX Spotting Session

Next up, we have a spotting session (p. 144) during which all parties (director, editorial, VFX supervisor, head of VFX for the studio) are present. We identify the pre-flagged VFX we marked during dailies. We make a spotting session timeline, which is the longplay with the scope of work displayed on-screen via SubCap, the creation of which I automate using FileMaker. There are tools available on various online resources that allow you to parse an EDL with markers and create a SubCap file (p. 266).

It's noted which shots are chromakey, paint, or other composites and which shots involve 3D work or need stock footage/graphics. Questions I ask include: "Which vendor should we assign the shot to?" and "Does the vendor have all the assets they need?" We discuss priority shots, which shots have good enough temps (or we can spend some more time refining), and which ones we need for the Preview screening.

This spotting session is also when we add shots we didn't initially flag and omit shots we now find unnecessary. We prioritize shots that we know will be difficult or time-consuming. I'm not privy to the explicit cost of shots or what deals get made, but comps are generally less expensive than 3D work. If there are stabilizations or re-speeds, doing them in VFX is more cost-effective than in the DI suite (because VFX teams are usually given more time to work on a shot than a finishing editor). A good rule of thumb to estimate the expense of a shot is how difficult it is for you to temp. I can tell when a stabilization will go from "fairly simple" to "holy heck, that requires paint and a minor set extension" when After Effect's Warp Stabilizer makes it look like Jell-O.

Cosmetic and DI / VFX Shots

NOW is the time to discuss what can potentially be promoted from DI to VFX (or vice versa). Some VFX shots don't start out as such. They might be a retimed shot or a paint out, which you initially marked for DI. Another example is extreme flicker; it might seem like something DI can handle but ultimately needs to be addressed using VFX.

Sometimes, a DI event needs to be promoted to VFX; At other times, a VFX shot is omitted in favor of addressing it in the DI. Generally speaking, the following can be considered DI events: Re-pos, resizes, stabilizations, simple paint outs, and constant retimes—more on tracking these effects in the DI chapter (p. 248).

NOW is the time to flag cosmetic shots. Odds are, no one wants to discuss cosmetic shots at this stage in the game since they're considered low priority and they're the last work order that's completed, but this is a good time to be proactive.

Once one shot in a sequence is flagged for cosmetic work, many typically follow. It's especially important to be specific and thorough upfront and be sure to scan the sequence and rest of the film for shots that will need the same attention. These kinds of shots tend to pile up. Even if no one wants to discuss them at this time, you can gently ask if there's any character the director intends to apply cosmetic work to.

> You can keep cosmetic shots flagged internally in the database as "cosmetic" (or "potential cosmetic") shots. It's easier to flag them now and omit them later, especially because everyone is present. None of these shots will come as a surprise to anyone. In my experience, addressing this now has been much better than suddenly adding 100 cosmetic shots at the 11th hour and assigning a bunch of new VFX shot codes. .

Assigning Shot Codes and Formatting Markers

We now formally assign Shot IDs (shot codes) and add more detail to the markers. This is all in preparation for bringing the clip data into the database and creating documents and QuickTimes for the vendors. Let's look at our VFX shot marker now:

```
=VFX=EFC_005_020===remove production equipment and stabilize=end
```

It's barebones still, and we'll dive into the formatting in a minute. For now, let's focus on the shot code. I use the format "*ShowCode_ SceneNumber_ShotNumber*" and increment in 10s. The first shot in scene 5 will be EFC_005_010, the second **EFC_005_020**, the third EFC_005_030... and so on, until you hit scene 6.

If there are no VFX in scene 6, you then go to scene 7; the first shot will be EFC_007_010. Incrementing in 10s allows you to be flexible when a new shot is added and falls between two others—split the difference (EFC_005_025, for example). If a shot is omitted, **never reuse the shot code**. I consider it "retired". All shot codes are **unique** to identify every VFX instance.

Using Clip Comments (Timeline Clip Notes)

When entering the shot code into the marker, I also **set the clip comment** on all elements with their respective shot codes. This will be nearly invisible (unless you show clip comments in your timeline view, which isn't a terrible idea) but will come in handy later. This method doesn't require me to make and carry VFX banners in the timeline. A single timecode generator effect applied to filler on a higher video track will be able to read and display the timeline clip note data where it's present. This makes all future exports that need VFX IDs burned in a snap to create. Not only will the timeline be cleaner, but the overall project size will be smaller because sequences have fewer effects. Every instance of a SubCap effect (multiplied by the number of versions and duplicated sequences) adds up and increases bin file sizes. Another disclaimer for readers furiously shaking their heads in disagreement: **This is just one guy's way of working!**

Identifying Specific Elements

I consider each segment of a shot in the timeline to be an element. A VFX shot may only have one element (which I like to refer to as the "Main Plate" or "MP"), but a complex shot can have many. Other element types I use are EL ("element"), FG ("foreground"), and BG ("background"), and I also make up other ones as needed—for instance, on one show we had firework elements, which I labeled as "FW." If there are multiple elements of the same type (EL, FG, etc.), they should be appended in the "type" field with a number (MP, EL1, EL2, FG1). The description can be specific to the element, or they can share the same description. This will be fleshed out later when it's all in the database. Let's add this information to our VFX marker:

```
=VFX=EFC_005_020=MP=1=remove production equipment and stabilize=end
```

Consider our shot, **EFC_005_020**. It only has one plate (MP) which the VFX artist will paint on top of and stabilize. Now consider a split screen (p. 75); two segments are in the timeline for this VFX shot—the foreground and the background (or the left and right sides of the split screen.) These two segments in the timeline will share the same shot code, but they will be differentiated by the "type" field in the marker. Furthermore, in a continued effort to *uniquely identify these elements* from each other, they will both have different sort numbers. This also allows them to be sorted in a specific order.

VFX Marker Formatting

VFX Marker formatting and EDL representation were broken down earlier (p. 83). It's **imperative** that the marker formatting is strict and uniform. I use macros to expedite typing all those equal signs. This not only saves me time but ensures consistency. All future work is based on tracking changes in these markers, so it pays off to have fine attention to detail in the first pass.

The order of information in the formatted marker is directly tied to how the database interprets the text, and the placement of "=" (effectively a delimiter) determines where the database will break off one chunk of text into a field—more on this in the FileMaker chapter (p. 76)—more on EDLs below and in the Turnovers chapter (p. 217).

Importing Elements into the Database

I bring an entire reel into the database, one at a time. Before exporting an EDL, I need to prepare the timeline. First, I commit multicam edits, which duplicates the active reel. If this is not done, any group clips or segments within submaster effects and their associated markers won't be present in the EDL. I then proceed to:

- Break apart all nested (submaster) effects.
- Rearrange markers as needed.
- Account for dissolves by removing them and extending heads/tails as needed.
- Delete all non-VFX markers from the sequence and delete the audio tracks.
- Double-check the remaining markers for formatting.
- Export one EDL per reel.

List Tool Settings for EDL Generation

I use File_32 EDLs with the "Source Name" and "Markers" checkboxes ticked. This ensures that the Tape name comes through formatted after "*SOURCE:" Technically, it's redundant because the source name is already included after the EDL event number, but I find it's easier to parse by looking for the pattern "*SOURCE:" Regarding markers, they show up after "*LOC:" a throwback to when Avid referred to markers as "locators."

The EDL Import Scripts

I import each reel EDL into the database, one at a time. This import script scans the EDL one line of text at a time and parses all the data it finds, including the formatted marker. Only events with a marker will make it through the import script. After the script finds all records with a VFX event, it loops back through them and parses the markers themselves (as outlined in the FileMaker chapter [p. 76]). I give the records a cursory look—a misplaced or missing "=" delimiter will cause a shift in data entry and not trigger an error. Here's your reminder: **Just because you're using automation doesn't mean you don't have to check your work.**

All the above happened in a table called "VFX EDL Import." It's related to another table called "VFX Elements," which I migrate data into once it's successfully parsed. The migration is performed using yet another script, which also creates an entry in the "VFX Tracker" table for any shot code that doesn't already exist.

The migration script creates all new records in both tables, save for any multi-element shots. In those cases, it creates one VFX Tracker record for the first element and skips subsequent elements related to the same shot code. To nerd out about this, it's because I'm using a script step called "go to related record," which, if one does not exist, there's an "IF" statement that will execute and create a new record.

Handles

By default, all elements have no handles added. I specify the head and tail handle length at this point. The default I usually use is eight frames on both head and tail, but I change it depending on the shot, element (if there's a long dissolve or a timewarp), or if we settle on a different number during the workflow call.

Timewarps

Speaking of timewarp effects, a good indication that one is applied to your clip is that the frame duration between source and record timecodes will differ. More frames of source than in record means the shot is playing back at a faster rate. The inverse is true for a sloweddown shot. There will also be an M2 comment in the EDL that expands on this, especially if the shot is running in reverse. If the shot is sped up, it's a good idea to double the handle length so the VFX artist has all the frames they need to provide the appropriate number of handles after re-speeding the shot.

When there's a timewarp applied, then you must fill out the counts (see "VFX Line-Up Sheet generated by custom FileMaker database [downloadable])" at (www.routledge.com/9781032843285), which is a representation of the speed changes throughout the shot. If it's constant, put the percent speed the element is going at on the first frame and write "ALL." If it's variable, the speed at the first frame should be noted, as well as all subsequent keyframes. A screenshot of the timewarp graph should be included in both cases.

Adding Individual Shots

For subsequent new shots, I wait until I can update the whole reel (which will automatically add any new shots it finds), or I do one of the following:

- Strip the EDL sequence of all segments and markers that are **not** the new shots.
  - Preferable when I have a handful of shots to add from the same reel.

- I take a subsequence of *only* the new shot(s).
  - Preferable when I only have one or two shots to add.

The reason why these are my two preferred approaches is because they retain the reel timecode. If you were to cut the new shots into a new timeline one after another, their location in the cut wouldn't be accurate.

This specific step of adding individual shots to the database is **additive** because it will only create new records and **not** *change* any existing ones. I bring this up because the aforementioned "updating the whole reel" will do just that; it will update other shots (which I usually don't want to do if I'm just adding a few new shots).

Filling Out the VFX Tracker

I now further clarify and add information to the description in the VFX Tracker. This is the main page for everything related to the shot. The VFX Tracker record will be the home for:

- Shot status
- Cut status
- Work order
  - Associated flags (key, comp, paint, etc.)
- Internal notes
- Elements and references that comprise the shot
  - Their related codebook data
- Vendor assignment(s)
- Versions that are submitted by the vendor
  - Vendor submission notes and our feedback to them

Since we just added a shot to the tracker, it's mostly empty. The fields we need to fill out now are the status (which is "Temp"), which flags are associated with the shot (for **EFC_005_020**, we'll flag it as "paint" and "comp," the latter of which I repurpose for any reposition/resize attributes), and the vendor assignment. We clean up (or expand on) the work order.

What's the Deal with These Flags?

I've talked a lot about the flags I use: Cosmetic, Graphic, ReSpeed, Composite, Key, Paint, (and Sync Sound and Matte). Why bother? Flagging these in the database makes it easy to call up all of one kind of effect in a snap. This is helpful when shots are moved from one vendor to another based on these criteria.

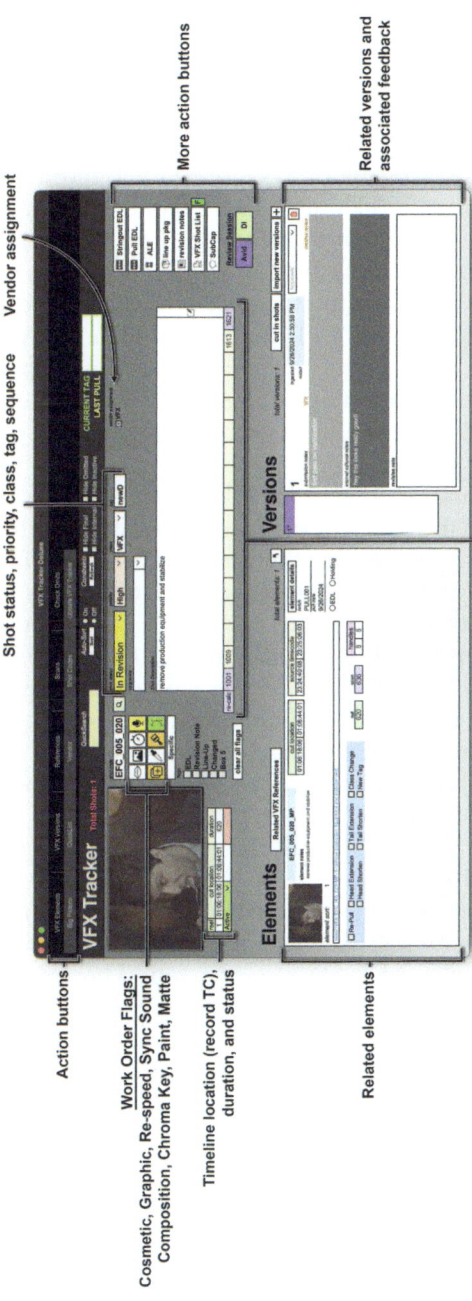

Figure 8.3 Custom FileMaker VFX Tracker layout. (See [www.routledge.com/9781032843285] for un-annotated high resolution illustration)

Imagine you are asked to turn over all your cosmetic shots to a secondary vendor halfway through the show, or a re-speed specialist is brought on, and you need to send them all the re-speed **only** shots. These flags make it easy to find *just* those shots very quickly.

Adding Representative Still Images—VFX Elements

Still images for the elements can be created via automation, and the workflow for doing so is the same as with dailies (p. 95). In FileMaker, I find all the elements I want to create stills for and run a script that creates an ALE on my desktop for those clips. This custom ALE not only renames the subclips to reflect the shot code and element (in our case: **EFC_005_020_MP**) but also adds an in-point halfway through the shot. This is why I create new stills as opposed to using the related codebook still image: I'll guarantee that the still image is representative of the section of the recorded take that's being used in the VFX shot.

In Media Composer, I'll open a bin that has all of the duplicate sequences that were originally used to export the EDLs that I imported into FileMaker. I'll then select *"Set Bin Display > Show Reference Clips."* This displays objects **referenced by sequences in the bin,** whether those clips were previously in the bin or not. This is why part of prepping the sequence in the first place is to delete the audio tracks first, lest we tempt Media Composer to crash (it's usually a lot of clips.) To further minimize the risk of a crash, save the project and set the bin view to a stripped-down one, which should match the ALE data columns (case sensitive, too). Sometimes, an ALE import fails, usually due to the bin view not matching the columns correctly or if I select **all** the clips in the bin (as opposed to *only* **the master clips**).

Now, with my master clips selected and my shot log import settings set to "Merge events with known sources and automatically create subclips," I drag the ALE file into the bin. The resulting subclips have an in-point marked halfway through, and their names are the exact concatenation of the shot code and element type—just as we specified in the custom ALE. By selecting all subclips and exporting to a still image (I use JPEGs with a small raster), stills get exported in bulk.

Back in FileMaker, I'll import the stills, and voila! The import script I use navigates to a related table (VFX Stills) and imports the images into container fields and the filename into a text field. A third field (which is a calculation) removes the file extension, leaving only the concatenated shot code and element ID, which is what's used to relate the still image to the element.

Adding Representative Still Images—VFX Tracker

The VFX tracker will represent the shot on most documents, but all these thumbnails make it easier to quickly know what you're looking at. Unlike with elements, I choose not to automate adding representative still images for the overall shots. This is because if the shot is re-temped, a new version is delivered, or if I want to annotate the frame, I can swap it out very quickly. You can use an element still for the VFX tracker image by dragging and dropping it into the still image area (or running "Replace Field Contents," which is faster).

Next Steps

At this point, I'm either ready to send vendors some files, or I'll skip to the "Checking the Cut" stage (p. 199), where I update the information in the tracker. Updating the tracker is fundamentally similar to importing new shots; I prep sequences, create EDLs, and import them into the database. However, it's different because instead of **only** adding new data, the "update" script looks for **changes** to already existing elements. We'll get into this shortly.

Line-Up Packages (Count Sheets)

Over the years, I've received requests for per-shot CSV, Excel, and EDL files to accompany the Line-Up Sheets. As a testament to building one's own database, I've been able to accommodate as needed. I've scripted into my database the ability to kick out a folder with subfolders per shot, and each shot's folder contains the above files alongside the Line-Up Sheet PDFs. I call these folders "Line-Up Packages."

A Line-Up Sheet, also referred to as a "Count Sheet," is a PDF that represents the VFX shot, all of the elements that comprise it, and any associated data. I view it as a document that condenses pertinent information from my VFX Tracker. (see "VFX Line-Up Sheet generated by custom FileMaker database [downloadable]" online) VFX artists work in frames, so it's helpful to break down the shot on the frame level to illustrate what should happen frame-to-frame. That's where the name of the document comes from—Counting frames or lining up elements.

When combined with a reference QuickTime, the Line-Up Sheet is the VFX artist's North Star. It contains most of the information from the VFX Tracker page regarding a shot—namely, the scope of work, duration, and elements. The elements themselves are packed with information—this is where the related codebook data shines, as it pulls in lens and camera data.

Bidding and Reference QuickTimes

There are two types of QuickTimes that we send: Bidding and Reference. They're similar in that they both represent the shots, but they might differ in their burn-ins, and they differ in color. All VFX QuickTimes should have source timecode, shot code, and frame count burn-ins, and color effects **must** be removed from reference QuickTimes. All video files have the usual identifying watermarks and burn-ins to uniquely identify the vendor (p. 210).

These QuickTimes can be sent on a shot-by-shot basis, but more common is to export sequences or scene ranges. I rarely send full reels out for VFX purposes. Vendors sometimes request that a sequence be turned over with sound for continuity purposes. Otherwise, I send everything MOS.

Bidding QuickTime Files

Bidding QuickTimes are meant for vendors to evaluate the cost of the proposed work. They are often requested before shots become official so VFX vendors can bid on asset builds and the scope of work. If the shots haven't been assigned to a specific vendor yet, they are exported and watermarked as needed for prospective vendors. If the shot is complicated, include a breakdown (or "decomp," short for "decomposition") at the end of the shot reference.

Reference QuickTime Files

Reference QuickTimes are created to guide the VFX artist and inform them of our creative intent after a shot has been assigned to them. Knowing that the artist will be working with the high-resolution plate and checking it against the reference, it could confuse them if you have a color effect applied within the reference file. It might be nested deep in a complex temp shot, so drill down and remove any and all color effects (p. 245).

Updated reference QuickTimes (and Line-Up Sheets) should be sent with any re-pull or update to the scope of work for a VFX shot.

VFX Pulls

A VFX pull is a turnover in which the highest quality frames for a shot are ordered from the lab and sent to the vendor. The pulls must be accurate because **each VFX pull costs money, time, and data.** Pulls need to be approved by the post supervisor before they're ordered. Each time a large pull (or "batch") occurs, I increase the tag. This means that I stop flagging new shots as "newA" and start flagging them as "newB" until the next pull occurs.

I use my database to generate an EDL for a VFX pull, but they can be made in Avid using the List Tool. I like using my database because it allows me to take advantage of custom and inconsistent handle length, it automatically logs the pulled frames in a related table, and it places simplified identifying markers in the middle of the EDL events. These are not easily achievable tasks using the List Tool. The database will sort the elements by name and string them out into one "timeline."

Alongside generating a VFX Pull EDL, I generate an ALE and Line-Up Sheets while I have the found set of elements in FileMaker. I use the ALE to create representative "scan" subclips in Avid, which can also be used to populate a sequence and export a "Pull Reference" QuickTime that the lab can use to verify that they're pulling the correct frames. Let's check in with our VFX shot and see what the scan subclip would be named:

> **EFC_005_020_MP**

Creating a Pull Reference QuickTime

The "scan" subclips are all renamed via the ALE to reflect their element names. I've also scripted it so these subclips have in and out marks set at the boundaries where the handles begin and end, and the duration of the clip represents the full scan. The in and out marks need to be cleared before making a pull reference file, as we do pull the frames that are in the handles.

I clear the marks, sort the clips by name, and then Option-drag these shots into a new sequence. Because I sort by name, this sequence mirrors the Pull EDL generated by FileMaker. I can burn-in the element ID by having a timecode generator read the clip name. I also burn-in the tape name and both record and source timecodes.

These subclips remain in the pull bin, but I can Option-drag them into an "All Pulls" bin for reference (perhaps adding the pull number in a custom column.) See the Turnovers chapter for more detail on a VFX Pull turnover (p. 232).

Checking the Cut

This is the "tracking" part that was mentioned in the VFX Editing section (p. 181) earlier. The process of checking the cut happens frequently and becomes more important after a pull. If there's a change to a work-in-progress shot or a new shot that needs to be bid on, it's time-sensitive. Likewise, if a shot gets omitted, the work should be stopped on it **as soon as possible.**

As far as my process is concerned, the idea is that I should be able to import an EDL of a reel into the database, and the database will highlight what has changed. The database should also update the cut location of all shots (the record timecodes)—even shots that have not been changed in any other ways. I have my database display three different found sets of records after importing an EDL of a reel:

- **Inactive yet not Omitted Shots**
  - Shots that exist in the database and do not have a shot status of "Omitted" and have not been found in the EDL.
  - *Reminder: Shots that aren't in the EDL are considered "Inactive."*
- **Changed Shots**
  - Shots that exist in the database, but there's something different in the EDL regarding the timing, scope of work, or elements that comprise it.
  - *Reminder: This includes new elements added to existing shots, head and tail extensions, and trims. These alert me if an element needs to be re-pulled.*
- **New Shots**
  - Shots that didn't previously exist in the database but were found in the EDL.
  - *Reminder: All new shots need handles, stills, and a vendor assigned—they should be treated exactly like the shots that were initially imported into the database.*

All other shots in the reel are silently updated with the timecodes of the cut location. Consider an unchanged VFX shot in a timeline that has been worked on. The location of the VFX shot in the timeline has changed, but the duration and scope of work haven't. This doesn't raise any flags in the database because the only update is the timecode *you* need in order to find that shot in the timeline (record timecode).

Now, let's dive into exactly how I update the tracker.

Updating the Tracker

Checking the cut begins by preparing sequences in the same way you would if you were importing them into the database for the first time. This means breaking apart all submaster effects, rearranging markers as needed, committing multicam edits, clearing all non-VFX markers from the sequence, and deleting the audio tracks. The EDL for each reel is imported into the database one at a time, consecutively. I rarely check only one reel in a day; I like to check the whole cut, just one reel at a time.

Note: **This script is a step that cannot be undone** *(as my database is currently designed)*. It might be wise to back up the database beforehand, just in case. The reason it can't be undone is because data is imported and committed, and there's no "undo" in FileMaker. There are ways to design a database to allow for checking a change before committing it; I just haven't had the time to build that functionality myself.

Once an EDL is imported and compared, it triggers a series of subscripts. These scripts update records by comparing the incoming EDL data to what already exists in the database. They primarily look for changes to already existing elements, but they do add new records for new shots they find.

As you keep checking the cut against what's in the database, a shot (or shots) could appear or disappear, and it could be at any given time. There are two statuses for any given shot: Cut Status and Shot Status (p. 76).

Inactive Yet Not Omitted Shots

These are shots that were in the database but didn't appear in the EDL. This could happen if, for example, a scene was dropped, and three shots no longer exist in the show. These events need to be investigated to determine if the shot status should be changed to "Omitted."

If the shot is flagged as inactive but is still in the timeline, the marker may not have made its way into the EDL. Multicam edits not committed? Submasters not broken apart? Did the editor trim the shot and roll out a marker, or restore a section from a previous cut before the shot was flagged? If an Inactive shot is, in fact, *not* omitted, I'll restore the marker, kick out an EDL of just that shot (p. 193), and run a script that updates and compares *only* that shot.

Trimmed Shots

Consider a VFX shot that has been trimmed by 15 frames on the tail. Assuming this shot has already been pulled with eight frame handles, the database flags it as "trimmed" and *adds* 15 frames to the tail handle length (23 frames of tail handles total). Note that any change in duration will require a new Line Up Sheet and QuickTime reference. Update the timewarp screenshot and counts if needed.

Extended Shots

Now, imagine the **opposite** situation, wherein the tail of a VFX shot is **extended** by 15 frames—that's seven frames outside the boundary of what was pulled and sent to the vendor; they don't have those frames! This is a good time to remind you that you can proactively avoid this by requesting extra handles on shots that you think might benefit from it, especially if that part of the film is particularly in flux or the shot itself is complex or re-sped.

First, let the editor know that this change affects a work-in-progress VFX shot. In some cases, the director and editor might want to revert or reduce the extension because it's likely to incur an added cost. Otherwise, the shot needs to be re-pulled.

Re-pulls

A re-pull is performed just like a normal pull. My database keeps track of how many times an element has been pulled and will label it in the Pull EDL accordingly, appending "REPULL_X" to the end of the element ID. Why don't we suspend our disbelief for a second and explore a hypothetical *within* a hypothetical? How would our VFX shot appear if it was extended and re-pulled?

> **EFC_005_020_MP_REPULL1**

Ok, good to know. But our shot doesn't need to be re-pulled. Phew, close call. The budget's getting tight.

Creative Changes (Tags)

Trimming and extending shots is all well and good, as it's easy to automate these technical changes by looking at the numbers. However, if there's a creative change, it needs to be drawn attention to. I handle this by using tags. The first field in the VFX marker string is for a tag that versions up alphabetically alongside VFX pulls.

After the first pull, we tag any new or changed VFX shots with the tag "newA." To avoid cluttering the editor's mind with any of this organizational stuff, I usually just ask them to leave a note in the notes track, and I'll update the VFX marker and take care of everything else. If I change the tag, that means the description has been altered. My database looks for a tag change, and if there's one, it updates the tag *and* the element description. This usually leads to an updated reference QuickTime and Line-Up sheet.

Whoa, it looks like our VFX shot has changed a bit! Let's look at the updated marker:

```
newA=VFX=EFC_005_020=MP=1=remove production equipment, stabilize, cosmetic=end
```

Our shot was flagged for cosmetic work. It doesn't need to be re-pulled, but the tag and description have both changed. The database will alert us of this; in a real-world scenario, we would be more descriptive of what specific cosmetic work needs to be done. In this case, the vendor is getting an updated Line-Up Sheet, which reflects the new work order. We don't need to send a new QuickTime reference because the only update is adding cosmetic work, which is likely something already apparent and easy to spot in the reference they already have.

Receiving Versions

Once the vendor receives the frames from the pull, they should send you a "version 0" or a "scan check." This is to confirm that they have all the frames for a given shot. If a timewarp effect is involved, you might need to re-apply it to the scan check, but after that, the vendor should send a version that runs at the same speed as in the reference. You will need to re-apply any temp color effects.

Batch Deliveries and Submission Notes

Vendors tend to deliver shots in batches. At first, they will arrive on designated days. When you're closer to meeting a deadline, the deliveries will be as soon as possible (ASAP), sometimes multiple per day. Each delivery should be accompanied by a CSV of submission notes (something to discuss with the vendor on the workflow call early on [p. 13]). It's now time to see what our VFX shot looks like in the submission CSV:

```
EFC_005_020,v002,[vendor name here],For Review,first pass on
         stabilization,no cosmetic work applied
```

The submission notes **need** to have the shot code, version number, and any specific notes the vendor wants you to know about while reviewing the work. Using the above example, we wouldn't want to give feedback on cosmetic work because they specified that this was only a first pass on the stabilization. Letting us know it's a first pass allows us to be more forgiving in any criticism, and in this case, we should ask for clarity on when the paint out is going to occur.

Upon importing the submission notes into my database, I bring the new versions into Avid. I used to request MOV files that matched the Avid project settings. In recent times, I've found it simpler to request MXF OP-Atom files (Avid Media) because it skips the import phase altogether and lets me better organize submissions on the Finder level.

In Avid, I use one bin per vendor, and all submissions are imported into it. Sorting by creation date (ostensibly the delivery date) or by name helps me find what I'm looking for, as does the Quick Find field. Upon importing the files, I sometimes choose to select all the new versions and "Sift Selected." This simplifies the bin by only showing me the clips I selected.

Cutting in New Versions

I cut the shots into the active reel timelines, A/B'ing the heads and tails of shots against the plate, then spot-checking the middle to make sure it's all frame accurate. If the naming convention allows, it's possible to point your sequence to the new VFX in the bin and relink the sequence to the new shots. This is a valid way of working, but I prefer to cut the shots in by hand because I like to get eyes on each shot one at a time.

If there's more than one version of a shot delivered at one time, I'll stack them in the timeline. I won't collapse them using a submaster effect until after a VFX review (we'll get to that shortly) to make it easier to toggle between different versions during the review. I cut all new versions in and then circle back to analyze and internally note them.

Analyzing New Versions

I like using the "difference" blending mode to spot changes between versions and check formatting issues. This blending mode compares the pixels on layer 1 to those on layer 2. If there's no difference, the resulting pixel will be black. The more different it is, the brighter the pixel will be. I disregard anything "snowy" looking, as it's likely a

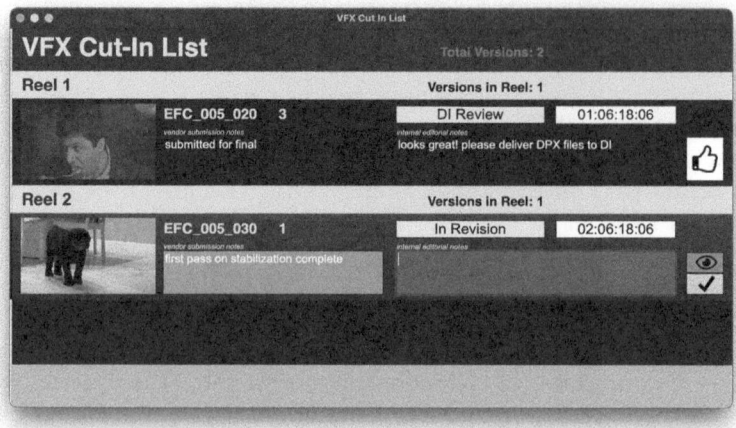

Figure 8.4 Custom FileMaker VFX cut-in list.

difference in grain structure. This might be different upon each render if the grain is added digitally using a random seed. If you don't have access to a blending mode plug-in, you can achieve something similar using an older methodology: Applying an "Invert" color effect followed by a "Superimpose" effect at 50%.

If I notice a discrepancy when I'm reviewing the shots as I cut them in (like missing handles or frames not aligning), I let the vendor know, mute the clip in the timeline, and color the source clip **dark yellow**. It might be a render error on their end or an issue that gets elevated to the lab. Still, regardless, I probably won't show the director or editor if the issue could distract them from giving valuable feedback. If there's no discrepancy but a thought I have that I want to bring up during the review, I leave an internal comment in my database.

Using our example shot, something I might note internally at this stage is if I think the stabilization is not smooth enough or if I notice there's some artifacting from the paintwork.

Once the shot is cut in and not problematic, I update the shot status in the database to "Avid Review" and change the source color of the clip in Avid to **purple**. Clip colors come more into play when reviewing VFX shots, but for right now, **purple** and **dark yellow** are the only important colors to me. I leave shots that have not been cut into the reel uncolored. I may choose to mute the shot in the timeline until the VFX review session to avoid any surprises if the editor and director start working on that reel ahead of a VFX review.

Reviewing VFX

There are two main types of VFX reviews that I participate in: Avid Reviews and DI Reviews. On shows with a VFX team or a high number of shots, there might be more frequent review sessions and different types of reviews depending on the many stages shots can be in. Ultimately, all VFX shots need to be reviewed by the director.

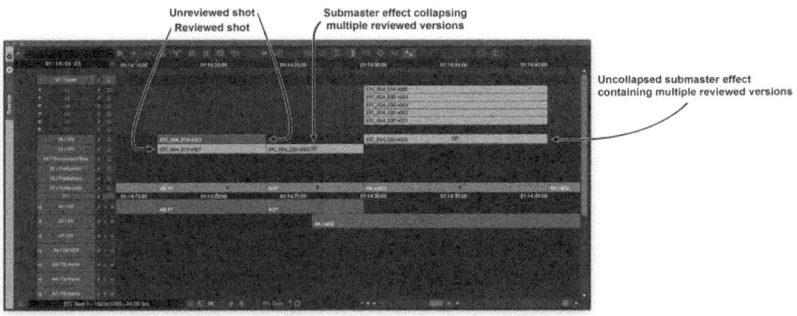

Figure 8.5 Collapsed and uncollapsed VFX shot versions in a timeline.

Avid Reviews

Avid review sessions are meant to provide creative feedback and shot review before rendering out high-resolution files for the DI.

When you have a moment to sit down and review the latest batch of submissions with the director, you, the editor, or a second assistant can run the review. This entails going to each clip on the "New VFX" track and playing it back. I usually keep the volume muted or very low during a review. I keep the bin with previous versions open so I can update the color of the source clip to reflect the status of the shot and play a previous version from the bin if needed. For the latter, I utilize collapsed tracks to reference old versions in the timeline.

Things to note during a review session are the shot code, version number, the date it's being noted, and who gave the note. Using my database, these are all semi-automatic things, so long as we're entering notes on the correct record. It becomes more about communication: I make sure to announce the shot code and version for the person taking notes. I clearly state which version is being viewed, especially if multiple versions of the same shot have been submitted in tandem.

When I run a VFX review, someone standing outside of the room might think I'm an optometrist because I say things like: "*Do we prefer version A or B? Again, here's A… and B. Let's look at the plate. And here's B again. Ok, so we prefer B. Fantastic.*" Upon settling on feedback for a shot, I announce the status of the shot, update the source clip color, and move the clip down to the "Reviewed VFX" track. I'll overwrite old versions with the latest ones *only* if it's approved for DI. Otherwise, I collapse tracks and keep the latest version at the top of the stack.

The person taking notes should change the status of the shot in the database accordingly. A typical session will have shots that are approved for DI Review and shots that need another revision. Sometimes, the director will ask us to approve any technical shots (like paint outs or cosmetic work) without them if the shots look good to us.

After the review, we send the vendor our notes so they can update their records. Regardless of whether it's feedback for a revision or a go-ahead to render out EXR files for a DI review, they get a note. Even when a shot is marked "Final" later down the road, they get a note from us confirming it. **It's important to keep a paper trail.**

We received a new version of our VFX shot, EFC_005_020. The stabilization looks great, the paint out looks good too, and they'll deliver the next version for final with the cosmetic work.

In-House High-Resolution Reviews

These reviews are becoming more common as hardware to process larger files becomes more accessible and typical VFX shot counts increase. The purpose of these in-house high-resolution reviews is to save time and money by tech-checking the VFX deliverables *before* reserving time in a DI suite with the colorist. The nature of these technical reviews means that the director and editor don't necessarily need to be involved, either. The software I've seen used to review high-resolution EXR files in cutting rooms includes Autodesk's RV and BlackMagic's DaVinci Resolve.

DI Reviews

DI review sessions are for signing off on shots in high resolution as "Final." They can be closer to a QC check than a creative review, as you're looking for any technical issues that present themselves in high resolution that you couldn't see in the Avid review files. Examples include render errors, cosmetic fixes, floor marks, and matting issues. You must expedite these and make sure they're necessary, approved, and pulled ASAP.

Before you get to the point of DI reviews, ensure that the VFX shots imported into Avid have an embedded timecode and remind the vendor to deliver holdout mattes upon DI delivery as specified. They might need to provide RGB+A files or EXR/DPX sequences, the former two of which are sometimes preferred. The facility handling the DI will have a spec sheet they give the vendor.

For a review session, DI wants a review sequence that contains all shots to be reviewed. Editorial sends an EDL, while VFX sends the high-resolution files for the online editor to link to. The colorist will have already applied a preliminary grade to the shot based on the plate that was turned over to them previously. The finishing editor will apply this grade to the submitted shot; they call this "color tracing." I'll give the DI a heads-up if there is a sequence we want to review in context, as they might want me to send a separate sequence (similar to a drop-in EDL) *in addition to* the stringout to make it easier for them. **Prepare to take notes during the session.**

Just before the DI review session, I'll send an email with the subject being the show title, the session purpose, and the date. I'll attach the EDL stringout of all shots to be reviewed and list them alongside their respective versions. See more about a DI review turnover in the Turnovers chapter (p. 231).

During the review, etiquette and communication are paramount because your time there is more expensive. It's helpful for me to have the database handy to quickly clarify any previous notes, confirm versions, take notes, and update shot statuses. Sometimes, the colorist has a quick fix or solution to an issue, but if not, I'm prepared to request a revision of a shot.

Let's say that we noticed that our VFX shot, **EFC_005_020**, had some tracking issues on the new cosmetic work during the DI review. It was imperceptible in the Avid QuickTime. We can't approve it as final, so we'll kick it back to "In Revision" and send a note to the vendor. When they deliver a new version to us, we'll follow the same steps up to this point, and if the issue is resolved, we can sign off on it as a final shot.

Final

If the shot looks good in the DI review, it's marked as "Final," and the vendor is told that their work is complete for the shot. Any non-final shot gets the same treatment as if it were noted in an Avid review. When we return to the cutting room, the clip colors and database are updated accordingly, and deliverables for the DI regarding the final shots are created.

The deliverables include updated QuickTime references for each reel, which reflect the latest VFX shots and EDLs (possibly also AAFs and Avid Bins) of the "Drop-Ins"— Drop-Ins are the final VFX shots as they exist in the timeline (as opposed to a stringout of shots to review). The finishing editor will load the Drop-In EDL as a track and then literally drop the final shots down to the VFX track, hence "Drop-In."

Our VFX shot, **EFC_005_020**, was approved for final. How fantastic!

And that's the lifespan of a VFX shot!

9 Outputs and Turnover

Now comes the time for things to leave the cutting room. I define "Outputs" as exported video files intended for review and approval (usually on PIX or similar services [p. 21]). I define "Turnovers" as one or more files sent to another department for work to be done on. For example, if the director wants to see a cut of the film, that's an **output** of the longplay. If the music editor wants the current cut, that's a **turnover** of all reels. This is part of the reason we work in reels: we don't always turn the whole show over—sometimes, it's just one or two reels at a time.

The most important thing to remember whenever anything leaves the cutting room is **content security**. Every video file absolutely must have a unique identifier that identifies the intended recipient and the date it was sent. To accomplish this, always use watermarks, try to put burn-ins **in picture** (these are both considered "spoilage"), and use secure passwords sent in a separate email to the recipients. See below for more on watermarks and burn-ins (p. 210). Use services provided or approved by the studio or production company, such as Aspera (p. 19). Get written permission to do anything other than the agreed-upon standards.

Basic Workflow

Regardless of whether it's an Output or a Turnover, here's the overview:

- Copy sequence(s) into a new output/turnover bin; label green.
- Commit multicam edits, label yellow.
  - This dupes the sequence—unless there are no group clips, in which case you should just dupe the sequence yourself.
- Rename the sequence to follow the established naming convention (p. 213).
- Apply mattes, watermarks, and overlays as needed.
  - The less applied in Avid, the better.
- Export, transcode, send, and archive.

DOI: 10.4324/9781003516491-10

Watermarks and Burn-ins

Everything Editorial sends out needs a watermark and/or a burn-in applied. **Period.** The only exceptions are cleared in writing by the head of post in specific instances, for example, playback on the stage or an overcut to marketing. Watermarks and burn-ins are added **in picture** (as opposed to within the matte) so that someone can't crop the file and share the content. The two terms can be globally referred to as "spoilage."

Watermarks

A **watermark** is anything that is applied over video at low opacity. It's usually a name or an image. Everything must be watermarked with something uniquely identifying the recipient(s). Sometimes, you have to move watermarks around on the screen, like to the bottom of the frame for the sound stage, to avoid covering mouths and aid in an easier viewing experience. A common request for watermarks is "Property of [**Studio Name Here**]," along with the recipient's department and initials.

I generate my watermarks using Photoshop. I create one PSD file, duplicate layers, and modify them per recipient. I toggle the visibility of any given layer and save individual PNG images. The PNG images get used in Media Encoder presets. What I like about this method is that I can modify and overwrite any given watermark PNG file, and the Media Encoder preset will automatically update since it still references the same file path and file name.

Burn-Ins

A **burn-in** is any piece of information that is rendered and encoded into the video file. Some burn-ins may already be present in the dailies media. Common burn-ins include timecode, tape name, clip name, sequence name, etc. I save all my turnover burn-in effects as presets in a bin, naming them with both the department they pertain to and the data the effect displays.

When it comes to burn-ins, I like to include as much information as I can to help myself identify footage if it's ever returned to me. Some departments will ask for metadata burned in within the matte, and that's fine. **The watermark can never be solely in the matte.** Burn-ins that are commonly requested are:

- Date/Reel/Version (easy to add all at once if you're burning in the sequence/file name)
- Tape name (source)

- Clip name (scene and take)
- Record timecode
- Source timecode
- Footage (feet+frames)
- LFOA (sound department)
- Total frame count (DI and VFX)
- VFX shot code

Making Use of Burn-Ins

Using a marketing turnover as an example, they take our watermarked/burned-in video files to edit the trailer. The trailer is then delivered to us, and we have to hunt down the footage to overcut their work with the dailies that have the actual metadata embedded so we can turn over the sequence. The burn-ins we apply with tape name and shoot day, or reel and version help expedite this process.

Source Timecode Burn-In

I want to note the importance of the source timecode burn-in on VFX turnovers—specifically shots with time remapping. Source timecode allows the VFX artist to look at the reference and identify which frames are being used. Nine times out of ten, frame blending will warp the dailies burn-ins, so letting Avid burn in the source timecode is more accurate and legible.

Scene and Take Burn-Ins: Clip Name vs Slate

The clip name contains the scene and take number. In my experience, the editor can rename subclips in the bin to add notes as they see fit. This means that displaying the clip name is not an option. Instead, the timecode generator effect can pull the scene and take data from their respective bin columns. Unfortunately, this means you might have to use more than one timecode generator to display all the data or, for more efficiency, the "Slate" column (as prepared during dailies). It contains the original clip name with no modifications.

Using Longplay Timecode Notes

When stitching reels or building the longplay for an output, people expect burned-in timecode (BITC). Due to how I build the longplay (p. 141) when I slap a timecode generator on the top track, it will start at hour 1, where I'm already eight seconds off (because I extracted the head leader from reel 1). It makes no sense after we're through the first reel. Timecode-based notes become difficult to navigate.

There are a few ways to get reel-specific timecode burned in besides the time-consuming act of creating a video mixdown per reel. One method I've used is the audio mixdown. Before building the show, create stereo mixdowns in the reels that you copied into the output bin. Then, for the mixed-down clips in the bin, copy the Start TC into the AuxTC1 column. Now, when you build the longplay or stitch the reels, have your timecode generator read AuxTC1 from the audio track that the mixdowns are on under "Other Counters." Voila! Just make sure you don't double-up the audio when exporting—*only* include the audio mixdown track. This is a fine option, but still time-consuming. The benefit is that these notes are remarkably easy to navigate through.

The method I prefer is as follows: I ignore everything I just brought to your attention. That's right! Instead of trying to force the timecode into relevancy, we can simply reference the sequence which the timecode originated from. To do this, I Option-double-click the sequence to open it in a separate source monitor. I can then type "minutes:seconds + . (double 0)" and **reverse match frame into the current cut**. This is helpful when you have to go to 1 hour and 6 minutes into the film and are working in reels.

Mattes

I've found that most departments are alright with receiving full-frame (non-matted) picture and that the only time I'm applying a matte is when we're prepping for a screening. Even for a DCP, I can provide full-frame picture files and tell them what aspect ratio matte to use. Still, when I need to apply a matte, I do so in Media Encoder or Compressor—not Avid. The parameters you're looking for are cropping and padding.

Cropping will remove pixels from the container raster (a cropped 1920x1080 file could be encoded at, for example, 855x1080), and there will be no black bars.

Padding will restore black letterboxing or pillarboxing to maintain the correct aspect ratio within the original container raster (a cropped and padded 1920x1080 file will always be 1920x1080).

Matting Different Aspect Ratios

One outlier scenario is if you're working on a project with multiple aspect ratios. While I haven't had to manage this myself, it has been considered on certain projects. I'd have proposed having a "hero" matte for general application and ensuring it's present yet transparent in turnovers. I had also planned to include the matte details (intended aspect ratio) in the metadata, which could be applied as a burn-in and on VFX Line-Up Sheets. For any screenings, mattes would have had to be applied manually. This is just food for thought.

File Naming Convention for Outputs and Turnovers

Naming convention: *[date] [film title/abbr.] [reel] [version] [tag(s)]*	
Longplay file for review	211105 EFC v2 longplay
Scene file for review - note: no version	190802 EFC sc 32-34 to TM
Folder of all reels - same version	241120 EFC R1-R6 v2.1 to [dept.]
Folder of all reels - differing versions	220222 EFC R1-R6 to [dept.]
Folder single reel	241120 EFC R2 v14 to [dept.]
Reel to the department, silent	190809 EFC R3 v3.3 MOS QT REF to [dept.]
Stem/guide	190803 EFC R2 v1.3 GUIDE DX [channel(s)]
AAF - music editor	191001 EFC R6 v2 MX AAF
AAF - DI	191001 EFC R6 v1 DI AAF
Sound EDL – picture sound EDL - sound	231001 EFC R4 v2 EDL V1 231001 EFC R4 v2 EDL A1-4
Change List	191215 EFC R1 v2.3 to v3.2 Change List
Portion of reel	190913 EFC R1 sc66A-77 v2.3 for Color to [dept.]

Tips, Tricks, and Reminders for Mindful and Efficient Encoding

This is part of "thinking at scale." When working on a project, exporting media is something that's done day in and day out. If we're going to be doing the same things repeatedly, we should make sure that we're doing them in the most streamlined ways possible.

Avid Video Exports

As of this writing, I've found that it's easiest to perform as few **video** exports from Avid as possible and utilize third-party programs such as Adobe Media Encoder or Compressor. Not only are the encode times shorter, but this workflow allows for greater flexibility when sending to multiple vendors.

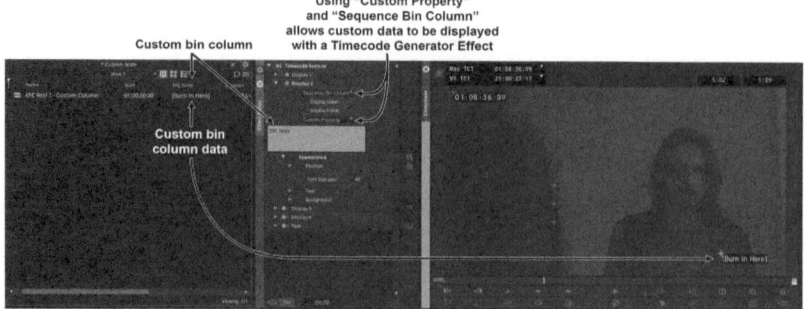

Figure 9.1 Custom bin column data, how it appears in the Timecode Generator Effect within the Effect Editor, and the resulting image in the Composer window.

Make sure your Avid export has the fewest number of effects applied to it. This means leaving the matting and watermarking to Media Encoder. Exporting with Mask Margins enabled is considered the same as exporting with a mask effect on the top track. Instead of using two Timecode Generator effects, make use of all four parameters within one effect.

Using the "Custom Property" bin column is a great way to get another static text watermark. This can be used as a "Property Of" watermark or, in my use cases, an LFOA burn-in. Consider using the "Slate" column in place of "Scene" and "Take." This frees up one of the four timecode generator effect display parameters (this is part of the reason why I dupe the name into the Slate column during dailies).

Parallel Encoding in Adobe Media Encoder

If you can convince multiple departments to accept the same burn-ins, you can use one file exported from Avid and then leverage parallel encoding in Media Encoder using multiple presets with individualized watermarks. Parallel encoding writes multiple files at the same time (in parallel) as opposed to serializing them (one at a time).

I tend to export files from Avid into a holding folder on my desktop and then set Media Encoder's default destination to the desktop itself. Once files are created, I spot-check them, send them out, and **move** them to the Nexis for archive.

The Translucent Matte

One neat trick I picked up is building a 50% opacity matte into the watermark. Oh, but why? Some departments ask for this; others might not know they want it. The benefit is that the person working on the file will know where the matte borders are the whole time (instead of having to reference the framing chart at picture start in the head leader), and they can still see the image—including metadata and burn-ins—below the matte. **I build it into the watermark** because (just like the water-mark) the matte is static and transparent. This reduces the number of "effects" that need to be rendered. It's elegant and lightweight.

Hot Tips for Exporting Files

- Try to get as many vendors/departments to accept the same burn-ins and as well as MOS picture files. Usually, the sound department, music editor, and composer can all share the same burn-ins, while DI, Marketing, and VFX might need another.
- For any review/approval platform, apply a "Property of [Studio]" watermark along the top of the frame.
  - Some studios won't require this if the platform can add a personalized watermark. I think it's a best practice to always include it regardless.
- It's faster to crop out the top and bottom, and pad with black within Compressor or Media Encoder than to render a matte over top as an effect in Avid. Export full frame from Avid whenever possible.
- A 50% opacity matte is best achieved when created **as part of the watermark**.
- As of this writing, Media Encoder can't downmix 5.1 audio to a stereo track. It only extracts the left and right channels from a 5.1 source. **Export as stereo from Avid.**
- Timecode Generators referencing an upper track (say, V4) will read whatever is on that track **or lower**. This means that if there are two empty tracks and a clip on V1, V1 data will be read.
- QuickTime Reference files *used to be* the fastest export method (despite a gamma shift) but it will not be compatible moving for-ward. UME exports seem to be the most promising and are likely to be the fastest export option from Media Composer.
- If someone requests split tracks embedded in the MOV file, I've had success linking guide tracks back into Avid and cutting them into a sequence instead of creating mixdowns. I mention this because, in these cases, I'm usually already exporting guide tracks anyway.
  - This being said, using Multiple Mixes can be a lifesaver, and I like using that as well.

The List Tool: EDLs, Change Lists, and Open Timeline IO

A handful of departments utilize these documents, and it's worth discussing and demystifying them briefly before being told to make one for a specific department. EDLs, Change Lists, and OTIO files are all created using the List Tool within Media Composer. All are human-readable plain text files that are generated from the data that comprise a sequence. They can be interpreted manually but are typically automated. Some programs exist (like Cargo Cult's Matchbox) which don't necessarily require Change Lists, but EDLs or AAFs instead to create a list of changes.

Let's take a quick look at some of the key differences between commonly exported files, what their main differences are, and how long they've been around:

	EDL	Change List	AAF	XML	OTIO
Full Name	Edit Decision List	Change List	Advanced Authoring Format	Extensible Markup Language	Open Timeline In / Out
Introduction	The 70s	The 70s	~1998	1996	~2016
Human Readable	Yes	Yes	No	Kinda	Kinda
Format	Plain Text	Plain Text	Binary File	Plain Text: XML	Plain Text: JSON
Information Contained	Metadata, limited	Metadata, limited	Metadata and Multimedia	Metadata	Metadata
Widely Used	Yes	Sort of	Big time	Yes, largely within other NLEs	Not yet, but soon
Primary Use	Transferring timeline data between NLEs	Linearly describing changes between two timelines	Transferring clip and timeline data and media between many applications	Transferring timeline data between NLEs	Transferring timeline data between NLEs

What are our takeaways? There's a similarity between all files in that they can all describe a timeline such that it can be recreated (except a Change List). Notably, AAFs are the only non-human readable files, **and** they are the only listed format that can contain actual media. Their predecessor is the OMF file, which you should feel empowered to look up its history. Most of these file types are relatively old! Their longevity attests to the simplicity of the data therein.

Also of note is that I consider XML and OTIO files to be "sort of" human-readable. I say "kinda" because, while they are text files that are possible to read (especially in a specialized text editor like Sublime Text, which color codes and formats the structure), they're not as easily broken down with the human eye like an EDL or a Change List. Their underlying structures are *very much preferred* to EDLs, though, because the thing that makes them difficult for the human eye to read is what allows a computer to parse them so much more easily. I like to think of XML and OTIO files as a sort of child between an EDL and

AAF. They contain more metadata than an EDL and can be read by simply opening them in a text editor, but they can't contain any media like an AAF. They're lightweight and full of data.

If you want to read an XML file, look into the XML language. Likewise, for OTIO, check out JSON. Because EDLs can be read by our eyes, let's break down one EDL event and see what we're working with.

Edit Decision Lists

An EDL contains a list of events. Each clip in the timeline is considered an event. An event contains—at the bare minimum—Event Number, Source Name, Track and Cut type, and Source and Record Timecodes. This fundamentally answers the following questions: What clip do I use? When do I start and stop using it? Where does it go in the sequence?

```
000001 A122C020_241215_ROW4   V   C
17:40:21:05 17:40:25:19 04:03:23:12 04:03:28:02
```

There can be more to an EDL than what's in the above example, which includes transition types and comments. But these are the basics. Check out an EDL event which has comments in the VFX chapter (p. 183). There are also different types of EDLs, such as File16, File32, and CMX3600. I use File32 formatting for my database EDLs because it allows for the number of characters I need when it comes to source names and marker comments.

Change Lists

A Change List is a list of instructions used to conform an old sequence to a newer one. It can contain the same information as an EDL but is generally kept a little simpler. The steps are *sequential* and must be followed in the exact order they are written. Again, there's more to a Change List than what follows, but here's a very basic example with two steps. The change is a rolled edit, hence why there's no duration difference at the bottom of the "Total Change" column:

		At This Footage	For This Length	Do This	Total Change
−	1.	0006+06 0006+13	-0000+08	Trim Head	-0000+08
−	2.	0006+06 0006+13	+0000+08	Lengthen Tail	+0000+00

A Change List compares one sequence to another, in our case, one version of a reel to another version of the same reel. As outlined below, a Rebalance Change List (p. 219) is created when moving or combining footage between reels (usually at the heads and tails). Rebalancing is not a frequent occurrence, but versioning up is.

Departments that received an older version of a reel will want a Change List to help them conform to the latest turnover. If they skipped a turnover, they might request a "**skip note.**" An example of this is if you turned over Version 1, then Version 2 (with a Change List from V1 to V2), and then Version 3 (with a Change List from V2 to V3). If they skipped Version 2 and never conformed, they'll need a "skip note" which is a Change List that compares Version 1 to Version 3.

The two departments that usually request Change Lists are the sound department and DI. The difference between the two is that DI wants to see the timecode while the sound department prefers footage (feet and frames). This is a selection you can make using the List Tool.

VFX-Only Change Lists

Change Lists are created by picture editorial by comparing **Video Track 1** of two sequences to each other—even for the sound department. The main purpose of a Change List is to track temporal changes in the cut, not necessarily the fine detail changes of each audio track. Creating a Change List that compares any number of audio tracks is usually too much information. Of course, a department may ask for this and, by all means, give them what they want. One more common request is a "VFX Only" Change List, wherein you compare the VFX tracks (in our case, let's say V5) instead of V1. You'll want to check the List Tool settings, of course, but enabling "Name" will allow the Change List to display the VFX version differences even if the duration of the reel hasn't changed.

Sound Department Change Lists

Before making a Change List, I'll prepare the sequence. Usually, if I'm tasked with making a Change List, I'm also making EDLs, so I'll use the EDL sequences to generate Change Lists. When the sound department receives a turnover package, they run the picture EDL or Change List through an automation application (as mentioned previously) to conform their session to the latest version of the cut.

When you create picture EDLs for sound, it's not necessary to collapse and organize the tracks or remove submaster effects as if you're preparing the cut for DI or for the VFX tracker. The most important thing is to keep things consistent when preparing reels from version to version: If you break your submaster effects apart and separate your tracks for one sound turnover, you'll need to *keep doing that for all subsequent turnovers*. If you don't, it'll all show up as changes (which can get confusing). For the sound department, I'll make the EDLs for picture using Video Track 1 and then make the Change Lists by comparing the previous version's Video Track 1 to the current version's Video Track 1.

DI Change Lists

After all this dismissal of organizing the tracks and breaking apart submaster effects, it's now time to admit that, in the realm of DI turnovers, this is very much important. When making EDLs for DI, they'll specify what type of segment should be on which track (drama, VFX, optical, etc.). When making a Change List for them, you'll need to be diligent about making sure that you're organizing the timeline in the same manner you did initially. An easy mistake to make is forgetting whether a certain shot was considered an optical effect or not. What I like to do to prevent this is to gang the old version's EDL timeline with the one I'm currently organizing. I can toggle back and forth and make sure I separate the tracks the same way.

Rebalancing Reels

Rebalancing is when you move sections of the film from the head or tail of a reel to the head or tail of another reel. Rebalancing is done when a reel gets too long or too short or if we need to avoid a music cue crossing through a changeover. It's good to consult the music editor if they're available when you're first breaking everything into reels.

When a rebalance is required, Change Lists are created from the last versions of the reels that went out compared to duplicates of the same sequences with **only the rebalance changes** applied. I drag **all the previously turned-over reels** into the "old sequence" drop zone in the List Tool, rebalance the duplicate reels (up-versioning them), and then drag **all the new rebalanced versions into the "new sequence" drop zone.**

If I'm rebalancing down a reel, I need to add a dummy sequence to the new reel versions, which represents the removed reel. The List Tool then creates one Change List, which outlines what moved from one reel to another, leaving nothing in the dummy reel. After rebalancing

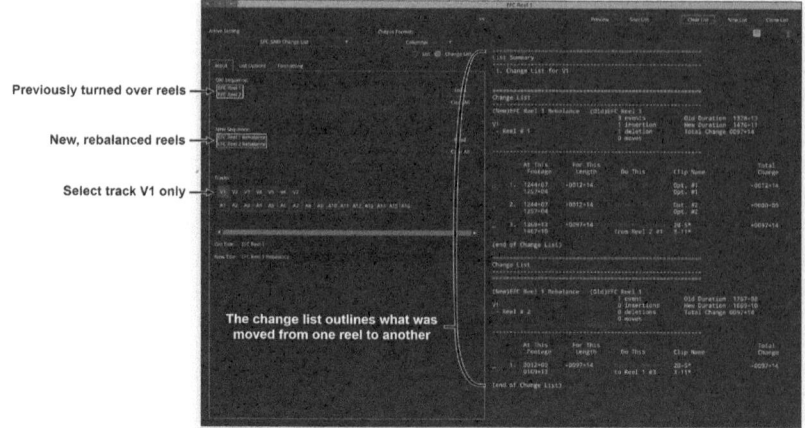

Previously turned over reels

New, rebalanced reels

Select track V1 only

The change list outlines what was
moved from one reel to another

Figure 9.2 List Tool showing multiple sequences for a rebalance.

down to fewer reels than I started with, I put an "x" in front of the old reel bin and archive it at the bottom of the Cuts folder, below "scenes deleted" and above "zOld Cuts" (depending on how the project is organized, of course).

> *Note: As mentioned earlier, I make change notes and rebalance lists with the same sequences I use for EDLs in turnovers. If you're making EDLs from **subsequences** as opposed to **duplicated sequences**, you'll end up stripping the sequence of its reel number (reel # column) metadata. This doesn't affect Change Lists, but the reel numbers **need** to be in there for the **rebalance Change List** to be created properly.*

Enacting a Rebalance

Let's pretend we need to rebalance Reels 1, 2, and 3 because we moved a scene from Reel 4 into Reel 2, and it's now running too long. Here's how I rebalance reels for a turnover:

1. Duplicate all reels **from the previous turnover.**
2. Mark the range at the beginning of Reel 2, which is being rebalanced into Reel 1.
3. Copy it to the clipboard.
4. Extract it from Reel 2.
5. Insert it at the end of Reel 1.
6. Repeat steps 2-5 for other reels as needed.

First frame of
head leader

2-pop
(seconds/footage)

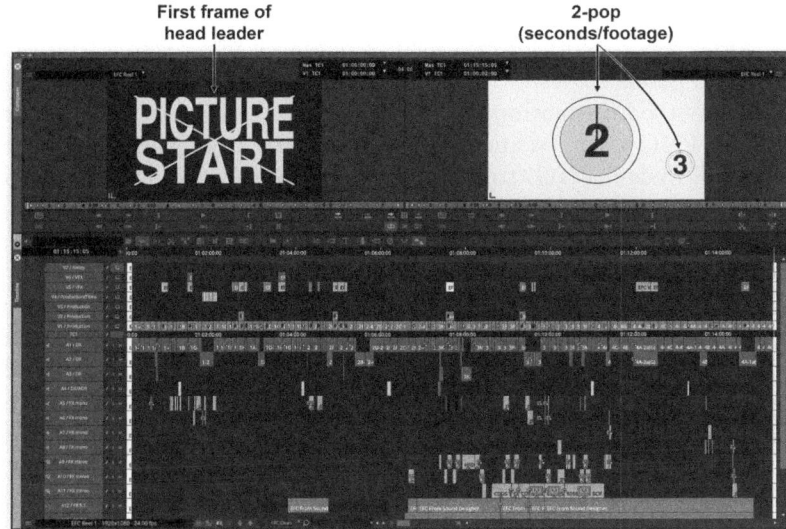

Figure 9.3 Custom head and tail leader in a timeline.

Let's say Reel 2 is now too short. We need to repeat steps 2-5 but with Reels 2 and 3 to achieve the ideal balance. Make sure to pay attention to the FFOA/LFOA markers when you're moving stuff around. Keep any defunct reels around for now. As mentioned earlier, you'll need dummy sequences with *only* head and tail leaders in them, as well as "Reel #" data, for when you make the rebalance Change List. By the way, the rebalanced Change List of all reels is the only one you need—not a Change List on a per-reel basis.

Head and Tail Leader

The purpose of leader in a digital environment is to provide sync points at the top and tail of every reel. 2-pops reside two seconds before and after the first and last frames of action (FFOA/LFOA).

I create custom head and tail leaders in After Effects for each show I work on. I like to add show-specific information, such as audio format, matte detail, and show title, to the head leader. Not only is it a great tool, but I like the level of professionalism it adds and how it represents the room. If I can, I'll even make the tail pop the show logo instead of a standard circle.

Creating Leader

Head leader has 192 frames (with the last second and 23 frames being black video), and *my* tail leader has 144 frames (with the first second and 23 frames being black video). The first frame of my tail leader has a film scratch on it, so I know it's a leader and not "program black."

I modify the information in the leader within After Effects and then export a PNG image sequence. I then export a Framing and Focus Chart still image (PNG) from Avid and replace the first frame of the head leader with this still image as a Picture Start frame, changing the name to match the old filename. Avid imports the image sequence as a single master clip, but then I need to add audio tracks.

I generate 36 channels of tone media at 1000 kHz and modify the channels to match the sequence track configuration (mono, stereo, and 5.1 tracks). I then cut in one frame of audio on the 2-pop across all tracks. It's important to lower the gain on each clip (I do so by 30 dB); otherwise, it'll be too loud, they all add up. I add channel IDs on 5.1 tracks before the 2-pop as well. I select the duration of the leader and export all audio tracks "direct out," so each track is discrete, re-import that file, and then modify the audio channels to match the track configuration again. I cut these audio clips into a sequence with the video leader master clips and then autosync *that* sequence to turn it into a clip.

This is done for both head and tail leader, separately, and it makes for one nice clean clip that also shows sync drift indicators. Every track of audio and video in a reel contains a leader with a pop. For video, this is as simple as duplicating the clip on every track. I stack them on all tracks (and color them white). Combined with FFOA/LFOA markers, it's easy to make sure everything stays in sync, accounted for, is turned over correctly, and makes building the show a breeze.

Outgoing and Incoming Indicators

Another thing I do once we're in reels and turning over is include grainy black-and-white footage from incoming and outgoing reels before/after the 2-pop.

If there's a change to the FFOA/LFOA, I make sure to update the grainy footage. This MOS clip informs the sound team where we're coming from and where we're going without them having to close the current session and load up a whole new reel. No one may request this, but it's always appreciated.

MediaFile Management Using MDVx

MDVx is a free-of-charge third-party tool made by an independent developer with a sense of humor (p. 266). **I love it.** MDVx is what I use to proactively chase Avid Media most frequently after turnovers, but I also use it as a general tool for managing Avid Media. I consider this a power user-level app, and it needs to be treated with respect. It will allow you to move or delete media, which can be dangerous if you're not careful. I use it mostly to facilitate file **copies,** so I'm never too concerned about misplacing or deleting media.

Using MDVx to Chase New Media Upon Turnover

Upon turning over, I open MDVx and click the Big Red Button. It scans all Avid MediaFiles directories it can find before showing you all the media files.

> *Note: You can drag and drop an Avid bin into this window, and it will filter the files to **only** show media that is referenced in the bin. It's super useful in some instances, but not what I'd do in this scenario necessarily.*

Then, using the filter button at the top, I select "Audio Media," so I'm only looking at **imported** and **rendered** audio media. I sort by

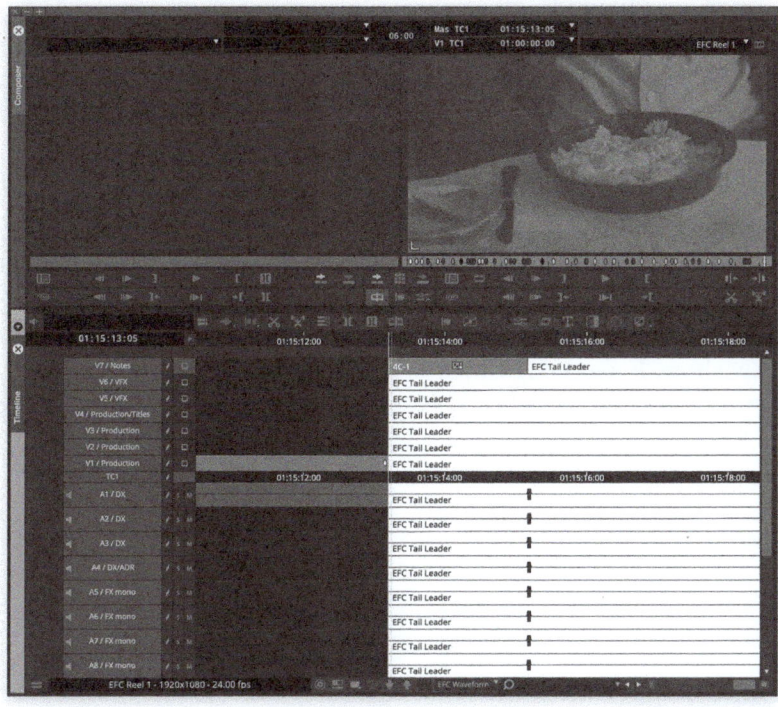

Figure 9.4 Timeline prepared for turnover. Note the grainy black and white outgoing footage before the 2-pop.

creation date and select all media files created since the last turnover. This catches everything from all reels, even media not currently being used. That's helpful if an old edit is restored or if an alternate music cue is used months down the line. I copy this to the desktop and send it to the sound department alongside "Link To" AAF or Pro Tools sessions. Now, the sound department has 1:1 Avid audio media to Editorial without you using too much brain power.

Using Media Composer to Chase New Media Upon Turnover

Regarding handling Avid Media *within Avid*, there's a checkbox within the export settings (both AAF and Pro Tools session files) to "exclude media from a previous sequence." In theory, you can keep all previous sequences in a bin, then upon export, point Media Composer at that (but the bin has to be **open,** and it becomes very large very quickly). There's no real alternative to MDVx; it's an incredibly useful utility that is perhaps rivaled only by the Media Tool within Media Composer (in combination with the consolidate/transcode commands).

> PS: The same developer also makes Blend-X, which is a free blending mode plug-in for when you want to use "Overlay" or "Screen," etc., without committing to the whole Boris suite.

Turnover Specifications and Notes

Here is a collection of output and turnover notes for each department. It's not exhaustive, and there will likely be turnovers requested of you that are outside the scope of what's contained here. I reference these (and update them) when I start turning over to departments on a new show. Even though each department has its own "boilerplate" standard specs, it's worth asking about a few changes if it could save you some time at scale.

PIX	Sequences or Longplays for review and approval		
When:	Anytime someone needs to watch the cut or segments of the cut but does not work directly with the file.		
Video	MP4 H.264 Matted	Burn-ins/ **Watermarks**	N/A **Property of [studio] (top center)**
Audio	Stereo	Guide Tracks	N/A
Other Files	-Continuity -Music Continuity		

Notes:

- This is more of an output than a turnover.
- H.264 should be 1080p at 5000 kbps.
- Entropy mode: **CABAC** vs **CAVLC** (Context-Adaptive Binary Arithmetic & Context-Adaptive Variable-Length Coding)
  - BAC = more specific, longer to encode, theoretically higher quality, less compatible.
  - VLC = common, less taxing to decode, more compatible (better choice usually).
- Export clean from Media Composer and feed into Media Encoder.
- Upload the file from the desktop, not the Nexis. It's significantly faster.
- **Slate details:** If exporting a segment for the director to review, add a four-second slate followed by one second of black. The slate should have the show logo, date, sequence name, and below all of that in red: "FOR [Director's Name Here] ONLY." Always keep a space between "sc" and the scene number (for example, "sc 108," *not "sc108"*).

SND	*Sound Department*		
When:	Anytime the editor makes a change that they want to share with the sound team		
Video	Quicktime DNxLB Unmatted	Burn-ins/ **Watermarks**	IN MATTE: Timecode, Footage, Scene/Take (Slate), Sequence name (date, reel, version), LFOA **Property of [studio] (top center), Initials (center)**
Audio	MOS	Guide Tracks	DX Mono, FX Stereo, MX Stereo
Other Files	-EDL V1 -EDL A1-4 -AAF/ProTools Export (Link to Media) -Chase the linked media using MDVx or a method that works for you. -**OR**: Copy All Media (exclude audio media from the previous sequence) -**OR**: Consolidated AAF (I am not a fan of this, and I'll explain why below) -Change List (or skip note, if requested) [VFX **only** Change List, if requested] -ADR cue sheets generated from Avid markers, including anything new since the previous turnover -LFOA list		

Notes:

- **Upon initial turnover**: send the full lined script, all sound reports, the cast list, and all audio MXF media (including the production sound rolls.)
- Parallel encode video file with music editor and composer file if possible.
- EDL sequence prep: remove head and tail leader audio (leaving the video leader to maintain duration), unmute all clips, and remove mixdowns.

- To create a VFX-only Change List, use the same Change List setting as usual and temporarily enable "Name" under the List Options tab. Compare only the VFX tracks to each other.
- Collect Avid media (if using a "link to" workflow).
  - One media collection option is MDVx. *I prefer this method.*
- Scan all drives and filter by selecting "Audio files only."
- Sort by Creation Date; further filter by selecting "Audio files only." Sort by Creation Date and copy any media created since the previous turnover.
  - **Missing Media workflow**: A "Missing Media" document is generated by the sound team after importing a "Link To" AAF, and any media they don't have appears as "missing."
    - The sound team kicks out a text export of the ProTools session (in timecode).
    - This "files in session" text document contains filenames and locations (that's a file path) formatted in a particular way. It can be parsed using online tools (see Evan Schiff, p. 188) or RegEx to reconstitute file paths and collect MXF media to send to the sound team.
    - One thing to look out for when working in a shared environment using this method is to find and remove "[*NexisNameHere*]/."
- Otherwise, use the Avid AAF export option "exclude media from previous sequence."
  - You can use an empty dummy sequence to point to if you want to copy all media without creating and using a different export preset.
  - I'll note that the above two media collection options are moot if you're using a consolidated AAF, which might be found to be simpler. I agree that it's fewer moving parts, but it creates a lot of redundant media with new UUIDs, **which is why I avoid that workflow when possible**.
- The LFOA burn-in is accomplished easiest by using the "custom property" sequence bin parameter in the timecode generator effect. I use a bin view, which displays an LFOA custom column. You can make as many custom columns as you want; just make sure to spell the column name correctly in the effect, or it won't work.
- When going to the stage, adjust the watermark to "**Property of [studio]**" upper center and "**STAGE**" bottom center. This should be **DNxSQ** (higher bitrate since it's being projected).
- They might want a clean picture on the stage **just for playback of the longplay** (when the executives come). Make sure to clear this with the head of post or the post supervisor *in writing* first. If they approve, bring the files on a hard drive the day of playback and make sure they're deleted right after. Otherwise, strip down the burn-ins/watermarks to reel/footage and "**STAGE**."

ADR	Automated Dialogue Replacement - Various Vendors		
When:	Before an ADR session (separate from a Sound Department turnover)		
Video	Quicktime DNxLB Unmatted	Burn-ins/ **Watermarks**	Same as SND, see above **Property of [studio] (top center), facility (center)**
Audio	DX Left, ADR/FX Right	Guide Tracks	N/A (or same as Sound Dept. turnover, if at all)
Other Files	-ADR cue sheets generated from Avid markers (or from Dialogue/ADR Editor)		

Notes:

- Send the full reel if it's warranted. Only send necessary reels.

- This can be subsequences of the scenes being looped.

  - Mark in and out, then go to the in-point and *subtract eight seconds*.

  - This makes it easier to slug in the head leader and maintain the correct start TC and footage.

  - Start TC can be changed in the "Start" bin column if needed. You just have to do the math.

- You might be able to send guides instead of the embedded split tracks. This is preferable because the guide tracks from the Sound Department turnovers can be repurposed. Just ask!

MX	Music - Editor		
When:	Anytime the editor makes a change they want to share with the music editor		
Video	Quicktime DNxLB Unmatted	Burn-ins/ **Watermarks**	Same as SND, see above **Property of [studio] (top center), Initials (center)**
Audio	MOS	Guide Tracks	DX Mono, FX Stereo (or Surround), MX Stereo
Other Files	-AAF copy all media (embedded) -Change List (*if needed/requested*) -LFOA List (*if needed/requested*)		

Notes:

- Parallel encode with SND and Composer file when possible.

- Remove muted music clips from the timeline.

- The muted status might not translate into Pro Tools and can be confusing because the recipients can't differentiate between what's muted and unmuted.

- **If carrying a temp mix**: Leave the corresponding music clips in the timeline, muted. If they come across, great. If not, then the music editor has what they need in the stem.

COMP	Music - Composer		
When:	After the first preview screening, possibly before then, depending on the schedule.		
Video	MP4 H.264 Unmatted	Burn-ins/ **Watermarks**	Same as SND, see above **Property of [studio] (top center), Initials (center)**
Audio	DX/FX Left, MX Right (embedded)	Guide Tracks	N/A
Other Files	-AAF copy all media (embedded) [same file as music editor]		

Notes:

- Parallel encode with SND and MX editor files when possible.
- Separate temp score from source music. Include source music in the left channel.
  - This is because the composer will want to work **without** any temp score but **with** all necessary playback music.
- If the Composer will accept MOS videos with separate guides, that's ideal. I've suggested it, but it usually gets denied. I believe the simplicity of a two-channel embedded file is preferred because it's less work for them and their team to prep a session and simply mute the stereo channel, which contains temp music.
- Use Avid's "Multiple Mixes" feature to create the guides or export them, link the guides back into the system, and pan them as needed.
- Subsequent turnovers occur when there are significant changes to sections that the composer is working on, if there's an added beat or scene that will need a theme, or if there's a rebalance.

IND	*Independent Theater*		
When:	Before any screening at an independent theater. This is only when there's no room in the budget to create a DCP.		
Video	Quicktime ProRes HQ Matted	Burn-ins/**Watermarks**	N/A
Audio	Direct Out, embedded (see below)	Guide Tracks	N/A
Other Files	-Direct Out: 16 channels; first six should be 5.1 SMPTE order		

Notes:

- Some independent theaters have systems that require ProRes HQ because of the bit depth, despite Editorial not working with that level of detail. These are the same systems that require 16 channels of audio, even if 10 of them are empty.
- I create a 5.1 mixdown of our sequence in Avid and break that out into six center-panned mono tracks in SMPTE order. I then add 10 tracks to the sequence, all with a 2-pop (just to populate them) but otherwise empty.
- **Request confirmation that the file has been deleted after the screening.**

DCP	*Digital Cinema Package (Preview Screenings)*		
When:	Before any preview screenings.		
Video	Quicktime DNxSQ Matted (or Unmatted)	Burn-ins/ **Watermarks**	N/A
Audio	MOS	Guide Tracks	5.1 WAV File (include channel IDs)
Other Files	-Prepare to upload to PIX when creating the DCP. The studio will want to see the cut after the preview screening. -**Include a continuity.**		

Notes:

- Can be turned over in Reels or as a longplay. Depending on the schedule, I prefer a longplay if there's time. A tighter turnaround time would have me preferring reels, as I can QC them piecemeal as they're ready. **You absolutely must QC these files**; DCPs are not cheap.

- For audio: use either a stage printmaster or Avid mixdown (export a 5.1 WAV file from Avid.)

  – If not creating a 5.1 Polyphonic file, include the audio channels in the file name.

- Include the head and tail pops.

  – They can separate the head and tail leader from the longplay, and they can keep the head leader (with channel IDs) as a separate file on the same drive.

- After QC'ing the DCP, you might need to make a patch to rectify a mistake or update VFX, ADR, music, etc. Patches can be sent for video or audio; just provide the start timecode of the clip and send them the media.

  – If sending an audio-only patch, send a still of the first frame the clip is being cut in on.

  – Make sure to check with the DCP vendor to verify there are no clicks or pops at the audio edit. They can roll the edit to account for this.

  – The DCP will need to be overwritten with any new media but only needs to be spot-checked/QC'd in the affected areas.

- Clipster is the name of the software commonly used to create these temp DCPs. If we provide a longplay, they break it into "reels" (their own defined 20-minute chunks); then, if we have a drop in (or patch), they only have to replace the "reel" that is affected on the DCP, not the whole DCP.

- DCPs are usually written to CRU drives and require two files to play if they're encrypted: A **KDM** (Key Delivery Message) and a **Cert** (Digital Cinema Certificate).

  – KDMs are created from a **DKDM** (Distribution KDM) and allow for the decrypting and playback of the media on the specific projector (information in the Cert) during a specified time window.

  – The post supervisor will coordinate these files in most cases.

TITLES	*Title House / Title Designer*		
When:	After a title spotting session and for any subsequently added or changed titles.		
Video	Quicktime DNxSQ Matted	Burn-ins/ **Watermarks**	Timecode, Sequence name (date, reel, version) **Property of [studio] (top center), Vendor Name (lower center) [try not to obscure title placement]**
Audio	Stereo, embedded	Guide Tracks	N/A
Other Files	-Provide two video files: Texted and Textless -PDF or list of all Titles in the show		

Notes:

- Include fonts used for temps in the list turned over to them.

MKTG	Marketing		
When:	After the first or second preview screening, and possibly upon picture lock.		
Video	Quicktime ProRes Unmatted	Burn-ins/ **Watermarks**	IN MATTE MARGINS: Timecode, VFX ID, Scene/Take (Slate), Source Timecode, Tape Name, Sequence name (date, reel, version), Shoot day **watermark per studio specs**
Audio	MOS	Guide Tracks	DX Mono, FX Stereo, MX Stereo
Other Files	-AAF (Link to Media)		

Notes:

- This changes from studio to studio and from vendor to vendor.

  – Sometimes the studio has you turnover unwatermarked files to them (only data burn-ins), and then they'll watermark it per creative vendor and distribute the files themselves.

  – Other times, you'll be in direct contact with the marketing agency, especially when they need an overcut performed or if they need something from dailies that isn't in the cut.

- DNxHR might be acceptable over ProRes; just ask. The burn-ins included in marketing are really for us in editorial to help track down the shots for if/when we need to overcut the trailer.

- **Export full frame** because the dailies burn-ins are in the matte.

- The marketing department usually has access to the dailies via PIX. That's how they know to ask for specific things that are not in the cut.

DI	Digital Intermediate		
When:	After the first or second preview screening and upon picture lock.		
Video	Quicktime DNxSQ 50% opacity matte (or unmatted)	Burn-ins/ **Watermarks**	Timecode, Sequence name (date, reel, version), Frame Count, Scene/Take (Slate), Source Timecode, Tape name, VFX ID **Property of [studio] (top center), Vendor Name (center)**
Audio	MOS	Guide Tracks	5.1 Full Mix
Other Files	- EDLs by track (V1 Production, V2 VFX Plates, V3 VFX Shots, V4 Opticals, V5: Titles) - Add more tracks as needed on top of this, but keep these consistent - AAF (Link to Media) - Avid bin of EDL sequence(s) (*if requested*) - DI Event list(s) generated from Avid markers, including anything new since the previous turnover		

Notes:

- Picture updates don't require new guide tracks, just the initial turnover.
- Leave temp color effects intact and apply in the reference MOV (unlike for VFX).
  - This is useful for troubleshooting color management, especially when various formats are shot.
- "Save list to several files" in the List Tool automatically saves EDLs as separate files by track.
- The "Production" track of EDL should contain any **non-effected clips**.
- "Opticals" are speed changes, re-positions, re-sizes, or any effects DI is expected to complete.
- If a VFX shot (final) is not present during the turnover, use the prominent plate in its place.
  - This allows the colorist to get a head start on color timing, and the plate will be replaced with the VFX final when it's available, and any color work will be traced.
- Remove non-DI/VFX markers (mainly ADR/MX and notes track markers) to generate a DI list.
- It's fine to leave the head and tail leader in the Bin/EDL/AAF sequences.
- Send AAFs, Bins, EDLs, and DI list(s) via email, unless content security prohibits it.
- **For VFX reviews**: stringout all shots to be reviewed and send DI an EDL. A supplemental turnover will be sent with all finalized VFX shots from this session; see below.

DI-VFX	*VFX Drop-Ins - Digital Intermediate (Supplemental Turnovers)*		
When:	After a DI VFX review		
Video	Quicktime DNxLB Unmatted	Burn-ins/ **Watermarks**	Same as DI, see above
Audio	MOS	Guide Tracks	N/A
Other Files	- EDL of **only** VFX to be dropped in at their appropriate points in the timeline - Avid bin of EDL sequence(s) (*if requested*) - AAF (Link to Media) (*if requested*)		

Notes:

- The version should be an alpha update because of the new VFX. Only needed for significant changes.
- Reverse drop-in: if a shot that's already been turned over and dropped in is omitted, the DI will want an update that reflects what should be in the show. It's like a VFX drop-in, but it only uses the plate instead of the VFX shot.

VFX-DI	*VFX Pull - (Send to Lab and VFX Vendor)*		
When:	During a VFX Pull		
Video	Quicktime DNxLB Unmatted	Burn-ins/ **Watermarks**	Same as DI, see above
Audio	MOS	Guide Tracks	N/A
Other Files	- EDL stringout of all VFX to be pulled. No filler between clips. Include a marker in each clip with shot code and element type.		

Notes:

- The VFX vendor should be copied on the email to DI (where the EDL is attached).
  - The vendor does not need to receive the QuickTime.
  - QuickTime is mainly used by the lab to verify that they pulled the correct frames.
- If using Avid to generate the EDL, make sure the list tool settings include handles. I say this because I use my database to generate an EDL instead of Media Composer.
  - My database kicks out an ALE alongside the EDL of all elements in a VFX pull. Then, I populate a timeline with subclips generated from the ALE to use as a reference QuickTime.
- If a shot is extended past the head or tail, it needs to be re-pulled, and that should be indicated in the marker (append "**_repull#**" to the marker name).

VFX	*VFX Bidding/Reference - VFX Vendor*		
When:	After VFX shots are identified or a temp has been updated.		
Video	MP4 H.264 Unmatted	Burn-ins/ **Watermarks**	Timecode, Shot Code, Frame counter, Source TC, Scene/Take (Slate) **Property of [studio] (top center), Vendor Name (center)**
Audio	PRN (as needed)	Guide Tracks	N/A
Other Files	-Line Up sheet -CSV of Line Up Data -XLSX of Line Up Data -EDL of elements per shot (*if requested*) -Annotated frame(s) (*as needed*)		

Notes:

- **Bidding QuickTimes** are provided before the vendor begins any work. They are used as creative references if the vendor moves forward on the shot.
- Updated **Reference QuickTimes** should be provided as the shots change throughout the edit.
  - **Strip any and all color effects from the references.** Step into nested effects to

ensure no color effects are applied to any part of the reference.

- Remove temp paint outs. It's easier for them to spot the issue if you're not hiding it.

- These can be per scene/sequence or on a shot-by-shot basis—whichever is preferred.

- Provide a decomposition (breakdown) of elements for a complicated shot.

- Source timecode burn-ins are most important for time remapping and motion estimation shots.

- Only include audio if the sync sound is relevant to the creative work (for example: Gunshots, lip-sync).

10 Screenings

After the director's cut and before we lock the picture, we ping-pong between temp dubs and watching the film. We screen the film internally and at test screenings called "Previews" (p. 236). Internal screenings are conducted in the editing rooms, in-house screening rooms within the post facility, independent screening rooms, or at the studio. The purpose of screening the film isn't just for us to keep re-evaluating our work, but to get fresh eyes and gain perspective after losing objectivity.

In-House Screenings

These are the most common screenings and happen as frequently as needed. It's vital to step back and see the forest from the trees. These are great opportunities for the assistant to take notes on what areas have changed (p. 142), what needs more sound work (p. 155) or temp VFX (p. 175), and to take stock overall of how the story is being shaped.

Keep it Secret, Keep it Safe

Everyone external to the team will need to sign a Non-Disclosure Agreement (NDA), so keep blank ones printed out and ready. These screenings happen under the "cone of silence." Agents and managers aren't typically allowed because these screenings are somewhat informal and represent a "work in progress."

Securing the Screen

Some post facilities will have you reserve their screening room ahead of time, and then they'll set the room up for you. Other times, you'll be entrusted to set it up yourself. This usually entails powering up the projector and computer. Once the projector has warmed up and the Avid project is loaded, check the speakers and framing. I build the framing chart and channel identifiers into the head leader (p. 221) for this purpose.

DOI: 10.4324/9781003516491-11

Prepping the Sequence

After building the show (p. 141), I perform an ExpertRender and lock the tracks. Using ExpertRender is faster and leaner than a full render, as it only renders the topmost track (which includes anything from lower tracks necessary for smooth playback). Ideally, I'd have rendered all the reels before this. That reduces the amount of rendering that has to be done now because the render files would remain linked to the "parent" sequences from which all subsequent longplays are built. I lock the tracks because we sometimes go back to these sequences to reference the screened cut, so the locked tracks prevent anyone from accidentally making changes in it, mistaking it for the active cut.

Running the Show

If the door to the screening room makes a lot of noise, place tape over the latch so it's less distracting when someone steps out. Hang signs on the doors that read, "Screening in Progress – Please Close Doors Quietly." If you have visitors (especially guests of the director or representatives from the studio), ensure everyone has directions and parking instructions ahead of time, as well as parking validation upon their arrival. Make sure the A/C is on if your screening is taking place after hours. Your PA should be able to help with all these tasks.

Shutting it Down

Once the screening is over, be sure to power down the projector and log out of the Nexis.

External Screenings

If you're not screening at the editing facility, odds are you're either at an independent screening facility or at the studio itself. Either way, the media is leaving the cutting room. Not only does the media need to be secure, but before each screening, it's vital to check the picture and sound (p. 238) at each venue with enough time to adjust as needed.

Family & Friends Screenings

The importance of an "F&F" screening lands somewhere between an in-house screening and a preview screening. It's higher stakes because it's people outside of Editorial (albeit, as you can imagine, family and friends of the editorial team), and you want everything to go smoothly. However, it's not so high that the state of the project hinges on the results.

It's all about gathering information, making sure the narrative is clear, and gaining some perspective from trusted individuals. The editor might choose to pass out questionnaires, or the director might want to have a little Q&A session afterward. Perhaps neither, but when you know a little more about your screening, you can be prepared to ensure it goes off without a hitch.

Studio Screenings

If you're going to the studio, you can likely playback through Avid (it's usually the case if you're at a studio screening room) and perform mixdowns ahead of time. Bake in the matte, if applicable, or plan to use Mask Margins. The mixdowns can be the longplay or in reels—the latter is better for flexibility, so you can QC reels as they become available from the editor and swap reels out later if needed.

There's an argument to be made for kicking out a single ProRes file in an MOV container, as it's simpler and, therefore, has fewer variables associated with it. I prefer to retain as much control as possible, though, and if I'm the one plugging the drive in and running the screening, then I'll do whatever gives me the most flexibility. If a lot is out of my hands—for example, if we're at an independent screening facility that won't let me touch their equipment—then I opt for the self-contained file.

In any case, load the media onto an encrypted drive and bring it to the facility. It's a good idea to spot-check the lightest, darkest, quietest, and loudest moments. These mixdowns should be clean of any spoilage and, once the screening is over, be deleted from the server or hard drive that the system projecting them uses. You either do this yourself or look on as the projectionist does. It's even better if your second assistant editor or PA is available to bear witness.

Preview Screenings

The largest screenings are previews. A preview is where you take the film to a real, operating movie theater and recruit an audience. A lot of money is spent renting out the theater, recruiting the audience, and analyzing the resulting data from the audience's feedback, so it's imperative that the screening goes smoothly. **That's in your domain.**

Another thing to recognize is that preview screenings are how the filmmakers and the studio determine their next steps. If people react favorably, the studio may be less inclined to get involved, whereas an unfavorable reaction might lead to conflicting opinions between the filmmakers and the studio. All this is **beyond your control**, and the only things you can do are keep a cool head and a positive attitude, ensure the screening looks and sounds good, and plays back smoothly.

Preparing for a Preview Screening

You can prepare for a preview screening by creating clean video mixdowns. You can matte them or not; if not, let the person creating the

DCP know what the aspect ratio is so they can properly render it with a matte. I usually let them do this because it saves me time, but matting the video files certainly reduces another variable of human error.

If you're screening using the Avid mix (assuming you're working in 5.1), create 5.1 mixdowns. Even if you're working in LCR, create a 5.1 mixdown. The rears will be empty, but you'll get the channel separation in the front. If you're not providing the audio, it's likely coming from the stage after a temp mix. The mix tech will either forward the printmasters (by reel) to the DCP vendor or editorial for you to forward.

It's imperative to QC all video and audio mixdowns created for preview screenings. Once I watch them in the Avid, I copy the media to an encrypted drive and get them to the DCP vendor.

Making and QC'ing a Temp DCP

Here are four possible paths to making a DCP (in my order of preference):

- They come to the editing room with a mobile rig, and you hand them an encrypted hard drive.
- You upload files to their facility via a secure Aspera Dropbox link and pick up the DCP from their facility at a later time.
- You physically take an encrypted hard drive to their facility and possibly QC the DCP there.
- You make the DCP yourself (*highly uncommon*).

I prefer it when they come to us, and then we can QC the DCP at the studio or a nearby screening room. This is usually an upcharge, which the budget may not allow. QCs need to happen early enough to make a change, should it be necessary, which is why we usually schedule them early in the day.

DCP Drop-ins/Patches

Changes made to the DCP after the files are sent are called "patches" or "drop-ins." This could be audio or video, like a segment where an audio file is improperly rendered, the music drops out, or there is an incorrect/missing VFX shot. For these patches, I include the start timecode of the patch in the filename and communicate what the visual should be. I sometimes follow this up with a phone call. While patches are possible, you want to avoid having to do them, as the vendor might charge more. Patches or not, the DCP needs to be QC'd after it's created.

Once everything verifiably looks and sounds good, the next time I'll see the DCP is during the run-through. All I have to do is make sure the keys and the certs are issued—something the post supervisor handles, but in some cases, could be assigned to me.

The Day of the Preview

On the day of the screening, we arrive around 9 a.m. for a run-through. The theater projectionist ingests the DCP by copying the files from the CRU drive onto the projector and plugging in the digital key. So long as the Cert matches, everything's good to go. While the files are transferring, I'll see if I need to get parking validation for the team and introduce myself to the security guards, audio tech, and projectionist. This small group watches the film in the theater, checking the audio levels and the picture quality, just like at any other screening room.

Checking the Image

Before the run-through, note the projection area and make sure the image isn't running off the screen edges. Spot-check an area that's particularly light or dark and adjust the gamma levels and/or brightness (measured in foot-lamberts, 14 fL is standard for 2D) if needed. If the picture looks milky, the gamma might be too high.

Ask if it's a silver screen or not, as this affects the brightness and saturation. Silver screens may come off too bright/dull and introduce hot spots when displaying a 2D image. I believe this is because 3D movies need to reflect more light due to compensation for the polarized glasses. It doesn't matter if your project is in 3D or not; theaters have different screens installed in their auditoriums for the flexibility of being able to project all sorts of different formats. There's not much you can do besides adjusting the picture to compensate appropriately.

Checking the Audio

In the projection booth, note the levels the amps are set to. In the auditorium, check an area of the film that should be firing on all six speakers and ensure everything is coming through as expected. I build channel identifiers into the head leader and ensure that they make their way onto the DCP as a separate file. It's a fast way to ensure that everything is coming across as we intended. If you don't have that, the audio technician should have pink noise they can play, which allows us to hear the full spectrum of sound coming through each speaker.

During the run-through, move to different parts of the auditorium periodically to ensure it's not too loud or soft. Tweak the projector settings and audio levels if needed. The Dolby volume knob is standard and has been in every preview I've ever been involved with. Typically, we play back at reference level 7 (standard), and the knob counts one click of a turn as 0.3 dB, so three clicks is 1 dB.

Post-Run Through, Pre-Preview

After the run-through, the auditorium is **locked and guarded** until the preview screening commences. No one should make any changes **whatsoever**. Now is a great time to go grab a bite to eat. Never forget to eat!

Later, just before the preview, we return to the auditorium and spot-check the film. We ensure everything is still in sync and that picture and sound are at the right levels. Right before the preview begins, I send the cut via PIX to the distro list provided and email the continuity to the post supervisor and studio contact.

Now, I run to the concession stand and grab a bag of Watermelon Sour Patch Kids and a bottle of water (or whatever it is that *you* need to snack on when watching a movie). I prefer this to popcorn because I can still shake hands and not get oil all over the volume knob. Also, Watermelon Sour Patch Kids rule.

Audience Capture

Audience capture refers to video recorded of the audience watching the film. I've heard that it's more prevalent in comedies and horror films. This can be one file with multiple angles baked in, multiple separate angles, or simply an audio-only file. They usually film the focus group as well. These files are physically handed to me on a hard drive immediately after the focus group concludes.

In the days following a preview, if audience capture is recorded, I take the recording and put it up against the picture. I link this file (instead of importing—it's a long file and rarely referenced) and cut it into a duplicate of the DCP sequence. I take the DCP video mixdown and make it picture-in-picture to focus on the audience's response.

No one has ever asked me to export this; we've only scrubbed to specific areas to see how people reacted to certain things. I usually read the cards people fill out while listening to the audience capture if I have the time.

The Focus Group and Score

Immediately after the preview and before a focus group is selected, there's an interval where the audience fills out feedback forms (either physically or digitally). The focus group is usually around 20 people chosen at random and moderated by a person from the research firm that recruited the audience. The studio executives and filmmakers sit in the back (unless you're asked to stay outside) and listen to the discourse.

The focus group sits in the front rows of the auditorium and is asked a handful of questions to gauge what was liked, disliked, and, most importantly, **what, if anything, was confusing**. They are asked to rate aspects of the film on a scale of 1–5, where 5 is excellent, 4 is very good, 3 is good, 2 is fair, and 1 is poor. I always found this interesting because I'd argue that three or four of those are positive-leaning words, and I think the psychology of this is fascinating.

The key numbers to look at after a preview screening are the score (a sum of the percentage of audience members who rated the film "Excellent" and "Very Good") and the percentage of people who said they would definitely recommend the film. **These numbers typically indicate the amount of work that lies ahead and what the schedule looks like moving forward.**

Preview Screening Specifics

These are notes I took on auditorium details during preview screenings over the years. Each theater was different, and I wanted to have a starting point as a reference. As mentioned, the gamma and screen type are things to pay attention to. **Amps should always be 100% and calibrated to 85 dB at level 7.** Note that the playback volume is some-times a bit higher.

	Seat Count	Media Type	Playback Volume	Screen Type	Gamma / Lamberts	Notes
Auditorium A	250	DCP	7.0	-	-	-
Auditorium B	223	DCP	6.6	Silver	2.6/20 fL	Contrast: +4.5
Auditorium C	60	Avid	7.4	-	2.2	-
Auditorium D	300	DCP	7.2-8.5	White	2.6/14 fL	Laser projector

After a preview, notes are addressed, and you might preview the new cut. The cut continues to be refined as more sound work is done (which entails multiple music and sound turnovers), and VFX continue to come in and be noted. This cycle continues until the film is locked.

11 Digital Intermediate

The Digital Intermediate (referred to simply as "DI") began as exactly that: An **intermediate** step in the filmmaking process. The film was scanned, digital files were edited "offline" (using proxy media), information about the offline edit went back to the DI, and then the physical film itself was used to finish the project. As digital files increased in quality, this became less "intermediate" and more final—and we still call it "the DI." Seeing as the digital workflow is more ubiquitous these days than the film workflow, this book is focused on the former.

DI Workflow Overview

Today, in a digital acquisition workflow, the images are captured in an acquisition format (like X-OCN XT or ARRIRAW). These Original Camera Files (OCFs) are backed up and stored at the finishing house and transcoded to high-quality proxy media for editing (like ProRes 422 or DNxHR SQ). The dailies lab and finishing house aren't always necessarily the same entity, but when they are, it's more streamlined.

When we've finished editing, we send information about the edit to the DI, who relink (or debayer and *then* relink) to the OCFs. They perform color grading and digital optical effects, ultimately finishing the film. The tape name and source timecode are used to relink Editorial's offline sequences to the online project. It's common to find a conform being done using Baselight and Resolve.

DI isn't *usually* involved until after previews (emphasis on "usually"). Exceptions include preview screenings or early festival submissions where a color pass is desired, when you need dailies re-transcoded without burn-ins (if you apply a re-po that brings them into frame), or if you manipulate the footage such that it breaks (p. 245).

The DI Team

There are a few people involved in the DI that you should be aware of: the DI producer, finishing editor (sometimes referred to as the online editor), and colorist. The director of photography (DP) usually

DOI: 10.4324/9781003516491-12

has a good relationship with the colorist going into a project, which might influence which finishing house you end up at.

The colorist's sole focus is to creatively work with the director and the DP on the look of the image. The finishing editor oversees conforming offline editorial timelines and prepping their sessions so that the colorist can work without distraction. They're also the ones applying and matching DI effects, dropping in VFX, and accounting for titles. The DI producer manages multiple projects that the finishing house has going on and will interface largely with the post supervisor. You'll be in touch with them and the finishing editor more than the colorist.

Color Pipeline (CDLs and LUTs)

Let's establish that the color pipeline needs to be non-destructive. The original camera negative always remains intact, and upon re-encoding them, color is transformed. CDLs and LUTs (Color Decision Lists and Look Up Tables, respectively) can be used to do this. CDLs are simpler and easier to transfer between software (slope, offset, power, and saturation values come across in an EDL). LUTs are easier to apply but more complicated to translate. Typically, they're used in conjunction with one another; the dailies will be run through a process that applies a CDL value, which is stored in the metadata. Then, a LUT will be applied, the name of which will appear in the metadata—but someone will need the LUT file to re-create the look, unlike CDL data. Most shows have one LUT, referred to as the "Show LUT," which is the easiest. Other shows opt for an interior and exterior LUT, or more, depending on the creative intent. That's more to keep track of, though—and when using multiple LUTs, this should be denoted on the slate. I generally don't have much to do with CDLs and LUTs aside from making sure I'm maintaining the metadata and passing it along as needed.

When plates are pulled, no CDL or LUT is applied. For a VFX vendor, the lab supplies the associated LUTs and .ccc files if needed, but in Editorial, we can also pass along CDL information in an EDL and on Line-Up Sheets. The VFX vendor needs to have the necessary files to recreate and apply the dailies color to their Avid references. Ultimately, they'll deliver frames to DI that have no color information baked into them, but they'll have been working with an accurate color reference and providing versions to Editorial that match surrounding shots. The colorist might use this as a starting point, and the LUT will likely be referenced but not used. It'll probably be rebuilt using the tools within the grading program.

Temp Color Correction

I always use Media Composer Ultimate, which you need if you work in a shared environment to enable bin locking. This also includes ScriptSync, PhraseFind, and an expanded color correction add-on known as "Symphony." I mostly stick with curves and HSL adjustments, jumping over to secondary color corrections as needed.

Monitor Calibration

These are all considerations to keep in mind when thinking about color and temp color correction. It would be a shame if you took a color pass on a scene and then went into the editor's room to review it, and everything looks slightly brighter and more orange.

Any screen calibrations I perform are highly unscientific. You should ask the company that is processing your dailies to come out and calibrate the editor's reference and client monitors, using their specialty tools (like CalMan and a colorimeter). They may agree to perform one calibration for free. If you can do more than one, prioritize the editor's monitors first, then all other assistants' client monitors, and finally, all other assistants' reference monitors. There may be no budget for this at all; in this case, you should just ensure the editor is happy with how their reference and client monitors look and then ensure all others in every cutting room match.

Every manufacturer uses different branding for their "special sauce" of image manipulation. You'll see things like "Game" and "Expert" modes, "Super Resolution," "TruMotion," and "Real Cinema." These are the kinds of settings that make the image look like a soap opera. There has been a push from the industry to standardize these terms. You should know that Game Mode usually refers to a higher refresh rate, which can improve sync, but this comes with the tradeoff of fewer color adjustment options. Expert Mode prioritizes total control over color and is generally preferred. All those motion settings with goofy names should be turned **off.** You might need a "service remote" to disable auto-dimming since it's a feature built into these displays to prevent image burn-in (something OLED panels are prone to).

Avid Color Correction Types

My biggest takeaway is the difference between Src Segment, Master Clip, and CC Effect options. The first applies a color correction to the segment in the timeline. The second applies the color correction to that segment and **all others in the sequence of the same master clip.** There's also a Src Tape option which will do the same, but across clips from the same tape name. There are more options than what I listed. Finally,

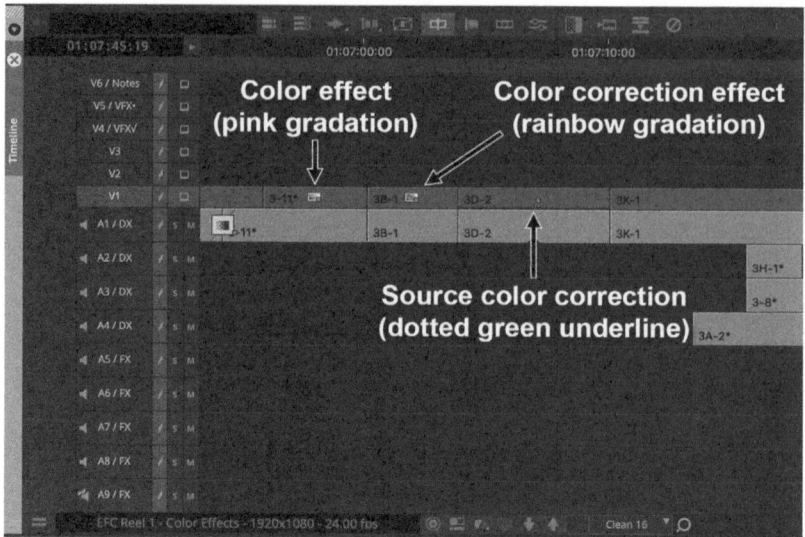

Figure 11.1 Color effect icon vs. color correction effect icon vs. source color correction green underline. (See [www.routledge.com/9781032843285] for un-annotated high resolution illustration)

the CC Effect applies a color *effect* to the clip, not a correction (which Media Composer treats differently.) The effect allows for shape-based color correction, "power windows," so to speak. You can tell at a glance whether it's an effect or a color correction because an effect presents as an effect icon with a rainbow design, and a correction appears as a simple green dot (and the whole clip is underlined if it's not rendered.)

Matching Color

Matching color is simple; it looks the same in the HSL tab as in the curves tab, but they match colors based on different criteria. The basic workflow is to click on the color "chip" on the left, then use the eyedropper to select the color in the destination clip you plan on changing (in the Composer window). Click on the right-side "chip" to sample the color you want to match. *Sidenote: You can Option-drag the color chip into a bin to save the color for later.* Now, clicking "match color" will do just that.

There's a "NaturalMatch" option that lets you match color when the clips have significantly different lighting. It compensates for the luminance and saturation qualities of the original image, adopts the new hue value, preserves the original luminance value, and adjusts the saturation value in relation to the other values.

Keyframing Color Changes

To change in color over time, add a keyframe in the effect editor under the category in which you're adjusting color (curves, HSL, etc.). Click on each keyframe in the composer window before making your adjustment. Subsequent changes will automatically create new keyframes (but you can create them manually if you wish).

Removing All Color Corrections in a Sequence

To remove all color corrections (not *effects*, mind you) at once, open the color correction window and right-click anywhere in it. Select "remove correction," then select the type of corrections you wish to remove. In my case, it's usually "Src Segment." When would you want to do this? Before turning over references to VFX, of course!

Resolution and Image Quality

Most films are finished in 4K as of this writing. This means they're shot in at least 4K, bumping up to 6K and 8K, depending on the project. Even if the film is mastered in 2K, they'll shoot in a higher resolution. Specific workflows for large format exist, but I won't cover them here in detail as they're the exceptions that prove the rule.

The image is usually framed for 5% safety (referred to as "slop" and intended for subtle reframing or stabilization in DI if needed) as opposed to shooting edge-to-edge.

A quick note: It's easy to blow up the size of the image digitally, but that doesn't mean it should be done in extremes. You can blow up a shot by up to 400%, but it's going to look noticeably different from

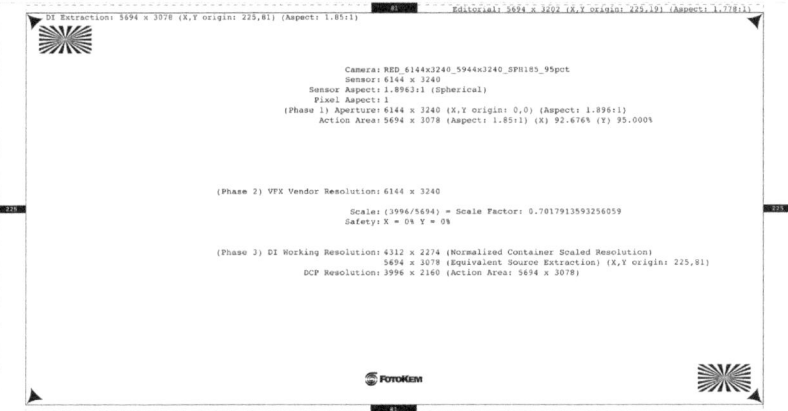

Figure 11.2 Framing and focus chart, displaying focus patterns and aspect ratio.

Photo credit: Bryan Golder, Senior Deployment Engineer - FotoKem the surrounding shots. In my experience, 30% is the upper limit of resizing without any noticeable visual degradation. Digital can handle more than physical film—and in cases of extreme resizes, the shot might need to be degrained and have grain re-introduced to match the surrounding shots. This is all also dependent on the original image, the sensor, and exposure. An underexposed image is more challenging to blow up because it gets noisier faster.

Another consideration is whether the film was shot in 6K but is being mastered in 4K. In this case, you might want to discuss with the DI producer about pulling and debayering the OCF in a higher resolution than the finishing format to allow for a higher-quality resize.

DI Review Sessions

There are two main reasons you'll find yourself at the DI facility: Color sessions and VFX review sessions. Before either of these—and again, this can be different from show to show—the DP will usually spend one-on-one time with the colorist to set looks. After that, the director works with the colorist and fine-tunes the color on a shot-by-shot basis.

Color Sessions

After we turnover to DI and they successfully "online" (relink) the show, the DP gets a pass to set looks. The director might allow the Editorial team to join a color session, but the rooms can be small, and capacity is sometimes limited. It might just be the editor that can attend.

The work done during this time is making sure the color is consistent and that the audience's eyes are drawn to the desired part of the frame. "Power windows" are utilized to brighten or darken specific areas. If you're able to take part, it's useful for you, as the assistant, to be prepared with a list of color notes and DI effects so you can speak up if something is out of place or missing.

Consider requesting that the colorist displays on-screen information such as the Record Timecode and VFX shot code. I've worked with finishing editors who had set it up so the shot code was pulled from our EDLs using the VFX plate track [V2] and our markers. It's possible to include the Shot Code in the EDL if using clip comments. If they're using Baselight, there's also a color-coded indicator they can put in the lower right-hand corner of the screen. The color coding I've seen in use includes red (dailies), grey (VFX plate), and yellow (optical). All this information can be toggled on or off at any given time and helps answer the director when they ask status questions.

VFX Review Sessions

A DI VFX review session is for reviewing any VFX shots that have a status of "DI Review." This means the shot has been approved creatively in the cutting room and now needs to be viewed in 4K before rubber-stamping its status as "Final." This session is dependent on Editorial having already reviewed the shots in Avid (p. 205) and the VFX vendor sending EXR files to DI for the approved version(s).

Ahead of the session, I send a list of DI Review shots alongside an EDL to DI. The EDL is easy to create if you're using source clip colors:

1. Select one DI Review shot in the timeline.
2. Right-click and select "*Select > Clips with Same Source Clip Color.*"
3. Right-click again and select "Create Sequence Based on Selection."

The resulting sequence can be used to generate an EDL for Drop-Ins. By removing the filler, this sequence can become a stringout. Here's how to do that using the sequence from above:

1. Select all to the right.
   - This will select all the VFX clips in the sequence.
   - Enable the yellow "Segment Insert" smart tool.
   - Consult the Edit tab within Timeline Settings to turn on "Select Filler with Segment Tools." (That's what makes the next step work.)
2. Shift-Option-click the same function to select **only** filler.
   - This will invert the selection so that only filler is selected.
3. Hit "Delete."
   - This removes all the filler and leaves you with a stringout of all the clips to review but without their slates or head and tail handles. This is why you can't just create this stringout using the master clips of imported VFX shots.

Stringouts are typically the way shots are reviewed, save special cases like reviewing a series of shots in context (which the director or editor may request). I give the finishing editor a heads-up if there's a particular sequence of shots that I anticipate we will want to review in context.

We play a shot back, looping it once or twice. Someone authorized to "Final" the shot (usually the highest-ranking person in the room—could be the director, editor, or first assistant) approves or rejects it. Having laser pointers handy helps draw people's attention to problem areas—more on VFX Review sessions in the VFX Chapter (p. 207).

Tracking DI Effects

I call DI-related items "DIOP" events—Digital Intermediate Opticals (Effects, Color and Titles.) This is anything with a re-po, re-size, re-time, or another effect that's not assigned to a VFX vendor. Color notes aren't considered opticals, but I lump them in for tracking purposes—more on those in a bit. I create, format, and carry green DI markers throughout the editorial process; I only assign the shot codes upon lock and turnover.

DI Markers and the Database

Here we go; let's break down an example DI marker:

newA=DI=EFC_1030=push in 100% to 110%, repo (to hide boom)=end

- **newA**: DI Marker added after the first turnover.
- **DI**: Identifies this as a DI marker.
- **EFC_1030**: Shot ID. Thousands place is the reel; shots increment in 10s. This is the third shot in Reel 1.
- **push in 100% to 110%**: The effect to be applied. If it's a color note or title, I'll start it out with that, like this: "color note:" or "title:"
- **end**: ensures the entirety of the marker has been parsed.

Remarkably simple, no? Especially when compared to an ADR or VFX marker. I track DI Effects more similarly to ADR lines than VFX shots. It's a marker list-based workflow as opposed to using EDLs. This doesn't give a shot duration or accurate start timecode, but I've found that the DI doesn't need that. So, if the timecode navigates them to anywhere within the body of the shot, I'm good.

My database checks the imported marker shot codes against what it already has in its system. It either adds new records, flags any omitted events or simply updates the timecode associated with the shot ID. Note that the shot ID is formatted differently from VFX shot IDs. It's a two-part structure with a four-digit number instead of a three-part structure with three-number padding. This is a distinction that I make purely to further differentiate between the two kinds of shot IDs.

DI Event Categories

I classify DI Events under three categories: **Effects, Color Notes,** and **Titles.** A script in the database scans the event descriptions for the words "Color Note:" and "Title:" and marks them as such, leaving all others as "Effect." This allows me to provide one master list of all events to the DI producer and send individual PDFs to three groups: Effects to the finishing editor, Color Notes to the colorist, and Titles to the title house.

DI Turnover

Every post house is different, but here's what I've done in the past. To prepare a sequence for turnover to DI, I break down the tracks as they request.

All non-effected clips are left on V1. VFX plates are placed on V2, and final shots from the vendor are put on V3. For VFX which will also have an optical effect applied, I move the plates for that shot to V4 and higher. I move all titles to V5 (or the highest track available past the stacked opticals).

Change lists to DI are run from the last turned-over EDL sequence (which I label grey in the bin) to the current EDL sequence. The notable difference between this change list and the one generated for the sound department is that the sound department wants to see footage (feet+frames), while DI expects a timecode. For more on DI Turnovers, check out the Turnovers section (p. 230).

Updating the Status of DI Events

Once turned over, I change the statuses of DI events in the database from "New" to "Turned Over." After receiving a Confidence Quicktime (p. 252), I *should* switch all events to "Avid Review;" more often than not, I pull up the list and switch them to either "Noted" or "DI Review" as I watch the ConCheck (see "Custom FileMaker DI list" [downloadable] at www.routledge.com/9781032843285). Noted means something is wrong, and I need to let DI know. DI Check means that it looks good in Avid, and we'll check it out again when we're at DI next. After a once-over in the DI, I can mark the status as "Final."

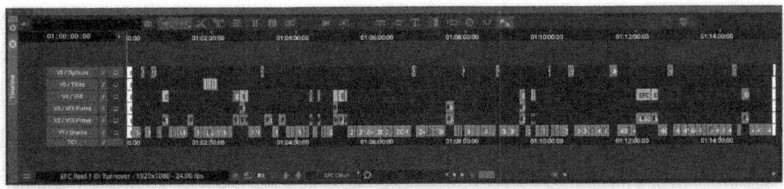

Figure 11.3 Timeline prepared for DI Turnover. Note the track names.

Titles

It's good to get a head start on titles, whether it's main titles, main on ends (MOE), or the crawl. All take time—especially the MOE, which requires a waiver (that is above our pay grade). Titles can dictate the length of an opening sequence and how much music is needed at the end of the film. Interstitial titles are necessary to place the audience in time, location, or both... Or maybe to serve a more creative need.

There are always three questions for deliveries: Font for **mains on end**, **subtitles**, and font used for **location cards/narrative titles** (interstitials). Temp titles are ultimately replaced with editorial renders from the vendor.

Creating Temp Titles

I create most of the simple titles in Media Composer using Titler+ (p. 49). I type out the designator, name, and affiliation one by one. Sure, there are ways of automating this using Photoshop and a CSV file, but it's something I haven't felt the need to explore, personally. It's a lot to type out, and after they're all timed and placed, it's nearly inevitable that someone asks for them all to be re-sized or re-positioned. This is easier to accomplish than one may think, using the trick of updating a single effect parameter (p. 177). Not only is it fast, but it's consistent (so titles are in the same spot from title to title).

Timing

Yes, timing and size are important to specify, even at the temp level. While the end crawl can speed up or slow down to accommodate (its speed is measured in pixels per frame, or "ppf"), there are contractual obligations that need to be adhered to. I've dealt with main titles where most titles had one name, and some had multiple names. A single name was **72 frames long**, and a double (or more) was **88 frames long**. Timing is measured from the first frame where the title is fully opaque, to the last frame where it's fully opaque; in other words, ignore dissolves when timing credits (though they should all be consistent if not identical).

Sizing

The sizing is ultimately something that the title house is accountable for, and they'll send a "checkers" document measuring everything for posterity once the dust settles. You should still be aware of this stuff so that you don't accidentally mockup titles that people get attached to when the legal requirements prohibit it. In addition to noting the font sizes, note the typefaces too.

Typeface

As assistants, we certainly help mockup the titles. This might include choosing a few typeface options to audition for the director and editor. Ultimately, this might change, or a custom typeface will be created for the show. If the typeface is custom-made for the show, be sure to archive it with the rest of the show documents. I keep the OTF or TTF (OpenType and True Type Font files, respectively) on the documents Nexis partition. If the font is Helvetica or Futura (personal favorites of mine that are both standard typefaces), you don't need to archive those files, but it should be documented somewhere that those are the fonts used. I put this information in my database, and the vendor should include it in their Checker file.

Creating a Temp Crawl

Assistants are often tasked with creating a temp crawl for end credits, which can be a daunting and time-consuming task. Instead of using traditional titling tools, I take a different approach, which makes it faster and removes some guesswork. Typically, someone (either the post supervisor or someone at the studio) will have already started compiling a spreadsheet formatted for end credits. I request that and then:

1. Import the spreadsheet into Apple's Numbers app (their version of Microsoft Excel).
   - Why Numbers? It's accessible, and it works. There's probably a way to accomplish all this in Excel, but I haven't tried it. I can't seem to get this done in Google Sheets, though.
2. Select all cells and remove any borders that may exist.
3. Set all cells to no fill and the text color to black.
4. *File > Export To > PDF*
   - Here's the key part: Under Page Layout, select "**Fit each sheet to a single page.**"
   - This ensures that you have one PDF instead of a multi-page one.
5. Import this PDF into After Effects and add it to a composition.
6. Apply an Invert effect to turn the "black text on white page" into white on black.
7. Add position keyframes (or use an After Effects expression) to animate the crawl.
8. Export from After Effects and import into Media Composer.

When there are any updates, I repeat the above, replace the file in After Effects, and re-render.

Working with a Title Vendor

The title vendor might want to see the film via PIX (or perhaps looped into one of many spotting sessions (p. 144)—probably not one for them *alone*, though). They'll want two "same-as-source" files with a watermark (below the center frame; basically, don't block any titles with the watermark), a record timecode, and the sequence name. One will be **Texted** (include any temp titles for reference) and the other **Textless** (only for sections where text is over picture instead of black). They don't need the whole film or all the reels, just the sections with titles (consider adding handles).

Titles sometimes get bid out similarly to VFX, wherein you send a sequence (texted *and* textless) for the vendors to apply proof of concept work on. Sometimes, different vendors will handle different types of titles, so it's not uncommon for the DI to apply subtitles using SubCap and to have a service like EndCrawl generate the, well, end crawl. Most end crawls I've seen run at around 4 ppf. Make sure to request that renders for Editorial include an alpha channel, but only for the titles that are over-picture. There's no need to render an extra channel when it's not needed!

Cutting in New Title Versions from a Vendor

A great tip for cutting in a series of titles, like main titles: Relink based on the source filename and ignore characters after the last occurrence of "_". If the formatting of the filenames is consistent (**Title_01_v03. tif**, for example), they'll relink based on everything *before* the version number. Talk to the vendor and see if they can accommodate.

Checkers (Galleys)

"Checkers" is a document that's delivered from the title house to the studio before finalizing the titles. It allows the studio to legally sign off on the sizing and order of the credits per contract stipulations. Checkers are typically delivered in PDF format with rulers, a grid, and percentage statements for measurement and reference. Editorial does not cut checkers in anywhere.

Confidence Checks (ConChecks)

Confidence Checks (or Conform Checks, either way, I call them "ConChecks") are sent to Editorial once DI has successfully relinked all the media from the offline edit and applied the DI effects. This is before any color work is applied, and the purpose is to ensure that the online edit matches the offline edit. They usually don't contain any of the color work, but they should always include the latest VFX that have been sent as drop-ins and all DI effects. Don't expect to see titles (unless finals of those have been dropped in). Request that they render the ConCheck with color, if possible. Be aware that there might be a cost associated with rendering out ConChecks and one or two sets may be included in the budget. If you're limited to two, I'd suggest requesting one after the first turnover and the second batch after 90% of the VFX finals have been dropped in.

I link the ConChecks into Media Composer instead of importing them (unless Avid media is provided). I cut them in over our reels and apply either a difference blend mode effect or a matte so I can see both the ConCheck and our timeline at once. I've become a massive fan of the difference composite mode (the same method I use to compare a new VFX version to an old one). I used to use a matte overlay or a split screen, but I find that I'm more efficient using the composite mode. I primarily look for any cuts that aren't aligned. I also look to make sure the frames themselves are aligned, and at the edges for QC black. While watching the ConChecks down, I place markers in the ConCheck clip on the timeline where there are errors. Red is if an edit is off or if there's a render or sync error. Green is for a DI effect that isn't (or is incorrectly) applied. Blue is any VFX or missing title. Magenta markers are internal notes that aren't shared. I export these markers to send them to the finishing editor. The most common note you'll have is a timewarp effect that can't be replicated with their motion estimation tools. These events will inevitably be pulled for VFX, so it's best to flag re-speeds for VFX early on (especially if they're not at a clean multiple of the project frame rate or if it's a dynamic [keyframed] timewarp effect).

Generally, I watch each reel once, and then go back to each DI effect event and inspect those shots more closely. I pull up the DIOP list in the database and update the status of the DI events. If there are no errors, I mark the event as "DI Review." Errors are marked as Noted. After reviewing in DI (it doesn't have to be an explicit review, just any DI session), if there are no notes, I mark any DI Review events as Final.

These ConChecks are left on the top track and muted to not be included in any export. This also allows me to check newer ConChecks against older ones with the notes we gave. It's also nice to have that in the timeline if changes are made, as you'll see an edit or gap in the ConCheck as a visual reminder.

12 Wrap

This is the last few days or weeks on the job. The studio will want to be given a list of all the titles in the film, for the PA to box and label everything up, and archive everything else. Be prepared to provide a backup of the Nexis. Shred any sensitive and non-archived documents. The studio will provide specs for their expected deliverables—they likely have a "wrap document" to complete.

Save any templates or settings that aren't sensitive and are useful in the temp editorial process. Templates and presets are helpful to reference in future jobs, especially when working for the same studio. Any physical items purchased along the way are considered "show assets" and should be delivered to the studio and accounted for (or sold to the crew at a discount. If there's a RAID or a light you want, ask).

Supplemental Material

Before wrapping, you might be asked to pull deleted or extended scenes. Ask the director if there are any scenes they'd like for you to include. The output for these is usually the Avid working resolution, and they don't need a formal turnover; they just need a clean export. There's a rule to remove music and sound effects, as they're not licensed. So, make sure to take those out before exporting. Some directors might want you to repurpose the final recorded score from the composer. This is kosher, as the show owns that music (it's not temp and was commissioned for the film).

Finishing Touches

After the last VFX shot is delivered, approved, and dropped in, the film goes back to the mix stage for final playback. In some cases, the final mix won't align with the DI on the schedule, so things get a little offset. As with everything in this book, let's continue using this scenario as an example.

The sound is printmastered, and the sound team delivers the final mix to both editorial and the company making the DCP. The picture files are sent from the DI to the DCP company, and a DCDM (Digital

DOI: 10.4324/9781003516491-13

Cinema Display Master) or IMF (Interoperable Master Format) is created. This is the master DCP/IMF, which will be duplicated for distribution. The director needs to sign off on it at the mastering facility, and then, there's one final QC viewing. And, that's it!

The Last Day

There isn't a "last day" because the editor might wrap before you, or the director might not come in during the last few weeks. All of this is schedule-dependent, but a good idea is to plan to celebrate together, perhaps after the final mix concludes or after the last DI review session.

Either way, I like to handwrite cards to each team member to thank them personally for their contributions. This includes the editor and director, who, often, have motivated, inspired, and given me the opportunity to work on the project.

Preparing for the Next Job

When you're winding down a project, it's time to start thinking about what's next. You might be jumping onto another gig or taking some time off (on your terms or otherwise). Perhaps you have a few job offers and must decide which fits you. Maybe you don't have anything lined up, so you take the opportunity to get out of town and travel.

Considering Prospective Opportunities

This part is *highly* subjective and specific to me at this point in my career. They're value judgments based on what's important to me. I'm including this section because I have often been asked what I think about when considering a potential job opportunity. Even if you disagree with it, I hope that outlining my thought process can, at least, encourage you to decide for yourself what questions need to be answered when facing such a scenario.

There are three questions (in no particular order) I ask myself when considering a job:

- Is it a good opportunity?
  - Will this job **connect me with people** who motivate and inspire me? Is it an environment in which I can learn and grow? Does it work with my schedule and commute?
- Is it creatively fulfilling?
  - Is this project *really cool?* Will I be able to contribute creatively? Is this something I think is **exciting, inspiring, or neat**? Will I learn a lot about something I'm interested in?
- **Is it financially beneficial?**
  - Will it allow me to **pay my bills**? Can I add to my savings?

If I can't answer "yes" to at least two of the above, I don't consider taking the job. The perfect job meets all three requirements. If a fascinating project comes along and it has wonderful good people, I'd be willing to take a pay cut. If it's not creatively fulfilling but a good opportunity, and they're paying above scale rate, I'll consider it. But if a job isn't paying enough and it's not a good opportunity, then working on something that's *only* creatively fulfilling won't be sustainable for months on end.

When you're starting out, *everything* is a great opportunity. You get out of any job what you put into it, and you should make it the best experience for yourself that you can. That means if the job pays your bills, it's worth taking. I'll admit, I did a job or two for free when I started out. I reasoned that it was both creatively fulfilling and a *very* good opportunity to prove my worth to people who didn't know me. However, out of necessity, I put a time cap on how long I could do this without running out of money.

Later in your career, you might want to start sculpting your resume more and perhaps prepare to jump into editing at some point. Hopefully, you've saved enough money to give yourself more flexibility between jobs and not stress about the downtime. Flexibility, to me, is being able to *enjoy* the time off, make the most of it, and choose the next job instead of having to take whatever comes up first.

Passing on an Opportunity

There's a saying about knowing what to say no to and how it's just as important as knowing what to say yes to. Someone re-phrased it in a way that resonated with me: "**Sometimes, you have to say no to something good so you can say yes to something great.**" The flip side is knowing when to take time for yourself. Avoiding burnout is crucial because any career is a marathon and not a sprint. Look out for your mental health and take the time you need outside the office so you can be at your best when you're in the office. Whenever you determine you need to pass on an opportunity, thank whoever reached out for thinking of you (and consider recommending a qualified peer!).

Nostalgia

One final note. If you're anything like me, the final weeks of a project are the point in the process where the realization that the project is coming to an end sets in. Some slower days and quiet time on the stage or in the DI can give you time to reflect. I wanted to write about this because I haven't seen anyone discuss it before, maybe because it's difficult to put into words.

What we get paid to do is beyond special. We work long hours and form bonds with our peers. Each project is like a little rock band that gets together to perform a couple of hits, and then suddenly… we disappear. I don't want to be overly dramatic about it, but it truly will never be the same, even if everyone reunites. It's a moment in time. The end of a project can be difficult, especially when it's a particularly good experience, and more so if you don't already have another project lined up.

When we whip out the camcorder and record home movies, we watch them with our families and remember what's on the screen and all the memories surrounding those moments. In my career thus far, I've experienced a very odd mix of emotions seeing the films I've worked on go out into the world. Once it's released, a film belongs to the audience. It's wild how a new audience reaction can change how you view the film you know so intimately. It's exciting when people connect with it. Sadly, the audience might not always like what you worked on. Critics might pan it. For an empathetic person who gives 110%, the film feels like a part of me. Early on, I'll admit, I took some of that criticism personally (which is *wildly* narcissistic for a second assistant editor). So, if you're like me, this is a gentle reminder to **not tie your emotions to the success or failure of a film.** Just like how tying your self-worth to your employment status can devastate you between jobs, correlating the performance of a project you worked on with your self-worth is an impossible and worthless feat for any artist.

I like to focus on the memories I made while working on the film. No amount of praise or criticism can change or erase them. People can rip a project up, saying, "Why was *that* scene even in the movie?" I'll still smile fondly thinking about the lunch we had at that great sushi place the day the dailies came in for that scene. Even in the absence of criticism or praise, each frame that passes reminds me of alt edits, or that time when this was a VFX shot or a scene that was lifted (silently thinking, "You're welcome," to the audience who is none the wiser).

Once, I was allowed to screen a work-in-progress cut of a film I was working on with a handful of its actors. Memories flooded in for us all; the actors pointed at the screen and laughed about things that happened between takes. It was exactly like watching a home movie. I hope you make some good memories.

Glossary

Affiliation	In a title: The post-nominal "ACE," "ASC," etc.
ALE	See "Avid Log Exchange"
Artifacting (picture)	Warping of the picture due to the duplication or combination of frames within the software. When a clip is slowed down and rendered using FluidMotion, the computer has to create frames that don't exist. Artifacting results from the computer analyzing the motion within a clip and erroneously guessing what should be there.
Avid Log Exchange	A file used for metadata exchange
Bounce	Usually, in reference to audio, this term originated in an early version of ProTools and is synonymous with "export." Bounced audio is usually a region within a reel, while a "stem" would be a bounce of an entire reel (pop-to-pop).
Camera Report	Notes from the camera department during production, which lists the recorded takes (by a camera), their associated equipment (lens, filter, etc.), and circle takes
CDL	See "Color Decision List"
Circle Takes	Takes selected by the director on that set are typically the preferred takes. Sometimes referred to as "circled takes" or "selects."
Codec	The "program" (or *method*) in which video and/or audio streams are encoded and decoded. That's where the term comes from; compression+ decompression, encoder+decoder. Common codecs include ProRes, DNxHR, H.264, PCM, AAC
Color Decision List	A file representing color values consisting of Slope, Offset, Power, and Saturation.
Comma Separated Values	A document containing data (values) separated by commas
Concatenation	The textbook definition would be "linking things together in series." In the context of this book, I concatenate data in FileMaker Pro. Data from two separate fields can be concatenated by a calculation in another field using an ampersand. Shot Code and Element Type are separate fields: **EFC_ 012_015** and **MP1**. Concatenating them would look like this as a FileMaker expression: ShotCode & "_" & ElementType. The calculated text would look like this: **EFC_012_015_MP1**.

ConCheck	A term I made up, which refers to a Confidence QuickTime or a Conform Check file from the Digital Intermediate. See "Confidence Quicktime."
Confidence Quicktime	An exported video file of the finishing editor's conformed timeline, which should match the offline editorial's picture.
Conform Check	See "Confidence Quicktime"
Container	The file format (extension) containing video and/or audio streams. Common containers include MOV, MXF, MP4, WAV, and MP3. Within every container resides a codec.
Continuity (document)	A document that outlines the scenes in the film in the order they appear, delineated by reel.
Continuity (film term)	The fluidity of action from one shot to the next.
CSV	See "Comma Separated Values"
DAW	See "Digital Audio Workstation"
dB	See "Decibel"
DCP	See "Digital Cinema Package"
Decibel	A unit used to measure the loudness of an audio signal.
Designator	In a title: The job title, as in "film editor."
Digital Audio Workstation	Programs such as Avid Pro Tools, Adobe Audition, Apple Logic, and Ableton Live
Digital Cinema Package	The final product for distribution and playback is primarily formatted as JPEG2000 compressed picture assets, along with a control file that allows a particular composition to be played.
Digital Imaging Technician	A position within the camera department which is responsible for corralling the footage for the dailies technician
Distribution Key Delivery Message	A security passcode that allows post facilities to unlock DCP's within their mastering station to localize content. See also: "Digital Cinema Package" and "Key Delivery Message."
DIT	See "Digital Imaging Technician"
DIT Report	Paperwork that identifies all received files upon production wrapping. It details the data size, take length, and any associated technical notes
DKDM	See "Distribution Key Delivery Message"
DX	Shorthand for "Dialogue;" is mostly used when labeling guide tracks.

Edit Decision List	A file that represents a sequence of media, the media sources, and associated metadata, including but not limited to source name, source timecode in, source timecode out, record timecode in, and record timecode out.
Editor's Log	Script supervisor paperwork, which lists all setups and takes in the order they were shot in on the day of production
EDL	See "Edit Decision List"
Facing Pages	Script supervisor paperwork, which lists all setups and takes, organized by corresponding script page. These have notes regarding continuity, potential VFX, and, most importantly, anything the Director may have said about the takes on-set. This paperwork also includes circle takes.
Fast Menu	Colloquially referred to as the "hamburger" menu, it's a button within Media Composer that invokes a contextual menu. Notably, it is found in the Project, Bin, and Timeline windows.
FFC	See "Framing and Focus Chart"
FFOA/FFOP	See "First Frame of Action / Picture"
First Frame of Action / Picture	Also sometimes referred to as "First Frame of Picture," this is the first frame of picture after the head leader ends. The inverse of this is the LFOA, or "Last Frame of Action," which is the last frame of the picture before the tail leader.
Flub	A line of dialogue that was delivered incorrectly.
Framing and Focus Chart	An image recorded by the camera that represents the full aperture being exposed to the sensor. Annotations and patterns represent the intended aspect ratio and ensure accurate focus.
FX	Shorthand for "Effects," mostly used when labeling guide tracks
Handles	Extra frames beyond the bounds of the clip being used in the cut. They allow for wiggle room should the shot be extended at the head or tail. I use handles on dailies clips for perf slipping, and handles are prominent in VFX to provide flexibility and avoid overages in the event of an extension.
IMF	See "Interoperable Master Format"
Interoperable Master Format	A standard package of picture, sound, and subtitle assets that allows the creation of multiple tailored versions of the same title for different audiences. Think of it as a DCP for streaming.

ISO	Short for "Isolated Microphone" or Lavaliere Mic. This is used when discussing which audio track to use: mix track, boom, or ISO.
KDM	See "Key Delivery Message"
KEM Roll	KEM and Steenbeck were two manufacturers of flatbed film editing machines. The order in which dailies film takes were organized when working on these machines consisted of all takes from one camera followed by all takes from a second camera, and so on. One roll is as much film fits on a reel of film.
Key Delivery Message	A text file that serves as a key to unlock prescribed content on a certain device for a certain period. See also: "Digital Cinema Package."
Last Frame of Action / Picture	Also sometimes referred to as "Last Frame of Picture," this is the last frame of the picture before the tail leader begins. *(The inverse of this is the FFOA, or "First Frame of Action," which is the first frame of the picture after the head leader.)*
LFOA / LFOP	See "Last Frame of Action / Picture"
LFOA List	A PDF list of all reels with their respective versions and LFOAs, referenced frequently on the mix stage. See "Last Frame of Action / Picture."
Lined Script	Script supervisor paperwork showing all takes as lines running through the script pages squiggled out whenever dialogue is not on camera.
Longplay	This refers to the build of the full show. All reels played sequentially without a head or tail leader. Sometimes abbreviated as "LP."
Look Up Table	(Very) simply put, it is a file that remaps color values.
LUT	See "Look Up Table"
Main on Ends	Main titles are presented at the end of the film (instead of the standard presentation at the beginning of the film). These require a waiver to be signed, and the decision is above the pay grade of the assistant editor.
Matchback	The "Match Frame" function locates the frame your playhead is parked on and loads the source clip into the source monitor. A crucial part of any workflow that utilizes subclips. Using Match Frame on a subclip will match back to the master clip from which it was created.
MDB file	See "Media Database"

Media DataBase	A file generated and maintained by Avid Media Composer that resides within any given MediaFiles folder. It stores all **metadata** of Media Objects within the folder. This file is continuously updated by the application.
Media Object	Any media file that Avid Media Composer can read—typically an MXF OP-atom file.
Mix Track	Usually, the first audio track in the files from the production sound mixer. This is a sum of all other microphones (boom mics and lavaliere mics). Editors like to cut with this track and dig into the ISOs if clarity is needed.
MOB	See "Media Object". If you see "MOB" in an Avid error message, the error is likely media-related.
MOE	See "Main on Ends"
MOS	Mit Out Sound (German for "Without Sound"). Denotes a silent clip.
MX	Shorthand for "Music." Mostly used when labeling guide tracks.
ng	Shorthand for "not good". Best when paired with a reason *why*.
NLE	See "Non-Linear Editor"
Non-Linear Editor	Programs such as Avid Media Composer, Adobe Premiere, Apple Final Cut Pro, and BlackMagic DaVinci Resolve.
OCF	See "OCN" and "Original Camera Negative"
OCN	See "Original Camera Negative". Also referred to as "OCF" for "Original Camera File."
Original Camera Negative	A file that was captured by the sensor and saved to the internal camera card, and then archived and/or delayered for use in Digital Intermediate. Original Camera Negatives are not used in the offline editorial process.
Perf Slip	Perforation slipping refers to a strip of film wherein a 35 mm strip of film contains four perforations per frame. Slipping refers to changing the timing of a clip. **Perf Slipping** is when you adjust the timing of the audio by one perforation (in this case, 1/4 of a frame) for better accuracy.

Persistent Media Record	A file generated and maintained by Avid Media Composer that resides within any given MediaFiles folder. It stores the **status** of Media Objects within the folder. The contents of the file are read upon launching the application and continuously while operating, but if another machine is showing media as offline when it's online on your machine, try restarting the application.
Pick-Up	Without cutting the camera or sound, a partial take *within* a take *after* a line of dialogue that was delivered incorrectly, or a cue was missed.
Plate	In VFX: A piece of footage without any effect or color applied—the base element.
Playback (On Mix Stage)	When everyone on the mix stage watches a reel (or the longplay) and takes notes to enact in the mix. Sometimes abbreviated as "PB."
Playback (On Set)	Typically, this is a music cue played back on set for actors to perform to. Think of a "live" band, but they're miming their performances to match the song so it's consistent across takes. Occasionally, playback music with live vocals.
plist	"Property List:" A preferences setting file used by the MacOS on the user level.
PMR file	See "Persistent Media Record"
Pre-visualization	Abbreviated as "pre-viz," roughly animated sequences constructed by a vendor ahead of the film shoot to help guide the production in obtaining the necessary shots.
PRN	Latin for "pro re nata," which means "as needed." Primarily used in a healthcare setting. I've adopted it because my father is a nurse.
QC	See "Quality Control"
Quality Control	Also referred to as a "Quality Check;" this involves watching and listening for any errors in exported files ahead of sharing them outside of editorial. Quality controls are also performed on DCPs before screenings.
QuickTime	In the context of this book, I usually use "QuickTime" to refer to a MOV-wrapped video file. Otherwise, QuickTime is a framework that has since been depreciated and replaced by AV Foundation in MacOS. Many people simply refer to video files as "QuickTimes" as shorthand.
Re-po	Short for "reposition"—when the image is moved on the x or y axis within the frame.

Re-size	When the size of the image has been altered. Usually, a shot is "blown up" or increased in size to compensate for a reposition (re-po), stabilization, or digital push-in/pull-out—both keyframed resizes.
Reset	Without cutting the camera or sound, a full take *within* a take.
Roll Edit	An edit in which frames are equally added/ subtracted to the tail of one shot and added/ subtracted from the tail of the subsequent shot. No overall duration change in the sequence.
rsync	A utility for copying and synchronizing files.
rxn	Shorthand for "Reaction"
Slide Edit	An edit in which a shot itself is unchanged, but the edit points of the clips to the immediate left and right are trimmed. No overall duration change in the sequence.
Slip Edit	An edit in which frames are equally added/ subtracted to the head of one shot and added/ subtracted from the tail **of the same shot**. No overall duration change in the sequence.
SMPTE Order	In the context of audio and channel routing, the standard audio channel mapping for 5.1 surround sound. This is: Left, Right Center, LFE, Left Surround, Right Surround. See also: "Society of Motion Picture and Television Engineers"
SMPTE Timecode	The standard used to identify and label each frame. Represented as HH:MM:SS:FF (hours, minutes, seconds, and frames). See also: "Society of Motion Picture and Television Engineers"
Society of Motion Picture and Television Engineers	An internationally recognized association that sets standards for the film and television industry. See also: "SMPTE Timecode" and "SMPTE Order"
Sound Report	Notes from the sound recordist during production, which lists the recorded takes, their associated equipment (microphone, etc.), and character designations
Stunt-visualization	Abbreviated as "stunt-viz," blocked out action sequences created by the stunt team ahead of the film shoot, which help guide the production in obtaining the necessary shots.

Texted	A reference movie file with text (titles) on screen. Often used as a reference for the title house or international spotting.
Textless	A reference movie file without text (titles) on screen. Often used as a backplate for the title house to overlay their work on while they design. Also, a possible deliverable request for international spotting.
Timewarp	Avid's name for its re-timing effect. can be rendered using a variety of computation methods, the default of which is "Duplicated Field." I often change this to "Blended Interpolated" or "FluidMotion."
Total Running Time	The length of any given file in time, usually the longplay
TRT	See: "Total Running Time"
Universally Unique Identifier	Sometimes, just "UID." This is a unique sequence of characters that allows files to have their identifier. The editorial's version of this on a day-to-day basis is a burn-in and/or watermark that uniquely identifies the intended recipient.
UUID	See "Universally Unique Identifier"
Wildlines	Also referred to as "Wild Tracks," these are audio-only takes recorded on set during production but not associated with anything shot on camera. This could be a requested line of temp ADR due to fuzzy production sound from a previous day or an off-camera line or ad-lib alts, which the Director wants to experiment with later.

Awesome! You successfully figured out how to navigate this book. If you're confused by this sentence, check out Navigating the Book (p. 2).

Recommended Resources

Name	Author(s)	Contents	Format
In The Blink of an Eye	Walter Murch	Editing Philosophy	Book
Avid Agility	Steve Cohen	Media Composer, advanced	
Avid Uncut	Steve Hullfish	Media Composer, comprehensive	
Make the Cut	Lori Jane Coleman, ACE	Assistant editing, breaking in	
Jump•Cut	Diana Friedberg, ACE	Assistant editing, transitioning to editing	
Master the Workflow	Lawrence Jordan, ACE Richard Sanchez	Assistant editing, comprehensive workflow, database development	Course
FileMaker Pro Essentials	Cris Ippolite	Database development fundamentals	
The Avid Assistant	Jack Brown	Assistant editing, Avid-specific tutorials	YouTube Channel
Let's Edit with Media Composer	Kevin P McAuliffe	Avid-specific tutorials, entry-level	
tools.shift-e.net	Evan Schiff	Tools to create SubCap files, copy media for ProTools, generate mattes, and more.	Website
doomsolutions.com	Rhett Finch & Beth Howe	Tools to streamline post-production and VFX workflows in television and film.	
djfio.com/mdv	Valentin Kubyshkin	Avid media manager (and other tools)	
alwaysediting.com/avid-mc-versions	Chris Bové	Avid-specific resource outlining versions, features, and compatibility.	
avidtech.my.salesforce-sites.com/pkb/articles/en_US/User_Guide/Avid-Media-Composer-What-s-New	Avid Customer Care	Every new feature added to Media Composer from version 8.0 through the current version.	

Index

For Product Safety Concerns and Information please contact our EU representative GPSR@taylorandfrancis.com Taylor & Francis Verlag GmbH, Kaufingerstraße 24, 80331 München, Germany

T - #0027 - 260325 - C72 - 229/152/16 - PB - 9781032843285 - Matt Lamination